God's Shining Forth

Princeton Theological Monograph Series

K. C. Hanson, Charles M. Collier, D. Christopher Spinks,
and Robin A. Parry, Series Editors

Recent volumes in the series:

Koo Dong Yun
*The Holy Spirit and Ch'i (Qi):
A Chiological Approach to Pneumatology*

Stanley S. MacLean
*Resurrection, Apocalypse, and the Kingdom of Christ:
The Eschatology of Thomas F. Torrance*

Brian Neil Peterson
*Ezekiel in Context: Ezekiel's Message Understood in Its Historical
Setting of Covenant Curses and Ancient Near
Eastern Mythological Motifs*

Amy E. Richter
Enoch and the Gospel of Matthew

Maeve Louise Heaney
Music as Theology: What Music Says about the Word

Eric M. Vail
Creation and Chaos Talk: Charting a Way Forward

David L. Reinhart
*Prayer as Memory: Toward the Comparative Study of Prayer
as Apocalyptic Language and Thought*

Peter D. Neumann
Pentecostal Experience: An Ecumenical Encounter

Ashish J. Naidu
*Transformed in Christ:
Christology and the Christian Life in John Chrysostom*

God's Shining Forth

A Trinitarian Theology of Divine Light

ANDREW R. HAY

Foreword by Ivor J. Davidson

PICKWICK Publications · Eugene, Oregon

GOD'S SHINING FORTH
A Trinitarian Theology of Divine Light

Princeton Theological Monograph Series 218

Copyright © 2017 Andrew R. Hay. All rights reserved. Except for brief quotations in critical publications or reviews, no part of this book may be reproduced in any manner without prior written permission from the publisher. Write: Permissions, Wipf and Stock Publishers, 199 W. 8th Ave., Suite 3, Eugene, OR 97401.

Pickwick Publications
An Imprint of Wipf and Stock Publishers
199 W. 8th Ave., Suite 3
Eugene, OR 97401

www.wipfandstock.com

PAPERBACK ISBN: 978-1-5326-0523-9
HARDCOVER ISBN: 978-1-5326-0525-3
EBOOK ISBN: 978-1-5326-0524-6

Cataloguing-in-Publication data:

Names: Hay, Andrew R. | Davidson, Ivor J., foreword writer

Title: God's shining forth : a trinitarian theology of divine light / Andrew R. Hay, with a foreword by Ivor J. Davidson.

Description: Eugene, OR: Pickwick Publications, 2017 | Series: Princeton Theological Monograph Series 226 | Includes bibliographical references.

Identifiers: ISBN 978-1-5326-0523-9 (paperback) | ISBN 978-1-5326-0525-3 (hardcover) | ISBN 978-1-5326-0524-6 (ebook)

Subjects: LCSH: God (Christianity) | Trinity | Light—Religious aspects. | Christian theology

Classification: BT148 H19 2017 (paperback) | BT148 (ebook)

Manufactured in the U.S.A.   04/21/17

New Revised Standard Version Bible, copyright 1989, Division of Christian Education of the National Council of the Churches of Christ in the United States of America. Used by permission. All rights reserved.

Scripture quotations are from the ESV® Bible (The Holy Bible, English Standard Version®), copyright © 2001 by Crossway, a publishing ministry of Good News Publishers. Used by permission. All rights reserved.

For my beloved Kendall

Dum spiro spero

From Zion, perfect in beauty, God shines forth.
   —Ps 50:2

I have come into the world as light, so that whoever believes in me may not remain in darkness.
   —John 12:46

In their case the god of this world has blinded the minds of the unbelievers, to keep them from seeing the light of the gospel of the glory of Christ, who is the image of God. For what we proclaim is not ourselves, but Jesus Christ as Lord, with ourselves as your servants for Jesus' sake. For God, who said, "Let light shine out of darkness," has shone in our hearts to give the light of the knowledge of the glory of God in the face of Jesus Christ.
   —2 Cor 4:4–6

The light or revelation of God is not just a declaration and interpretation of His being and action, His judgment and grace, His endowing, directing, promising and commanding presence and action. In making Himself known, God acts on the whole man. Hence the knowledge of God given to man through his illumination is no mere apprehension and understanding of God's being and action, nor as such a kind of intuitive contemplation. It is the claiming not only of his thinking but also of his willing and work, of the whole man, for God. It is his refashioning to be a theatre, witness and instrument of His acts. Its subject and content, which is also its origin, makes it an active knowledge, in which there are affirmation and negation, volition and decision, action and inaction, and in which man leaves certain old courses and enters and pursues new ones. As the work of God becomes clear to him, its reflection lights up his own heart and self and whole existence through the One whom he may know on the basis of His own self-declaration. Illumination and therefore vocation is the total alteration of the one whom it befalls.
   —Karl Barth, CD IV.3.2:510

Contents

Foreword by Ivor J. Davidson | ix

Acknowledgements | xiii

Abbreviations | xv

Introduction | xvii

1. In the Beginning: The Concept of Light in Scripture and Theology | 1
2. God's Shining Forth: The Light of the Father, the Son, and the Holy Spirit | 29
3. The Light of the Gospel: God's Radiant Event of Love | 55
4. *Pro Ecclesia:* The Saints in the Light of God | 86
5. The Illumined Mind: Theology in the Presence of the Radiant One | 121

Conclusion | 150

Bibliography | 153

Foreword

THE ANNOUNCEMENT "GOD IS LIGHT" EPITOMIZES THE CHRISTIAN GOSPEL. According to that gospel, God is essentially radiant; in the radiance that is all his own, God shines forth towards us, his creatures. God determines his own luminosity. The light that he is does not acquire its identity by our ascription to him of some infinite expansion of light as we know it, a symbol of our imagining at its fullest stretch. Nor may we equate uncreated light with created, as though God were necessarily to be found within creation's light. God is light; light is not God. The light that is God is his alone—exclusive source of all creation's light, certainly, but in itself unapproachable by creatures: in strictest terms, unlike any they know. Yet, *as* this incomparable light, in the plenitude of the splendor that is uniquely his own, God shines forth. God is not locked up in the light he is; *as* the One he is, he makes himself known. This is the news, the best imaginable.

The declaration dazzles. Creatures, made for the light, have opted for darkness; perversely, self-ruinously, they have repudiated the glory for which their Creator purposed them: they shrink from the exposure, the judgment, his entrance entails. Yet enter he does: impelled by the love of his own glory, he, the light, will not be prevented in his shining forth; for the sake of his name, he will scatter the darkness and all that it involves; refulgent, he will bring his creatures to the exquisite honor he has determined for them—intimacy with the glory that is his. His arrival in their midst is, in a real sense, much too much for them; confronted by him, they are overwhelmed. Faith's only response is to bow down, to wonder, to confess—and to wonder again.

Theology exists in that posture: it has no other. It must ask for light to see the light, to think and speak of it—of him—as well as it can. Yet it dares to speak of an infinite mystery: he, this eternal light, is indeed known, and known by us, and committed to go on illumining us with the infinite radiance of his presence. And so: theology must wait upon the means by which he sheds that knowledge abroad, the Word that is generated, sanctified, and brought near as instrument of his luminosity, effective in his Spirit's power for all that he intends. It must wait in expectation that he goes on meeting us there, and changing us as he does. It must seek, in the strength he grants, to set forth, declare, enact whatever it is he shows: to point it out—staggering, all-comprehensive as it is—over and again. As theology so attests, it worships; worshipping is its task, and its delight.

In as much as the scriptural declaration of God as light is so fundamental to the gospel, it has naturally occupied a substantial place in the history of theology and of Christian spirituality. The language has played a major role in historic exposition of the doctrine of God, in Christology, and in pneumatology; it has featured extensively in the depiction of salvation and eschatology, and of the church and its vocation; it has shaped an array of spiritual, moral, and aesthetic images, symbols, and practices. Yet in all this there has, perhaps, been something of a lack of attention to what we might call an overall dogmatics of divine light—to what it might mean to set forth a general account of divine luminosity as Scripture's gospel presents it to us. It is to this important task that Andrew Hay has given himself in this study.

The work makes, I believe, just the right kinds of moves. Conceiving of dogmatics as the church's necessary submission of all its teaching to Scripture's holy rule, Dr. Hay considers the concept of light as we encounter it there, and as we do so with help from those who have met it before us. According to the biblical picture, he argues, God's light is first and foremost the light that God is in himself in his unique and essential triune identity as Father, Son, and Holy Spirit. God's light is his triune glory in himself, in the plenitude of the relations in which his perfect life eternally subsists. It is because God is radiant in and as himself that he is able to shine forth from himself: to elect, to reconcile, and to illumine creatures for fellowship with himself. In this great radiant occurrence of his eternal love, God shines into the darkness in which creatures have chosen to dwell, estranged from their Creator. In mercy he gathers a people to himself, summons them out of their ruined state, scatters and abolishes its effects; he constitutes them children of light, appoints them in turn to shine for him, grants them the immeasurable privilege that their present calling and future destiny is to be with him where he is, in the light. Those who once were darkness are now themselves "light in the Lord" (Eph 5:8); summoned to walk in the light, they must proclaim and reflect his splendor. No small part of that is their work in theology itself: here not least, they read, think, speak, pray, act as those for whom divine *illuminatio* is no vague or nominal hope, but a promised reality in the Spirit's power.

I had the great pleasure of working with Dr. Hay on his project in its initial form as a doctoral dissertation, and I am delighted to commend this revised version of that study warmly. It has instructed me; it has a great deal to teach all who recognize the importance of dogmatic theology in the church's praise. The theme is as good as it gets. The invitation is framed with clarity, insight, and joy. Join in the praise.

Professor Ivor J. Davidson
University of Aberdeen

Acknowledgements

THE FOLLOWING STUDY IS AN OUTWORKING OF MY DOCTORAL THESIS COMpleted at St. Mary's College, University of St. Andrews, Scotland. Were it not for Steve and Bonnie Mason I would not have turned my eyes to St. Andrews in the first instance. It was here that I was placed under the very capable supervision of Ivor Davidson. Ivor's many helpful insights in Christian dogmatics and patristics, and his guidance and encouragement in the writing process itself, deserves special thanks. For his timely advice, pastoral comfort, and unfailing friendship I am forever grateful. After all, his were the words that stirred in me the courage to embark on such an intrepid journey: "God really does shine forth, dispelling creaturely darkness by the sheer potency of his inner splendor, reaching us as he really is." I am extremely blessed to have had him as a *Doktorvater*; I am humbled to call him a friend.

I wish to thank the examiners of this study in its initial form, John Webster and Donald Wood. Each offered constructive readings of the work, and each embodied the meaning of a "conversation full of grace" during the *viva voce* examination. Their critical insights were especially incorporated throughout the eventual completion of this study. Alas the former, John Webster, passed away before the publication of this work. Continual correspondence with John before his unexpected passing revealed a generous and accommodating man willing to calm the theological anxieties of a young scholar—all the while deflecting any praise I offered for his monumental work in the field. Surely the loss in the Western church is very great; yet John's gain is joy unspeakable. *Plenus annis abiit, plenus honoribus.*

Those residing inside the "bubble" of St. Andrews who encouraged me during the writing of the thesis were many: Sven Ensminger, Jamie Davies, Micah Snell, Christina Larsen, James Andrews, Steve Duby, Jon Mackenzie, Ian Church, Shawn Bawulski, Ash Cunningham, Sean Cook, Kevin McConnell, Matt Gibb, Alden McCray, and the Reverend Alasdair Macleod. However, special mention must be made of two colleagues. Sam Adams, who challenged me daily during our many discussions in the Rutherford Room, and whose wonderful family brightened many a dark day in the Auld Grey Toon, shall remain forever in my gratitude. And another, Travis Buchanan, proved not only a fierce friend of quick wit but also a delightful playing partner on our many (needed) loops around the Old Course. *Clarior hinc honos*! I am honored to have these two as loving friends and fellow sojourners in life.

I attribute my sober introspection to my wonderful children, Amelie, Aaron, and Isla, who arrived throughout the various phases of writing this study, spectacularly shattering any sense of academic snootiness that remained personally intact. Moreover, our siblings and their families—the Hodgeses, Hays, Sparkmans, Gardners, and Stolls—provided much needed love and friendship throughout our stay over the Pond and the years since. Many thanks are due to our parents—Les and Pam Hay, Jimmie and Leesa Hodges—who offered love and support at every turn.

As the manuscript turned from a thesis into a book, I have many to thank at my past and present places of employment, Hillside Christian Church and Denver Seminary. Besides my duties within the church and surrounding community of Amarillo, Texas, Hillside Christian Church allowed the space and time to devote to research and writing. And the many wonderful elders, staff members, and lay members of this church—alongside its energetic, studious, and perceptive senior pastor, Tommy Politz—daily humbled the ecclesiologies I had foolishly built up in my mind. The collegial support from Denver Seminary has also been invaluable during this current moment of initial lecturing and administrative duties at the newly formed West Texas campus. Don Payne, Doug Fombelle, Randy MacFarland, Mark Young, and the postgraduate students of the West Texas campus have been an unending source of wisdom and guidance in my infancy at the Seminary. In all, I am humbled by this "great cloud of witnesses," and so very grateful to have the opportunity to come alongside such co-laborers for the "Kingdom of the beloved Son."

But above all I wish to thank my lovely wife, Kendall. Without your unwavering love and encouragement, without your tireless joy and support, without your faithfulness and godly example, without your beautiful smile amidst the ups and downs of life—without you, Kendall, this journey would have never found its mark. It is to you, my love, that this work is dedicated.

Non nobis, Domine, non nobis, sed nomini tuo da gloriam.

Abbreviations

ANF *The Ante-Nicene Fathers*. Edited by Alexander Roberts and James Donaldson. 10 volumes. Reprint. Peabody, Hendrickson, 1994.

CC   Calvin, John. *Calvin's Commentaries*. Edited by the Calvin Translation Society. 22 volumes. Reprint. Grand Rapids: Baker, 2009.

CD   Barth, Karl. *Church Dogmatics*. 4 volumes. Edited by G. W. Bromiley and T. F. Torrance. Edinburgh: T. & T. Clark, 1956–75.

CO   Calvin, John. *Ioannis Calvini opera quae supersunt Omnia*. Volumes 1–59. In volumes 29–87 of *Corpus Reformatorum*. Edited by Johann W. Baum, August E. Cunitz, and Edward Ruess. Brunswick: Schwetschke, 1863–1900.

Inst. Calvin, John. *Institutes of the Christian Religion (1559)*. Translated by F. L. Battles. Edited by John T. McNeill. Vols. 20 and 21 of Library of Christian Classics. Philadelphia: Westminster John Knox Press, 1960.

KD   Barth, Karl. *Die Kirchliche Dogmatik*. 4 volumes. Munich: Chr. Kaiser, 1932; Zürich: Evangelischer Verlag, 1938–67.

NPNF *The Nicene and Post-Nicene Fathers*. Edited by Philip Schaff. 2 series. 28 volumes. Reprint. Peabody: Hendrickson, 1994.

OS   Calvin, John. *Joannis Calvini opera selecta*. Edited by Peter Barth and William Niesel. Vols. 3 and 4: *Institutionis Christianae religionis 1559*. Reprint. Eugene, OR: Wipf & Stock, 2010.

PG   *Patrologiae graeca*. Edited by J. -P. Migne. 161 volumes. Paris: Garnier, 1857–66.

PL   *Patrologiae latina*. Edited by J. -P. Migne. 221 volumes. Paris: Garnier, 1844–55.

PPS *The Popular Patristics Series*. Edited by Jhn Behr, et al. 49 volumes. Crestwood, NY: St. Vladimir's Seminary Press, 1996–.

ST   Aquinas, Thomas. *Summa Theologiae*. Edited by Thomas Gilby and T. C. O'Brien. 60 volumes. Reprint. Cambridge: Cambridge University Press, 2006.

WA   Luther, Martin. *D. Martin Luthers Werke Kritische Gesamtausgabe*. 120 volumes. Weimar: Böhlaus Nachfolger, 1883–2009.

WJE Edwards, Jonathan. *The Works of Jonathan Edwards*. 26 volumes. New Haven: Yale University Press, 1957–2008.

Introduction

> For who would dare to say that there is darkness in God? Or what is the light? Or what is the darkness? God is light. I know that any man might say, "The sun is light, and the moon is light, and a lamp is light." But it ought to be far greater than these, far more excellent, and far more surpassing. How much God is distant from the creation, as far as the Maker from the making, from Wisdom and that which has been made by Wisdom, far beyond all things ought the light of this One be. And, perhaps, we shall draw near to it, if we know what this light is, and apply ourselves to it, so that from it we might be illuminated, because we ourselves are darkness, and only when we are illuminated by it can we become light.[1]

THIS STUDY SEEKS TO TRACE THE RADIANT PRESENCE OF GOD AS IT IS PROclaimed in the gospel and confessed in the praises of the gathered "saints in light" (Col 1:12).[2] This study is not concerned, therefore, with aesthetic or mystical theology, which might be an expected course of inquiry. Rather, our concern involves the strange rhetoric of Christian theology, namely, "that movement of believing intelligence by which the church today attends to the instruction of the church past, submitting its received teaching to the rule of Holy Scripture."[3] In submitting the "received teaching" of the church to "the rule of Holy Scripture," this study therefore tries to voice several soundings regarding the doctrine of God, ecclesiology, and the nature of trinitarian theology in view of the declaration that "God is light and in him there is no darkness at all" (1 John 1:5).

---

1. Augustine, *In Ep. Joh.* 1.4 (PL 35:1980–81): "Et forte vicini ei erimus, si quae sit lux ista cognoverimus, et as eam nos applicaverimus, ut ex ipsa illuminemur; quia in nobis tenebræ sumus, et ab illa illuminati possumus esse lux."

2. All scriptural references will be in the NRSV unless otherwise noted.

3. Wood, "Maker of Heaven and Earth," 381–82.

Our constructive study is concerned with offering a trinitarian account of God's light which makes two proposals throughout its course: *God is light in himself*; and *from himself God shines forth his light*.[4] The first proposal, *God is light in himself*, centers on the doctrine of God proper, namely, that *God is light* as it is the light of his own radiant identity as Father, Son, and Holy Spirit. God's light is the radiance and unity of the Holy Trinity. The image of God's light is therefore a conceptual articulation of the biblical witness that *God is light in himself*. Second, however, *from himself God shines forth his light*. That is, this second proposal arises in the forthcoming chapters as the ascription of God's "shining forth," which encompasses the divine movement of election, reconciliation, and illumination—that movement of God to his human creatures that is proclaimed in the gospel. And God's triune light includes, though it is not exhausted by, his shining forth in which he makes himself present to human creatures.

Alongside, and often reinforcing, our study will be several attendant voices from the ancient and modern heritage of the Christian past. The coming chapters are deeply marked by the "pro-Nicene trinitarian theology" of the fourth-century church; that is, the dogmatic terminology developed in the debates surrounding Trinity and Christology by Athanasius, Gregory Nazianzen, Gregory of Nyssa, and Basil is vital to our reflections offered here. Reference to the work of John Calvin and post-Reformation Protestant orthodoxy is also a premium source of our study, particularly with the important contributions to the doctrines of God and Scripture voiced in the sixteenth and seventeenth centuries. And modern voices also have their place, perhaps best figured in Karl Barth's handling of the concept of light in his third cycle of the doctrine of reconciliation in *Church Dogmatics*.

Such ancient and modern sources allow this study to join various uses of the concept of light in expressing the reality of the triune God's radiant self-revelation. However, found over and above these historical soundings is the *principium theologiae* of such expressions of God's radiant reality, clearly announced in the prophets and apostles of Holy Scripture. It is here that a clarification arises regarding the relationship between exegesis and the theological statements that occur throughout our study. In short: the *locus* of theology is exegesis. And such a location will be sustained in the following chapters as we offer a "trinitarian theology of divine light." The reason for the occupation of theology with exegesis is quite simple: its subject matter is the risen and ascended Christ as he speaks through Holy Scripture. And the details of this notion will be duly examined in later sections of our study.[5]

---

4. Cf. Ps 50:2 and 1 John 1:5. We concentrate more fully on this theme in chapter 2.
5. See, e.g., chapters 3 and 5.

Yet in attending to Holy Scripture and the historical soundings of theology, we ought to note, at the outset of this study, that there is much that the proceeding chapters avoid. They do not offer any lengthy handlings of the primary concepts of trinitarian theology, such as "persons" or "unity"; nor do they give any extended account of the debates surrounding the different models of trinitarianism currently residing within the realm of analytic theology. Though this study certainly engages with such concepts, critiques such models, and participates in several related questions *passim*, the trajectory here is much more precise: we will try to show how a trinitarian account of God's *light in himself* includes a particular way of thinking of God's *shining forth his light* upon human creatures, one that arrests their plunge into the confusion and darkness of sin and death.

Our study follows a rather narrow route. Chapter 2 seeks to reflect upon God's light as the light *in himself* as Father Son, and Spirit, as well as God's economic, covenantal *shining forth from himself* to creatures in the darkness of sin. Chapter 3 offers a much more detailed rehearsal of this *shining forth* by an account of God's loving election, reconciliation, and illumination of creatures. Chapter 4 proposes that with the treatment of God's shining forth there belongs a treatment of the light of the church called out of darkness, gathered into the "marvelous light" of God, and set to proclaiming the "excellencies" of God. Chapter 5 concludes this study by examining what bearing the reality of God's shining forth as Father, Son, and Holy Spirit might have on the human work and vocation of theology as an activity of the "illumined mind." As we approach this route, however, we must first pause in chapter 1 and offer a study concerning the historical and scriptural use of the concept of light—with the admittedly perplexing images it invokes—in order to fix its conceptual boundaries for the way forward.

I

In the Beginning
The Concept of Light in Scripture and Theology

> He may most properly be termed light, but he is nothing like the light with which we are acquainted.[1]

AS WE REFLECT UPON THE DECLARATION THAT "GOD IS LIGHT," WE ARE seeking to answer the question: Who is God? Who is this One who is *light in himself,* and *from himself shines forth his light* to his human creatures? A trinitarian theology of divine light, we shall soon see, points to this radiant identity of God the Father, Son, and Holy Spirit. And such a radiant identity is, further, to be regarded with respect to the divine distance—"he is nothing like the light with which we are acquainted"—and with regard to the divine approach—"He may most properly be termed light"—in God's turning towards human creatures in the darkness of sin and death.

In speaking of the light of God, this first chapter seeks to give an initial grounding to a trinitarian theology of divine light by marking a conceptual boundary. This will be primarily accomplished in three ways: first, by a survey of several scriptural instances of the concept of light; second, by a brief examination of the dogmatic gloss upon these scriptural instances from Nicene trinitarian theology; and third, by an inquiry into the "contingent" misuse of the concept of light.

---

1. Irenaeus, *Adv. hær.* 2.13.4 (PG 7a:744; ANF 1:374): "Sensus enim capax omnium bene et recte dicetur, sed non similis hominum sensui et lumen rectissime dicetur, sed nihil simile ei, quod est secundum nos, lumini."

The Scriptural Foundation of the Concept of Light

The basis for a trinitarian theology of divine light is found in reading the prophets and apostles of Holy Scripture. That is, the guiding action for our study is straightforward: a *"conversation* in which One *speaks* [i.e., God through Scripture] and the other *listens* [i.e., the reader of Scripture]."[2] Of course, *listening* to scriptural witness is necessary for our present exegetical context: tracing the biblical use of light as the "best figure or representation of the Divine Majesty."[3] Yet before giving a select reading or, indeed, *listening* to several scriptures, we must at once caution that each instance of the image of "light" or "glory" in the biblical canon is situated in a unique context and *locus*.[4] It is not our aim here, therefore, to overlook such contexts; rather, again, we seek to listen to the scriptural witness of the light of God so as to provide the necessary boundary for the forthcoming theological movements of our study. We will initially retrieve several major themes about the concept of light by tracing three vital scriptural instances—namely, in the book of Genesis, the Synoptic Gospels, and various Johannine materials—before moving to examine how such scriptural occurrences might inform our way forward in this study.

"Light" in Genesis

We might first say that the standard text for any *listening* to the biblical occurrence of the image of light is often found in the narrative of the creation account in the book of Genesis.[5] It is here that we find a clear instance of God and his creation, the creative speech of God, and the creation of light by divine speech. That is, we find at the head of the Pentateuch the astounding fact that even before making the heavenly luminaries (Gen 1:14–15), in the primal chaos of darkness God spoke and created light.[6]

---

2. Barth, *Theologie Calvins*, 526.

3. Luther, *Genesisvorlesung* (WA 42:14).

4. A classic study on the history of the biblical notions of "glory" in their textual setting remains Ramsey, *Glory of God*, esp. ch. 2. Cf. Kittel, *"doxa,"* in *Theological Dictionary of the New Testament*, 2:242–55.

5. Additional instances in the Pentateuch and wisdom literature are common (e.g., Exod 3:1–6;12:21; 20:18; 24:16; 14:10; 16:19; 40:34–35; Pss 9:2; 19:8; 27:1; 36:9; 80:1; 88:12; 94:1; 104:1–2; Eccl 2:13).

6. It is worth noting that a recent study by John Walton ultimately bypasses several foundational elements in this section of Genesis. For instance, Walton seeks to render v. 3 as "Let there be a period of light." This appears a rather material reading of the verse under question, over against the more "functional" interpretation that Walton

> Then God said, "Let there be light"; and there was light. And God saw that the light was good; and God separated the light from the darkness. God called the light Day, and the darkness he called Night. And there was evening and there was morning, the first day. (Gen 1:3–5)

We hear in this principal passage of how God has surrounded himself with light, the "ornament and glory of the whole visible creation."[7] By this first creative utterance of v. 3, we see that created light is not itself God but a "creature" and an "ornament" of God's creative utterance.[8] That is, this ornament of God's creative power rests wholly on the fact that God, by the power of his Word, spoke light into existence and "saw that it was good" (v. 4). This means that God wills to uphold and preserve this light.[9] The fact that God "saw" his work, that he continues to see it, keeps the world from plummeting into chaos (v. 2). This "seeing" is followed by an allusion to the existence of darkness; but just as it does not state that God created darkness, so it does not state that he saw that this darkness was good. This can be said of light only—that is, of the light that was set apart from darkness. In finding light worthy of this separation, God sees how the light is good, namely, that it is good as his symbol and ornament; that it is a bulwark against darkness and confusion; and that it forms God's "basic principle of 'separation.'"[10]

This initial divine utterance, therefore, unmistakably differentiates between that radiant identity of God as Creator over against any so-called "god of light"—or, indeed, between the light spoken of here and an admittedly close hermeneutical connection with the Son of God.[11] Consequently, any

---

seeks to offer. Thus, Walton's reading of Gen 1:3 and its image of light gestures towards "solving" interpretive problems in the text, rather than following the doctrinal or exegetical backcloth behind said problems (see *Lost World of Genesis*, 54–55).

7. John Damascene, *Exp. Fidei* 2.7 (NPNF 9:23).

8. We say "creature" here to denote the creaturely qualities associated with created light—apart from and unequal to its Creator. See Luther's insistence that these verses should not be rendered allegorically into "light" and "dark" *beings* (see *Genesisvorlesung* [WA 42:15]), which is in contrast to Augustine (*Gen. litt.* 1.17).

9. Westermann (*Genesis 1–11*, 1:113) draws a connection between the Creator's positive self-evaluation and subsequent human worship given to the Creator because of these "good" works. In addition to Westermann's example of morning stars and heavenly beings giving praise to God (cf. Job 38:7) one could reasonably add Ps 136 where there is a repetition of the "good" punctuation, this time beginning a litany of praise for God's mighty acts including creation and liberation from Egypt.

10. Von Rad, *Das erste Buch Mose*, 31: "Grundbegriff des 'Scheidens.'"

11. This has been the classic interpretation of *Fiat lux*, as seen in, e.g., Tertullian (*Ad. Prax.* 7.12) and Augustine (*Gen. litt.* 1.6). The following centuries of creedal confession, namely the Niceno-Constantinopolitan Creed, concluded as much in placing

commingling of light—this "firstborn commandment"[12]—with a divinization of light, or with the Word itself, is wholly unwarranted. "Light is not somehow an overflow of the essence of deity," says von Rad, "but rather an object . . . of God's creation." Created by God, light therefore not only points to the radiant identity of God over creation, "the absolute distance between Creator and creature," but also to God's gracious turning to his creation in communion.[13] Whereas the darkness is seen as that which God has utterly rejected as the threat of death, light, on the other hand, functions in the creation narrative as overcoming darkness. This is why any interpretation of such biblical images as being *coincidentia oppositorum*—that is, as being a "mingling" of concepts—is to be rejected.[14] Such identifications lead some to mistakenly posit that God's "uncreated Light . . . does not seem to have the need of differentiation [from] thick darkness";[15] or that God's "dazzling light and deep darkness balance the clarity of truth."[16] According to this seminal occurrence at the head of the Pentateuch, however, the essence of darkness is unlike that of light.

Seen at the beginning of the book of Genesis, light is therefore an image of God's covenant- and communion-creating purposes with his creation. The light that shines in darkness and overcomes darkness gestures towards God's guarantee that creation is not abandoned, but that its term is to meet with his grace. In the center of creation, light is the symbol and ornament of the revelation of grace; with its creation there has been made known the judgment of the goodness of God formerly obscured. As this first work of

---

Christ synonymous with *phōs ek phōtós*. Of course, there are often modern distortions of this notion. In a recent commentary, R. R. Reno states that the "light" referred to in these passages should strictly be interpreted as "the Word" (*Genesis*, 46).

12. Gregory Nazianzen, *Or.* 40.6 (PG 36: 410; NPNF 7:361).

13. Von Rad, *Das erste Buch*, 32, 34: ". . . der Distanz zwischn Schöpfer und Geschöpf redet." Von Rad's comments come at the end of his thoughts on the second day in vv. 6–8, but the same obviously applies to the first day narrative. This "distance" also guards against the well-known dualistic notion between light and darkness, as found in further intratextual instances from the *Dead Sea Scrolls*. See, e.g., Vermès (trans.), *Complete Dead Sea Scrolls in English*, 1QS 1:9, 18, 24; 2:5, 16, 19; 3:13. Cf. the title of 1QM: "War of the Sons of Light against the Sons of Darkness." See also the edition of Yadin (trans.), *Scroll of the War*.

14. Palamas, e.g., takes up the *coincidentia oppositorum* from the Dionysian writings in stating that the divine light is rightly termed both radiance and darkness: "In the strict sense it is light [but] by virtue of its transcendence" it is experienced by us as "darkness" (*Triads*, 2.3.51). A discussion of Palamas and the Hesychasts occurs below.

15. Yeo, "Light and New Creation," 47.

16. Brown, "Darkness and Light," 181. See below for our hesitations with similar positions.

his occurs, and in it God annunciates his own glory as the Creator of light, God thus gives a mighty testimony of his concern for the human creature.

"Light" in the Gospels

The light of the covenant- and communion-creating God in the primordial creation narrative of the book of Genesis is gathered up and given further conceptual weight in NT occurrence. We might limit our *listening* of the NT to two instances found in the Gospels.[17]

First, an episode recorded in the Synoptic Gospels regarding Jesus' ministry is worth pausing over for a moment, not least because it is an expansion of the identity of Jesus and the revelation of his glory. On Mt. Tabor, in the presence of Peter, James, and John, Jesus was "transfigured" (*metemorphōthē*) and his clothing became "radiant" (*stilbonta*, Mark 9:2–3). Standing at the commencement of the journey to Jerusalem, the transfiguration story occupies a strategic position in Mark's Gospel, namely, a height at which "the reader looks down on one side upon the Galilean ministry and on the other side upon the *Via Crucis*."[18] The story is situated in the context of Jesus' teaching at Caesarea Philippi (cf. 8:27—9:13), which has the effect of claiming that Jesus is not only the "earthly" human messiah, but also the "beloved Son" from heaven (9:8). This "two-level Christology" at the heart of the Markan narrative finds its peak in the revelation of Jesus' identity in relation to Moses and Elijah.[19] In the account recorded in Matthew's Gospel, we find a different view of the scene when we hear that the face of Jesus "shone like the sun" and "a bright cloud overshadowed them," though Moses and Elijah are still recorded as present (Matt 17:1–8).[20] Luke goes further in his account by saying that the disciples saw "the glory" of Christ and of the

---

17. Of course, the Synoptic Gospels have further examples of the image of light (e.g., Matt 4:16; 5:13–16; 17:2; Luke 1:78f; 2:9, 30–32; 11:34–36), and the Pauline corpus is likewise replete with the concept (Rom 13:12; 2 Cor 4:4-6; Eph 5:8-14; Phil 2:15; Col 1:12; 1 Thess 5:5; 1 Tim 6:16; and, epistolically, Heb 1:3). We find the historical background for much of the Pauline (and other) epistolic emphases on the image of light in the description of Saul's luminous encounter on the road to Damascus (Acts 1:9–11; 2:33–35; 9:3; 26:13), and the catholic epistles together with the book of Revelation use the concept of light with increasing precision and depth (e.g., Jas 1:17; 1 Pet 2:9; 1 John 1:5–7; 2:8–10; Rev 21:23–24; 22:5).

18. Ramsey, *Glory of God*, 101.

19. Lee, *Jesus' Transfiguration*, 10.

20. Indeed, as Craig Keener notes, the placement of these two patriarchal figures is important for implying that "Jesus is the glorious Lord before whom all other heroes of the faith must bow" (Keener, *Gospel of Matthew*, 437).

two heavenly companions who had appeared with him, Moses and Elijah (cf. Luke 9:28–36).[21]

However, the modern career of this luminous event from the Synoptics often finds itself labeled a "misplaced narrative"[22] or a story of the "Hellenistic divine man."[23] But perhaps closer to the point, the story of the transfiguration is one whose importance is regularly underestimated by contemporary biblical scholars, who emphasize the message of suffering, that is, the way to the cross that commences at the height of Jesus' Galilean ministry.[24] Undoubtedly, proleptic suffering and glorification are clear christological themes in the Synoptics; yet the necessity of Jesus' suffering cannot be isolated from this instance of God's self-revelation on the mountain. That is, the accounts of the transfiguration in the Synoptics portray suffering *and* glory as being at the heart of Jesus' person and work. What this glorious moment of "two-level Christology" shows us, then, is a glimpse behind the human flesh and blood of Jesus Christ to the radiant identity of God. This "Jesus only" is at the same moment the "beloved Son" of the Father (Mark 9:7–8).

Second, we inevitably come upon the seminal set of texts regarding the image of light in the Johannine writings. The prologue to the Gospel of John offers a unique reading of the pre-existence of God the Son and his mission in and for the world.

> In him was life, and the life was the light of all people. The light shines in the darkness, and the darkness did not overcome it. There was a man sent from God, whose name was John. He came as a witness to testify to the light, so that all might believe through him. He himself was not the light, but he came to testify to the light. The true light, which enlightens everyone, was coming into the world (John 1:4–9).

From the first, we might note that the Gospel of John differs from the Synoptic account of transfiguration by identifying Jesus as "the light" (vv. 4–5, 7), by announcing that "In him was life, and the life was the light of all people" (v. 4), and by stating that "the true light, which gives light to everyone, was coming into the world" (v. 9). And as with the Genesis occurrence, so here: the connection between "light" (*phōs*) and "life" (*zōē*),

---

21. For more regarding the event of the transfiguration in its Lukan instance, see the insightful commentary of Marshall, *Gospel of Luke*, esp. 380–88.
22. Bultmann, *History of the Synoptic Tradition*, 259–60.
23. Collins, "Rulers, Divine Men, and Walking on the Water," 207–27.
24. See Bock, *Luke*, 1:863.

namely, that the life that dwells in the Son is the light of all people, and it shines in the "darkness" (*skotia*).

In contrast to this reading—and found within the contemporary intellectual activity surrounding the prologue—there are those biblical scholars who seek to push the pressure of interpretation of these verses in an entirely different direction.[25] For instance, some state that v. 4 is the response to a question apparently asked in v. 3: "How can all things have come into being from the Son?"[26] Likewise, others set the question in its linguistic divergence:

> Should we read the phrase with the rest of v. 3, as in, "apart from him nothing came into being that has come into being; in him was life?" Or should we read the phrase with v. 4, "apart from him nothing came into being; what came into being through him was life?"[27]

However, a proper listening to this heavily debated section of Scripture allows for a simple reading: The Son's life is the incorruptible redemptive life. Thus, the exposition of v. 4b appears to follow: the power of life that comes from the Son is a means of illumination in association to the creaturely world.[28] Yet some have pursued this thought, finding in *zōē* the general life of creation (with a reference back to v. 3), and in *hēzōē* the life that is the "illuminator of all humanity."[29] But the Son's light and life are not

---

25. The scholarly activity surrounding the "source" of the prologue and its image of light is diverse. See, e.g., Minear's contention that the image "light" (and others), beyond being used in NT literature, draws from the earlier sources of ancient thought in the OT, rabbinic, apocalyptic, Essene, hermetic, and gnostic writings (*Images of the Church*, 128–29). Rudolf Schnackenburg famously argued for a prototypical *Grundschrift* ("Logos—Hymnus und johanneischer Prolog," 76–82). Still others traced the generation of the prologue to three sources: (1) Judaism or Jewish wisdom hymns (e.g., Witherington, *John's Wisdom*, 47–58); (2) Christianity or pre-Christian hymns (e.g., Brown, *Gospel According to John*, 18–20; and Käsemann, "Aufbau und Anliegen des Johanneischen Prologs," 75–99); and (3) A "pre-Christian gnosticizing Judaism" (Bultmann, "Der religionsgeschichtliche Hintergrund des Prologs zum Johannesevangelium," 2–26; *Gospel of John*, 17–18, 107–8). For more on this interpretive history, see Painter, *Quest for the Messiah*, esp. ch. 3; and Keener, *Gospel of John*, 1:333–63.

26. Miller, *Salvation-History*, 14–15. Miller answers this question by pairing it with the incarnation.

27. Keener, *Gospel of John*, 1:381–82.

28. See Bultmann (*Gospel of John*, 39–40): "[The *Logos*] is the power which creates life." Thus, Bultmann states that something like Keener's distinction of the question is irrelevant, for in "both cases it is stated that life is not inherent in creatures as creatures."

29. Von Wahlde, *Gospel and Letters of John*, 1:29. Cf. Bultmann, (*Gospel of John*,

something inherent to creation, as we heard in the Genesis narrative. In line with Genesis 1:3–5, there seems no passage in the Gospel of John in which this "light" is the same that was uttered and formed in the creation narrative. Rather, John's Gospel is stating that this light is present as the uncreated, revelatory light of the created world.[30] God's gracious self-revelation is a separate action that goes beyond creation. Thus, we are told in the "scandal" of the prologue, God has worked the miracle that the "light of life" appeared on earth and did not remain hidden.[31] And this one, this "true light," was present to those that had eyes to see his glory: "the Word became flesh and lived among us, and we have seen his glory, the glory as of a father's only son, full of grace and truth" (John 1:14).

These themes are reaffirmed with a closer *listening* to the Johannine letters:

> Concerning the word of life—this life was revealed, and we have seen it and testify to it, and declare to you the eternal life that was with the Father and was revealed to us—we declare to you what we have seen and heard so that you also may have fellowship with us; and truly our fellowship is with the Father and with his Son Jesus Christ. . . . This is the message we have heard from him and proclaim to you, that God is light and in him there is no darkness at all. If we say that we have fellowship with him while we are walking in darkness, we lie and do not do what is true; but if we walk in the light as he himself is in the light, we have fellowship with one another, and the blood of Jesus his Son cleanses us from all sin. (1 John 1:1–3, 5–7).

These affirmations clearly repeat the opening movements of the prologue to the Gospel of John. It therefore appears that the purpose of the First Letter of John is the reiteration of the proclamation of the Son as the eternal,

---

40): "the light for men." We need to distance ourselves here and throughout from Bultmann's thought that *phōs* is merely the existential indicator of what creatures require, namely, a right orientation in this world and in relation to each other. This seems a rather one-sided account of the image of light, which in its more canonical range bears witness to God's gracious turning to human creatures in the darkness of death.

30. That is, we wish to avoid Peder Borgen's thought that, in view of the parallelism between the prologue and Genesis 1, the theme for John 1:4–9 may be presented thus: "primordial light and nightfall in primordial time, vv. 4–5, and light's entry into history, prepared by the coming of John [the Baptist]" (*Logos was the True Light*, 101). For our division of uncreated light and created light, see below the sub-section "Created and Uncreated Light."

31. Ernst Käsemann sees this verse as the paradigmatic and scandalous summary of the Gospel not because "the Word became flesh" but because "he dwelt among us" ("Aufbau und Anliegen des johanneischen Prologs," 93–6).

pre-existent Word, who had been with God from the beginning, had become flesh in recent history.[32] And the heart of John's proclamation is of extreme importance for our present study: "This is the message we have heard from him and proclaim to you, that God is light and in him is no darkness at all" (1 John 1:5). And, moreover, those who "walk in the light, as he himself is in the light" have communion with one another, and the blood of Jesus purifies them from all sin. It is this humble confession of the need for the cleansing blood of Jesus Christ that enables human creatures to continue "walking in the light" and thus to enjoy communion both with God and with others "in the light."

There are several features of the Johannine use of the concept of light worth highlighting. We note that John emphasizes Jesus as the fulfillment of the OT hopes and expectations: the light and life of the Son are not something inherent to creation, but rather the revelation of the "true light," who is the source of spiritual light for every person. Light is thus part of John's juxtaposition between communion in light and living in sin and darkness.[33] Such a notion is vital to the Johannine proclamation that the God who "is light" is the very One who seeks and rescues human creatures from the darkness of sin and places them in the light of life through his Son. It is no surprise, then, that we find in the closing passages of the NT a Johannine image of Christ standing among the seven lampstands of gold, his eyes flaming like fire and his face shining "like the sun at full strength" (Rev 1:13–16). Those in communion with this radiant one belong to a city that does not need the sun or the moon to shine on it, "for the glory of God gives it light, and its lamp is the Lamb" (21:23). And this Lamb, we finally hear, declares himself to be "the bright morning star" who is "surely coming soon" (22:16, 20).

The Sweep of the Survey

Listening to the sweep of the biblical survey of the image of light has yielded a clear development by the shift from the language used in Genesis to the Gospels. When saying "Let there be light," God creates the symbol and ornament of his glory. Yet this light is other than God and wholly dependent

---

32. Regarding the "Johannine double entendre" of the pre-existent Word and the life-giving message of Christ, see Yarbrough, *1–3 John*, 38; and Jobes, *1, 2, and 3 John*, 46. Of course, the pre-existence of the Word might also be found in the Synoptics, if one follows a particular reading of the "pre-temporal" sayings and titles of Christ (cf. Matt 5:17; 8:29; 9:13; 10:34–35; Mark 1:24, 38; 2:17; 10:45; and Luke 4:34; 5:32). For an intriguing study of this theme, see Gathercole, *Preexistent Son*.

33. On this division, see Schnackenburg, *Gospel According to St. John*, 2:352–61.

upon God for its existence. Still, the divine utterance moves beyond this symbol to also include a distinction in created light and uncreated light, the latter being an indication of God's radiant identity. In the Johannine linguistic turn, then, "God is light" suggests that this particular uncreated light, God's light, is not the created light that is manifest in the creation narrative, but rather the light of God's gracious revelation and his communion- and covenant-establishing concern for his human creatures. With the NT clarification and expansion of the concept of light, God's shining forth is seen as a separate action that goes beyond creation. And it is precisely from this NT bedrock, coupled with the OT occurrence, that the image of light finds its eventual emergence in the creedal confession of Jesus Christ as "Light from Light." It is to this historical, dogmatic emergence of trinitarian theology in the Christian tradition that we now turn for additional clarification and limitation of the concept of light.

Pro-Nicene Trinitarian Theology

The crystallized dogmatic use of the image of light was developed in the trinitarian theology of the fourth-century church.[34] The use of the image by the Nicene fathers was primarily prompted by the danger facing the early church, which came in the form of the fourth-century Arian controversy over the Son's *anomois* status with the Father. Are the terms "father" and "son" to be understood as images mirrored in creaturely relations? And, moreover, is the Holy Spirit to be worshipped along with the Father and the Son as God? These were several questions faced by the Nicene fathers, and they answered them in their unqualified acknowledgment of the divinity of Jesus Christ as Lord, Savior, and light, and of Holy Spirit as Lord, "life-giver," and "light-giver."[35] The resulting Nicene-Constantinopolitan Creed represents the dogmatic work of the Greek fathers in reaching a careful, exegetical expression of crucial points in the gospel over against the concepts found competing viewpoints.[36]

---

34. It is important to note that the second- and third-century ante-Nicene theologians often used the image of light to preserve the doctrine of the unity of God against competing notions of their day. For additional background on early "*Logos* theology," see McGuckin, "Apostolic Fathers to the Third Century," 256–70; Mark Edward's treatment of the "Gnostic Beginnings of Orthodoxy" in *Catholicity and Heresy*, 11–34; and Beeley, *Unity of Christ*, 3–45.

35. Gregory Nazianzen, *Or.* 41.9 (PG 36:444; NPNF 7:382).

36. More precisely, the fathers sought to establish the doctrine of the Trinity and unity of God, preserving the Trinity from Judaizing tendencies in a Sabellian contraction of the three persons into an undifferentiated unity, and preserving the unity from

And as with the preceding centuries of the church, the Nicene fathers knew that they could make use of creaturely concepts in expressing their understanding of the relation of the Son to the Father, and of the identity of the Holy Spirit, which were made to point to what God reveals of his own inner personal relations.[37] This means that, according to the Nicene fathers, we must interpret the concept of light according to its narratival sense given in OT and NT occurrence. It was in this way that the fathers of Nicaea brought the scriptural concept of "light" and "radiance" to help them elucidate, first, the relation of Christ as Son and Word to God the Father, and, second, the identity and works of the Holy Spirit.[38]

The Relation of the Son to the Father

According to the Nicene fathers, the concept of light had the effect of clarifying that as light is never without its radiance, so the Father is never without his Son. Of course, such language was in reaction to the Arian notion of the being of the Son and the being of the Father; namely, is the kind of eternity attributed to creatures brought into existence by the will of God to be associated with that of the Son, since "there was once when he was not"?[39]

The "pro-Nicene" reply came in the form of the concept of light.[40] Just as light and radiance are one and undivided, so the Father and the Son are one and undivided, that is, the Father and the Son are *homoousion*. And just as God is eternal light, so the Son of God as eternal radiance of God is himself eternally light. It was on biblical grounds, Athanasius stated, that the pro-Nicene position could "take divine Scripture, and thus discourse with freedom of the religious faith, and set it up as a light upon its candlestick,

Hellenizing tendencies in an Arian severance of the three persons by a diversity of natures. See, e.g., Gregory Nazianzen, *Ors.* 1.37; 18.16; 21.13; and Basil, *Adv. deos tres* [*On Not Three Gods*](PPS 47:269–77). For a good account of the historical issues at hand, see Williams, "Arius and the Melitian Schism," 35–52; and Anatolios, *Retrieving Nicaea*, ch. 1.

37. See Athanasius's comments in *In illud* 3 (PG 25:216; NPNF 4:89).

38. It is curious that Anatolios's recent study of Nicene theology, *Retrieving Nicaea*, makes no mention of the use of the biblical image of light with regards to the development of trinitarian terminology during this period. This does a disservice to the reader, particularly when he omits the concepts of *apaugasma* and *phōs* from Athanasius's thoughts on *homoousion* (cf. 129–30). These concepts are essential to understanding his points regarding the identity of the Son and the Father and, moreover, his pneumatology.

39. See Theodoret, "Letter of Arius," 1.4 (NPNF 3:41–2).

40. On the label "pro-Nicene" as relating to Athanasius and his Cappadocian heirs, see Ayres, *Nicaea and its Legacy*, 236–40.

saying. ... He is the expression of the Father's Person, and Light from Light, and Power, and very Image of the Father's essence."[41] The words "Light of Light, true God of true God" were therefore inserted into the Creed at Nicaea in order to clarify and define the unique nature of the relation of the incarnate Son to the Father.[42] Thus, the Son "and the Father are one in propriety and peculiarity of nature, and in the identity of the one Godhead," says Athanasius.

> For the radiance also is light, not second to the sun, nor a different light, nor from participation of it, but a whole and proper offspring of it. And such an offspring is necessarily one light; and no one would say they are two lights, but sun and radiance two, yet one the light from the sun enlightening in its radiance all things.[43]

These preliminary considerations reflect the Nicene reliance on the belief that the fulfillment of the Son's pre-existent life and the subsequent promise of life and light, as recorded in Hebrews 1:3, was requisite for using the concept of light to distinguish the first and second persons of the Trinity.[44] With regards to the Son's pre-existence and co-equality with the Father, Athanasius asks, "Is it reasonable [that] a man should say that the Son is not always?" Again, the response to this Arian notion was in the negative: "Who can even imagine that the radiance of light ever was not, so that he should dare to say that the Son was not always, or that the Son was not before his generation."[45] Here, in his gloss on Hebrews 1:3, Athanasius traces this light to its foundation in the Son's eternal relation to the Father. If there is indeed

---

41. Athanasius, *c. Ar.* 1.9 (PG 26:26; NPNF 4:311).

42. It is imperative that we interpret the phrase "light from light" as being *one* light, rather than as one light kindled from another. This latter form of the metaphor is criticized by Athanasius: "For the saints have not said that the Word was related to God as fire kindled from the heat of the sun, which is commonly put out again, for this is an external work and a creature of its author, but they all preach of him as radiance" (*De decr.* 23 [PG 25:456; NPNF 4:165]). It was, however, used by several ante-Nicene theologians (e.g., Titian) on the grounds that it safeguards the real subsistence of the Word. But Gnosticism seems to have used it in several forms of the radiance of the eons. For more on the ante-Nicene position, see Ayres, *Nicaea and its Legacy*, 248–50.

43. Athanasius, *c. Ar.* 3.66 (PG 26:464; NPNF 4:395).

44. Heb 1:3 was a seminal text for Athanasius and many of the fathers in establishing and defending the pro-Nicene logic of the identity of the second person of the Trinity, namely, the vocabulary of *homoousion*. See Kannengiesser (ed.), *Handbook of Patristic Exegesis*, vol. 2; and Edwards, *Catholicity and Heresy*, esp. 132–34.

45. Athanasius, *De decr.* 12 (PG 25:441; NPNF 4:157–58).

a present illumination for human creatures, it can only be because the life of the incarnate Son of God was "very light (*autophōs*) . . . and brightness."[46]

How, then, does the Son have light which, in turn, he imparts to human creatures? Athanasius proves a good guide here, especially in his constant use of "radiance" (*apaugasma*):

> The blessing was secure, because of the Son's indivisibility from the Father. . . . And this one may see in the instance of light and radiance [*apaugasma*]; for what the light enlightens, that the radiance irradiates; and what the radiance irradiates, from the light is its enlightenment. So also when the Son is beheld, so is the Father, for he is the Father's radiance; and thus the Father and the Son are one.[47]

The Son therefore has light *en autō* as the Father has light *en autō*. The Son's having light *en autō*, as a mode of divine light, at one and the same time, for Athanasius, distinguishes the Son from creatures and grounds the believers as being "'delivered' to him . . . as to light, to illumine the darkness."[48] This is light as the eternal existence of the Father and Son. Yet to this immanent reality there corresponds the Son's work; the light that the Son receives and has in himself is that which he in turn shines upon human creatures, for "Christ has come, and . . . he illumines absolutely all with his light."[49] Athanasius is, of course, acutely aware of the gap between God and human creatures, as he states against the Arians: "He indeed has gained nothing from us." Similarly, human creatures only have light in Christ, not in themselves; *autophōs* or *apaugasma* is entirely inexpressible, and so the identity of "Son" and divine "light" and "radiance" cannot be replicated in the creaturely realm. But if light differentiates the divine Son from human creatures, it is also at the same time the soteriological ground of the fact that he has "shone in our hearts to give the light of the knowledge of the glory of God" (2 Cor 4:6).

These important christological claims from Athanasius resulted in the influence of additional interpretations of the Son's relation to the Father. At the end of the fourth century, for instance, the Cappadocian heirs to Athanasius were beginning to read Nicaea in a particular way, one that insisted upon the logic of the *homoousion*. In perhaps a retracing of Athanasius's earlier Christology, Gregory Nazianzen argued against the Arian concern that "ingeneracy" (*agenēsía*) constitutes divinity. He therefore highlighted

---

46. Athanasius, *c. Gen.* 46 (PG 25:93; NPNF 4:29).
47. Athanasius, *c. Ar.* 3.13 (PG 26:349; NPNF 4:401).
48. Athanasius, *Illud Omnia, etc.* 2 (PG 25:212; NPNF 4:88).
49. Athanasius, *Inc.* 40 (PG 25:163; PPS 44b:93).

two key elements in this understanding of the relation between God the Father and God the Son. First, the Father's timelessness made his relation to the Son one that did not involve priority in any temporal sense.[50] Second, the Son's being "begotten" (*gennēsía*) of the Father is wholly spiritual, devoid of the notions of passion and division which the Arians read into the act.[51] In consequence, the Father's relation to the Son, Gregory says, cannot contain any priority in the sense of superiority or inferiority. Rather, the *gennēsía* of the Son "reflects" the *agennēsía* of the Father. In doing so, we find that the relations of the Holy Trinity have "internal ordering known only to itself,"[52] much like a "threefold light forms one single radiance."[53] Concluding against the "Arian quibbles," Gregory states that it is thus evident that the Father is not necessarily prior to the Son (and the Holy Spirit), "just as the sun is not prior to its light."[54]

Such foundational dogmatic language regarding the relation of the Son and the Father did not, however, reside solely in its Eastern expression. Set squarely in the generation following Nicaea, the Western interpretation of Nicene Christology came from the capable pen of Ambrose.[55] For Ambrose, the image of light—particularly found in Hebrews 1:3 and 1 Timothy 6:16—was an essential concept for affirming the relationship of the Father and the Son: "the Son is the Radiance of his Father's light, co-eternal, because of eternity of power; inseparable, by unity of brightness."[56] The anti-Arian rhetoric here is evident, especially as Ambrose moves to address the Homoian notion of "there was once when he was not" residing at the surface of the debates in the West:

> As one who is for ever, as the Word, as the brightness of eternal light, for brightness takes effect in the instant of its coming into existence.... Think not, then, that there was ever a moment of time when God was without wisdom, any more than that there was ever a time when light was without radiance.... So, then,

---

50. See Gregory Nazianzen, *Or.* 29.3 (PG 36:77; NPNF 7:301–2).

51. See ibid., 29.4.

52. Ibid., 6.22 (in Vinson [trans.], *Select Orations*, 20; cf. PG 35:749).

53. Ibid., 40.41 (PG 36:417; NPNF 7:375). For more on the image of light in *Or.* 40, see McGuckin, *Gregory of Nazianzus*, 340–44.

54. Ibid., 29.3 (PG 36:77; NPNF 7:302).

55. Moreover, it is evident that Ambrose was heavily influenced by Basil and was acquainted with Athanasius's early arguments against Arianism. See, e.g., Basil's letter to Ambrose from 375 AD, *Letter 197* (NPNF 8:234–5).

56. Ambrose, *De fide* 4.108 (PL 16: 38; NPNF 10:276 [N.B. the incorrect numbering in NPNF as 4:109]): "... quia splendor paternae gloriae lucis est Filius: coaeternus, propter, virtuis aeternitatem: inseparabilis, propter claritudinis unitatem."

since God is Light, and the Son of God the true Light, without doubt the Son of God is true God.[57]

Like his Cappadocian counterparts, Ambrose displays a particular indebtedness to the conceptual range offered in the image of light as he rebutted the Western Homoian confusion with orthodox Christology.[58]

From Athanasius, the Cappadocians, and, indeed, the Latin West, we see that the fathers of the fourth century deemed that Christ alone is "very light" (*autophōs*), true God of true God, and that he alone is properly the Son of the Father; but through his divine activity, his shining forth, human creatures are reconciled in him. Pro-Nicene theology, thus broadly construed, applied the image of light to reject the notion that the Son is a created intermediary. Rather, as *autophōs*, the Son is the "one living Word," says Athanasius. Thus:

> there must be one perfect and complete living activity and gift whereby he [the Son] sanctifies and enlightens. This is said to proceed from the Father, because the Spirit shines forth [*eklampsousin*], and is sent, and is given from the Word, who is confessed to be from the Father.[59]

The Identity and Works of the Holy Spirit

Yet the concept of light was used with equal force in affirming the identity of the third person of the Trinity.[60] Pro-Nicene theology of the fourth century shows a deep conviction that the Holy Spirit reveals the identity of the Father in the Son, and the Son in the Father. Thus, it could be said by Gregory of Nyssa that the Holy Spirit

> ever "searches the deep things of God," ever "receives" from the Son, ever is being "sent," and yet not separated, and being "glorified," and yet He has always had glory. It is plain, indeed, that

---

57. Ibid., 1.79 (PL 16:547; NPNF 10:214): ". . . quia simul splendor operatur nascitur"; *Sp. sanc.* 1.14 (PL 16:706; NPNF 10:112).

58. For an insightful study of Ambrose's use of light in his theology (and hymnology), see Morgan, *Imagery of Light*. See also Davidson's commentary on Ambrose's use of the image of light in Ambrose, *De Officiis*, vol. 2. On the seemingly different nature of the Western Arian controversy to that of the East, refer to Williams, *Ambrose of Milan*.

59. Athanasius, *Ad. Ser.* 1.20.5 (PG 26:577; PPS 43:85).

60. Indeed, the later Constantinopolitan Creed affirmed the emphasis of the Spirit: ". . . the Holy Ghost, the Lord and Giver of life."

> one who gives glory to another must be found himself in the possession of superabundant glory; for how could one devoid of glory glorify another? Unless a thing be itself light, how can it display the gracious gift of light?[61]

Moreover, he is the one Spirit in whom the Father communicates himself to human creatures through his Son, and in whom human creatures have communion through the Son with the Father. For the pro-Nicene position, the Holy Spirit is the light in whose shining forth human creatures see the radiant light of God manifest in Jesus Christ. For, again, the Holy Spirit is

> Life and life-giver; light and light-giver ... the Lord, the Sender, the Separator ... by whom the Father is known and the Son is glorified; and by whom alone he is known. ... All that the Father has the Son has also, except the being ingenerate; and all that the Son has the Spirit has also, except generation. And these two matters do not divide the substance, as I understand it, but rather are divisions within the substance.[62]

The Holy Spirit—"the Lord, the Sender, the Separator"—is indeed present among human creatures, Nyssa reminds us, but he is present in his radiant way of being, who as co-eternal with the Father and the Son, is therefore

> the place of the saints, and the saint is the proper place for the Holy Spirit. ... So, then ... we speak of worship in the Spirit as worship in him who manifests the divinity of the Lord. Therefore, in worship the Holy Spirit is inseparable from the Father and the Son. ... For it is impossible to see the Image of the invisible God, except in the illumination of the Spirit, and it is impossible for him who fixes his eyes on the image to separate the light from the image [except by the Spirit].[63]

In this way, God the Father, God the Son, and God the Holy Spirit in their indivisible triunity shine through to us in their three-fold light.[64] For "No sooner do I conceive of the One than I am illumined by the splendor of the

---

61. Gregory of Nyssa, *Sp. sanc.* (NPNF 5:233–34).

62. Gregory Nazianzen *Or.* 41.9 (PG 36:442; NPNF 7:382).

63. Basil, *Sp. sanc.* 26.62, 64 (PG 31:183; PPS 42:101, 103); cf. ibid., 22.53.

64. Cf. Athanasius, *Ad. Ser.* 1.30.5: "And when the Spirit is in us, the Word who gives the Spirit is in us, and the Father is in the Word. And so it just as has been said: I and the Father will come and make our home with him. For wherever there is Light, there is also Radiance; and wherever there is Radiance, there is also its activity and luminous grace" (PPS 43:10; PG 26:601).

three," says Gregory in a well-known passage. "No sooner do I distinguish them than I am carried back to the One. When I contemplate the three together, I see but one torch, and cannot divide or measure out the undivided light."[65]

For pro-Nicene trinitarian theology, the Holy Spirit is the seal that while the eternal being of God transcends creaturely understanding he is not distant from human creatures, for the Holy Spirit is the radiant movement of his being whereby he makes himself available to creaturely knowing. Basil could thus state that "in the illumination of the Spirit . . . he shows in himself the glory of the only-begotten and furnishes to true worshippers the knowledge of God himself. The way, then, to knowledge of God is from the one Spirit, through the one Son, to the one Father."[66] Yet at the same time, he warned, "we ought to know about what we can speak and about what we must keep silent. Not all words can be uttered by the tongue. For fear that our intellect . . . will lose even the light that it has."[67]

It is through communion with the Holy Spirit, who is in Christ and is himself God of God, "Light and light-giver," that human creatures are therefore lifted up to have a share in the knowledge of God, and yet at the same moment are confined by the majesty of God's being from transgressing the bounds of worshipful and biblical analysis. Thus the fourth-century fathers, in tracing the pattern of the concept of light as used in Holy Scripture, could summarily echo the apostle Paul:

> For what we proclaim is not ourselves, but Jesus Christ as Lord, with ourselves as your servants for Jesus' sake. For God, who said, "Let light shine out of darkness," has shone in our hearts to give the light of the knowledge of the glory of God in the face of Jesus Christ (2 Cor 4:3–6).

What our summary of the dogmatic use of light by pro-Nicene trinitarian theology shows us is that the concept was imperative for defining the relationship of God the Father and God the Son and for conveying the guarantee of the radiant nearness of God in the activity of the Holy Spirit. This language was one wholly beholden to the scriptural witness and, in the minds of the fourth-century fathers, necessary for the proclamation of the gospel. The fathers necessarily retrieved the concept of light for the doctrine of the Trinity, namely, for witness to and indication of God's way of being—Father, Son, and Holy Spirit. Such theological utterances about

---

65. Gregory Nazianzen, *Or.* 40.41 (PG 36:417; NPNF 7:375); cf. *Or.* 39.11.
66. Basil, *Sp. sanc.* 18.47 (PG 31:154; PPS 42:82–3).
67. Basil, *Adv. deos tres* 4 (PPS 47:275).

the Trinity had to "employ images or representations from the visible or tangible world to point out divine realities that cannot simply be reduced to words," Torrance rightly clarifies. Thus, they "arise under the activity of divine revelation and are adapted for special purpose."[68] Therefore, it was not that the fathers tried to define the Trinity by the "visible or tangible world," but that they tried to define the "visible or tangible world" *by* the Trinity in order to be able to speak about the Trinity in this world. The fathers did not believe that the Trinity is immanent *in* things—such as the sun, rays, or radiance—or that created light thus has *tertium comparationis* in the Trinity itself. Rather, the Trinity was "just like" these things—namely, light—though at the same moment "nothing like that light with which we are acquainted."[69]

Light, Contingency, and the Divine Economy

What are we to make of this dogmatic claiming of the scriptural occurrence of the image of light? How might our study proceed from such conceptual boundaries and trinitarian definitions?

We might initially state that light is an essential concept in Christian theology that is defined positively by the form of God's radiant way of being. More precisely: the concept of light points to God's radiant form as Father, Son, and Holy Spirit. But the theological undertaking of the concept is not found in an apologetic venture imported into certain cosmologies in order to serve an Aristotelian "First Cause" of the universe.[70] Rather, the concept of divine light endeavors to give a description of the God who self-reveals *a priori* to the cognitive efforts of his human creatures. That is, God is objectively radiant, shining forth himself, outstripping any and all conceptual notions *in toto*, and yet making himself graciously perceptible and "speakable." At this point the repeated idiom from Irenaeus is worth committing

---

68. Torrance, "The Problem of Theological Statements Today," 49–50.

69. Irenaeus, *Adv. hær.* 2.13.4 (PG 7a:744; ANF 1:374). Prior this statement Irenaeus affirms that if God is light then he is *totus lumen* (2.13.3).

70. Most recently, John Polkinghorn uses the concept of light to speak of the primordial "electromagnetic radiation" that is present in the universe. That is, the universe is bathed in "Cosmic Background Radiation," a universal symbol of cosmic circumstances after the Big Bang ("Some Light from Physics," 17–27). Along the same lines, the underlying assumption in Iain M. Mackenzie's work is that through created light, God has "bestowed on creation a rationality which corresponds in its created dimension to the uncreated Rationality which he is as uncreated Light" (*'Obscurism' of Light*, 3). We return to several of these concerns in sub-sections below and also in chapter 2.

to memory: "He may most properly be termed light, but he is nothing like that light with which we are acquainted."

Yet the concept of light does not suggest that God is in a predicative "beyond" and thus cannot be found; nor is the Johannine confession "God is light" rendered a subservient Dionysian concept, making apophatic statements "more suitable" and cataphatic ascription of the language of light "unfitting."[71] The "speakability" of the concept of light does not ferry a set of ascriptive freight that, in effect, somehow lessen God's divinity. On the contrary: although God is "incomprehensible and invisible," he nevertheless "made himself visible and comprehensible within the capacity of the faithful, that he might give life to those who receive and see him through faith," says Irenaeus.[72] The concept of light, that is to say, is a positive concept applied to God by his gracious rendering of himself "visible and comprehensible," yet at the same time, God totally transcends the notion of the term.

We are therefore content to say that trinitarian theology is simply concerned to ensure that its thought and speech of divine light concentrates on that which is proper to the One that "may most properly be termed light." Therefore, concepts developed and metaphors used in articulating a trinitarian theology of divine light, must point to the divine reality of the triune God as he has given himself to be known. In short from Webster: concepts "must be converted, made serviceable by correction, above all through being filled out by descriptive reference to the event and name of God whom they attempt to indicate."[73]

Created Light and Uncreated Light

The use of the concept of divine light is therefore not primarily spoken of in a "contingent" manner, but rather as "descriptive reference" to the God

---

71. Pseudo-Dionysius, *De coel. hier.* 2.3 (PG 3:141); cf. *Works*, 150. Denys, in his use of the paradoxical pairing of apophasis and cataphasis in theological predication, nuances the images of "darkness" and "light" well beyond his example *here*. And it appears that the subsequent Byzantine tradition from Denys—namely John Damascene and Maximus the Confessor—used such terms in a qualified manner as well. However, we shall see in the following pages that the terms "darkness" and "light," when applied to God, are often transposed into making several theological claims that work against the positive pattern of ascription we find in much of Scripture.

72. Irenaeus, *Adv. hær.* 4.20.5 (PG 7a:1035; cf. ANF 1:489): ". . . et incomprehensibilis [et invisibilis] visibilem se, et comprehensibilem, et capacem hominibus [fidelibus] praestat, ut vivificat percipientes et videntes se [per fidem]. . . . Quemadmodum enim videntes lumen, intra lumen sunt, et claritatem ejus percipiunt."

73. Webster, "Immensity and Ubiquity of God," in *Confessing God*, 94.

it seeks to indicate. That is, the content of the term cannot be determined simply by analysis of the difference between God and creatures, between the Creator and creation, or between the "parallel in the nature" in which created light "corresponds . . . as a pointer to the nature of the uncreated Light which God is."[74]

The worry of correspondence and contingency arises from several interpretations of the ancient discussion of "uncreated light" (*agenetos phōs*) and "created light" (*epoiēsen phōs*) in the Eastern interpretive tradition of the church. For instance, echoing much of Gregory Nazianzen's work,[75] Byzantine Hesychasm affirmed that the light of Jesus Christ in his transfiguration on Mt. Tabor is identical with the eschatological light of the coming kingdom, a light that likewise "transfigures" the human creature and all creation.[76] According to Palamas, once the human intellect has been winnowed through mental and physical asceticism, it is thus graciously illumined by God, beholding divine light and becoming light in that vision.[77] In this mystical experience, the subject and the means of vision are light: in the vision of this divine uncreated light, everything becomes luminous in the union with light. The transfiguration of Christ, therefore, was the instance of the paradoxical vision of the uncreated light by human eyes. Thus, Palamas: "This mysterious light, inaccessible, immaterial, uncreated, deifying, eternal, this radiance of the Divine Nature, this glory of the divinity, this beauty of the heavenly kingdom, is at once accessible to sense perception and yet transcends it."[78] Human creatures are to see the divine light of God's self-revelation with their physical eyes, but eyes as they have been transformed by the Holy Spirit; the immaterial light of God will be seen by material eyes, but through a power other than the human power of vision. Thus, for Byzantine theology, "light was a way of saying something about

---

74. Mackenzie, '*Obscurism*' *of Light*, 109.

75. See Gregory Nazianzen, *Or.* 21.1 (PG 35:1084): "What the sun is in the realm of the senses, God is in the noetic realm." Gregory employs the concept of light to compare the created light with the uncreated light of God: like the physical sun, God is dangerously bright to human perception (cf. *Ors.* 2.76; 12.4; 17.8; 20.1; 32.15). See also Beeley, *Gregory of Nazianzus*, esp. chs. 2 and 4.

76. For further background, see Meyendorff, *Byzantine Theology*, 76–8; *Gregory Palamas*, 52–70; and Hunt, "Byzantine Christianity," 73–93. Regarding the philosophical nuance of the light of Tabor in theophanies, see Louth, "Light, Vision, and Religious Experience in Byzantium," 85–103.

77. Palamas, *Triads* 2.3.36. It must be noted that this is the Taboric, eschatological light.

78. Ibid., 3.1.22.

the reality of the encounter, rather than a way of describing its psychological modalities."[79]

But ancient Byzantium does not strictly reveal the worrisome "contingent" notion we are after in our examination of the use of the concept of light, although the intellectual world of the fifth-century provides a rich foundation for contemporary use of the concept.[80] That is, the Hesychast use of the image of light employs the *agenetos phōs* as a literal image for both the glory of God and the resulting illuminating power present in the mind of the human creature. It is not, to the contrary, a substance or somehow a collapse into the *epoiēsen phōs*. But confusion arises when a contingent comparison between uncreated light and created light is allowed to wholly define the concept.

This point is worth highlighting, not least because the use of the concept of light is often marked by contingent or comparative interpretations, particularly by theologians with deep investments in natural theology. What this often means for the concept of light is that created light is conceptually collapsed into the uncreated, divine light of the triune God.[81] And the assumption of a collapse of created light and uncreated light into a contingent notion of light rests on the same logic as is found in the notion of natural revelation and the doctrine of the works of God *ad extra*, as classically relayed by Bonaventure:

> In the world there are traces in which we can see the reflection of our God. For since the apprehended species is a likeness produced in the medium and then impressed upon the organ itself, and by means of that impression leads to its principle and source. This clearly suggests that the eternal light generates a likeness of itself.[82]

79. Louth, "Light, Vision, and Religious Experience in Byzantium," 100.

80. For a detailed survey of the history of Christian mysticism, see Louth, *Origins of the Christian Mystical Tradition*.

81. See, e.g., Begbie regarding the notion that the "diverse particulars of creation" are like the "threefoldness of the creator" ("Natural Theology and Music," 576). Regardless of recent attempts to make natural theology more "complex" in its approach to revelation—and thus less capable of being maligned—the conclusion still holds true for theologians of natural religion, as relayed by Paul Ewart: "the order and disorder of nature reflects the character of the creator" ("The Physical Sciences and Natural Theology," 428).

82. Bonaventure, *Itinerarium* 2.7 (*Opera* 5): ". . . omnia sunt vestigia, in quibus speculari possumus Deum nostrum. Nam cum species apprehensa sit similitudo in medio genita et deinde ipsi organo impressa et per illam impressionem in suum principium, scilicet in obiectum cognoscendum, ducat; manifeste insinuate, quod illa lux aeterna generat ex se similtudinem."

Such soundings in the history of theology might trace their pedigree back to a seminal theological resource, namely, to a trajectory of arguable Platonist influence in Augustine.

Augustine's theological interpretation of Plato proves influential for contemporary contingent notions of light. We might stress the word *interpretation* here in order to caution against the reading of Augustine's approach to Platonic *loci* simply as an instance of "ancient thought baptized," as some have suggested.[83] Rather, Augustine's reading of several Platonic images—including light—reveals both the conceptual interrelation of Plato and the Western father, and also the contextual separation of the two into the spheres of philosophy and biblical exegesis.[84]

Thus, in turning to the doctrine of creation in his exegesis of the book of Genesis, *De Genesi ad litteram*, Augustine offers a watershed reading of uncreated light and created light—the latter he understands as both physical light and the light of the human mind. Though Augustine calls it created light, he nevertheless holds that it is a reflection of the divine, uncreated light, and that it involves a participation by the human mind in that divine light. He could therefore propose a non-material substance; that is, in terms of his concept of light, both uncreated light and the *habitus mentis*, the capacity of the mind, could be understood as "true analogies" with physical light.[85] Thus, for Augustine, the words of Genesis 1:9 indicate the already illumined existence of the first created *intellectualis vita*, which when "turned to its Creator to be illumined . . . the decree, 'Let there be light,' spoken by the Word of God has been fulfilled."[86] The creation therefore contains within it archetypal divine ideas, or *rationes aeternae*, of the identity and light of the Creator. It also bears a closer resemblance to the Creator in the higher levels of the *analogia entis*, granting that the higher the order of the creature, the closer it stands in relation to the divine being. Augustine had found significant ground for the notion, moreover, in the first chapter of Genesis, where the revealed action of the entire Trinity in the creation of light was described. The questions surrounding the connection between these passages in the first chapter—that is, the connection between created and uncreated light—were posed by Augustine in the following manner:

---

83. See, e.g., Rist, *Augustine*.

84. Regarding Plato's influence on Augustine, see Nash, "Philosophic Sources," 47–66.

85. See our brief overview of the Augustinian approach to the theory of illumination below in chapter 5.

86. Augustine, *Gen. litt.* 1.17 (PL 34:252–53): ". . . quae nisi as Creatorem illuminada converteretur. . . . factam est quod in Verbo Dei dictum est. *Fiat lux*."

> What is the light itself which was created? Is it something spiritual or material? In this supposition, we must understand that when God said, "Let there be light," and light was made, the creature, called by the Creator himself, underwent a conversion and illumination.[87]

It is here that several problematic modern interpretations of the image of light find their conceptual grounding.[88] One particular proposal worth noting is found in the "Radical Orthodox" approach of Catherine Pickstock, whose work betrays a retrieval of certain contingent leanings in Neo-Platonism which fatally collapses created light into the uncreated light of God.[89]

Pickstock begins her study by stating that God is "light," indeed as uncreated light and, in company with Augustine, as "the pure light of love."[90] This light is said to be "invisible and spiritual," yet it is integrally linked with created light. "For the light we now see," says Pickstock, "is *literally*, and not merely analogically, 'a glance of the glory of God.'"[91] Moreover, God's light and created light are said to be "shared without diminution," and, as such, the eternal light of God "perpetually shines."[92] This seems to imply that God's being is incomparable at some level, at least in terms of his self-revelation, yet at the same time "God is at once the things we seek to

---

87. Ibid. (PL 34: 218–19): "Creatore, conversion ejus facta atque illuminata intelligator."

88. Cf. the studies already mentioned above: O'Collins and Meyers (eds.), *Light from Light*; and Vaux and Yeo (eds.), *Theology of Light and Sight*. Yet Mackenzie's study is once again before us in the following pages. Of note is his insistence that light is "the creaturely reflection, the created reflection, of the will and purpose of the uncreated light" ('*Obscurism*' *of Light*, 63).

89. Without belaboring the point, "Radical Orthodoxy" supposes that the Neo-Platonic ontology of participation is the ground *par excellence* for a Christian ontology of participation, which, in turn, founds the proper conditions for the doctrine of the Trinity. This seems a rather upended reading of Augustine. An example of this is seen in the notion of participation in the trinitarian life as relayed by Michael Hanby's reading of *De trinitatis*: "[B]oth 'form' and 'content' of our participation are doxological, and this marks at once *both* our participation in the Son's response to the Father and our reception of the gift of the Holy Spirit shared between the Father and the Son" (*Augustine and Modernity*, 55). For an outline and, in some cases, critique of Radical Orthodoxy, see Smith, *Introducing Radical Orthodoxy*.

90. Pickstock, "What Shines Between," 118. Cf. Augustine's thought that love is equal to dwelling in God's light (*Trin.* 8.12–13).

91. Ibid., 118–19 (emphasis mine). Pickstock is here quoting Smart, *Jubilate Agno*, 372.

92. Ibid., 111–12.

know and His own mediation."[93] The world of creation, Pickstock continues, is said to have its own rationalities, which are summed up under the headings of various Neo-Platonic terms: "pathway," "rationality," "desire," and seminally, *metaxu*.[94] The creation is finally said to possess properties of rationality and noetic resolution in the image of created light.[95] Created light is thus conceived as visible, intelligible, stable, contingent, and reliable in a way that creates a "pathway" to these features as eminently instantiated by God. In a passage from Pickstock, we find the Platonic lineage: "Mimicking the imperceptible rapidity of light's own diffusion . . . one's own . . . inner-illumination discloses something, but what it discloses is things of this world disclosing God."[96]

"What was the light itself that was created?" we might ask Pickstock on behalf of Augustine. "Is it something spiritual or material?" Pickstock's answer follows: Created light *necessarily* mediates knowledge of God. And as created light perpetually shines in the world, so our discernment of objects reflecting the knowledge of God likewise shines. Created light therefore "shows the way," both in its refracting to us objects that "desire" to be known and also "beaming forth from us as desire," so too does God's eternal light meet with created light in the "lives of particular people who follow Christ under the prompting of His Spirit."[97] There is thus a contingent relation between created and uncreated light: "The manifestation of light in the diverse particularities of creation—consummated in Christ—co-belongs in equal measure with the source of light."[98] The noetic status of created light is therefore paramount for human knowledge of God, for "whenever we know anything at all, we already (whether we know it or not) recognize, know and love God."[99] Thus physical light itself, in a rather Socratic way, "shocks" the learner into recollecting the divine already apparent around human creatures.

Pickstock's ideas regarding God and creation, we might say, seem to trace their course in a rather *ad hoc* manner. Pickstock affirms God as

93. Ibid., 112.

94. Ibid., 109. When Pickstock uses the term "metaxu," she is referring to William Desmond's concept, where analogy expresses something of reality. Desmond, and subsequently Pickstock, affirm a "metaxological" reality, where a participatory metaphysics best preserves "reality" (see Desmond, *God and the Between*, 116–58). Of course, *metaxu* (the "in-between") is an important term from Plato's *Symposium* 203b–c.

95. Ibid., 117.

96. Ibid., 109.

97. Ibid., 118.

98. Ibid (emphasis mine).

99. Ibid., 118–19.

uncreated light; however, she wishes to coordinate the uncreated light of God with the created light of the world. Moreover, it appears that what is missing from Pickstock's thought is an integration of her ideas of uncreated light with that of divine unity and triunity. If divine unity, or *simplicitas*, logically requires the idea that God's difference from the world is absolute, then "the light of this One" would need to be, in the words of Augustine, "far beyond all things."[100]

Indeed, we may stay with Augustine as a critique to Pickstock, as he expressly added to his exhortation that dissimilarities are to be found even in the similarities; or, put in our terms, by the fact that the concept of light is to be defined by the radiant identity of the triune God:

> For the sun also is a light, but it is corporeal; and the spiritual creature is also light, but it is not unchangeable. The Father, therefore, is light, the Son is light, and the Holy Spirit is light; but together not three lights, but one light.[101]

Therefore, Augustine again:

> God is light. I know that any man might say, "The sun is light, and the moon is light, and a lamp is light." But it ought to be far greater than these, far more excellent, and far more surpassing. How much God is distant from the creation, as far as the Maker from the making, from Wisdom and that which has been made by Wisdom, far beyond all things ought the light of this One be.[102]

We seek to clarify, pace Pickstock, that God's radiant being does not need this association with the creaturely realm and its "lights." Rather, God's light "ought to be far greater than these." God's light is "far greater" by the sheer fact that he exists; he exists namely as "a creative agency of unrestricted power and undiminished glory."[103] Once again, therefore, the contrast between divine light and creaturely "light" is colloquial, merely a corollary of the essential confession: "God is light." God's light is not a reflection of contingency; nor is it interchangeable with the concept of darkness, as we heard in the sweep of our scriptural survey above. Rather, God's light is a feature of the radiant identity of God.

100. Augustine, *In Ep. Joh.* 1.4 (PL 35:1981).
101. Augustine, *Trin.* 7.6 (PL 42:938–39): "Est enim et sol iste lumen, sed non incommutabile. Lumen ergo Pater, lumen Filius, lumen Spiritus sanctus: simul autem non tri alumina, sed unum lumen."
102. Augustine, *In Ep. Joh.* 1.4 (PL 35:1981).
103. Wood, "Maker of Heaven and Earth," 385.

God's Economic Activity

Easing the tension between uncreated light and created light might be further accomplished by looking at how the concept of light is deployed in articulating God's economic activity. A model from the interpretive tradition is useful here, not only for exhibiting a further chastening of the "contingent" notion of light, but also for a glimpse into the forthcoming theological discussions of our study.

In his *Commentarius in evangelium Ioannis*, John Calvin turns to expound upon the radiant activity of God as found in John 1:4.[104]

> God, therefore, is the one who gives us life; but He does so through the eternal Word. . . . But because God kindles their minds with his light, it follows that they were created to the end that they might acknowledge that he is the sole author of such a unique blessing. And when the light of this One permeated us from the Word its source, it ought to be a kind of mirror in which we may see clearly the divine power of the Word.[105]

For Calvin, the Son's life *in se* is a light that "permeates us" from on high. Therefore, created light is a "borrowed light," whereas "Christ is *the light*, shining from himself and by himself, and enlightening the whole world by his radiance; so that no other source or cause of splendor is anywhere to be found." That is, "Christ, as the eternal light, has a splendor which is natural [to him]."[106] Calvin's imagery indicates the practical aspects of divine light, specifically that:

> God . . . is called the Father of light, and also light, [and] we first understand that there is nothing in him but what is bright, pure, and unalloyed; and secondly, that he so illuminates all things by his brightness that he lets nothing vicious or perverted, no spots or filth, no hypocrisy or fraud, lie hidden. Hence the sum of what is said is that, since there is no agreement between light and darkness, we are separated from God so long as we walk in darkness; and that therefore the fellowship which he mentions can only exist if we also become pure and full of light.[107]

The radiance of God is actual, for "there is nothing in him but what is clear, pure, and unalloyed." But the light in which God alone lives "illuminates all

---

104. "In him was life, and the life was the light of all people."
105. John Calvin, *Comm. Ioannis* 1.4 (CO 47:5; CC 17:32).
106. Ibid., 1.9 (CO 47:8; CC 17:37): "Erat lux vita."
107. John Calvin, *Comm. Ioannis ep.* 1.5 (CO 55:303–4; CC 22:163).

things by his brightness." The form of this life-giving abundance of God's light is the Son, the *lumen vivificum*. "Yet this meaning must be grasped," Calvin clarifies, "that as the sun discovers to our eyes the most beautiful theatre of earth and heaven and the whole order of nature, so God has visibly displayed the chief glory of His work in His Son."[108] Thus, the divine will is not simply to retain light as something hidden and dark, but rather "to dispel the darkness and to kindle in us the light of God."[109]

Calvin's thoughts on this image propose several themes that will occupy the remainder of our study. First, light is not only the absence of an external illumination but the eternal light of God *in se*.[110] Second, this light cannot be understood without the relations of Father, Son, and Holy Spirit; its radiance comprises the mutual light of the Father, Son, and Holy Spirit. Finally, this light cannot be regarded apart from its brightness in shining forth to human creatures.[111] God's light, although it signals God's utter difference from human creatures, does not entail his utter isolation; rather, God's light includes an outshining of love.

Yet as we viewed with Pickstock, a misunderstanding of the divine identity occurs whenever a collapse of uncreated light and created light determines the notion of divine light itself. Instead of pointing towards the radiant being of God, the concept instead seeks to reflect the nature of contingent reality; it becomes a matter of God's "creating light" so as to "make visible" his "uncreated Light";[112] it becomes a matter of the "natural bond . . . between created light and uncreated Light";[113] it becomes a merely "mundane" metaphor or analogy snatched from the "perceived properties of light" and predicated about God.[114] The content of the concept of light is therefore distorted; it is no longer a positive proclamation of God's glorious being and his gracious action in the economy, but rather a generic utterance regarding "the god of this age" (2 Cor 4:4). With this abstraction, light is expounded in terms of the contingency of the world. As Calvin reminds us, however, we must always keep before us the fact that created light is a "borrowed light," whereas God in his triune identity is *the light*, "shining from

---

108. Calvin, *Comm. Ioannis* 8.12 (CO 47:240; CC 17:369).

109. Calvin, *Comm. Ioannis ep.* 1.6 (CO 55:304): ". . . ut discussis tenebris lucem Dei in nobis accendat."

110. See chapter 2.

111. See esp. chapter 3.

112. Yeo, "Light and New Creation," 47.

113. Mackenzie, *'Obscurism' of Light*, 167.

114. This is Tanner's concession in "Perceived Properties of Light," esp. 130.

himself and by himself, and illuminating the whole world by his radiance; so that no other source or cause of splendor is anywhere to be found."

Conclusion

Our initial exposition sketched here argues that the concept of divine light must be grounded in the setting and logic of the Trinity and the gospel. When a separation from the trinitarian *antepraedicamenta* takes place, the content of light is made into something merely contingent. However, if our study seeks to offer a constructive revision, then we can only do so as the notion of divine light is articulated together with the doctrine of the Trinity. Yet as our study progresses in reflecting upon the image of light and Christian *loci*, we must keep before us the fact that theological concepts are truthful only as they are graciously granted to human creatures in service to the logic of the gospel of Jesus Christ. As Barth reminds us, such "illumination" must be "*granted* to the creature" from the very "presence of the Creator."[115] The concept of light, therefore, must become a matter of *granted* illumination by God, for "he is nothing like that light with which we are acquainted."

---

115. Barth, CD II.1:647 (emphasis mine); cf. KD II.1:730: "Wo Licht ist und leuchtet, da findet ja ein Belichten statt und also ein Belichtetwerden und also ein Lichtwerden auch eines Anderen, das als solches nicht Licht ist und ohne jenes Belichtetwerden nicht Licht werden könnte. . . . sondern eben aus der der Kreatur geschenkten Gegenwart des Schöpfers."

2

God's Shining Forth

The Light of the Father, the Son, and the Holy Spirit

> Contemplate the divine nature: permanent, immutable, inalterable, impassible, simple, incomposite, indivisible, unapproachable light, ineffable power, uncircumscribed greatness, supereminent glory.... There we find the Father, Son, and Holy Spirit, the uncreated nature, the lordly dignity, the natural goodness. The Father is the principle of all.... The Son shone forth from the Father's substance ... his equal in goodness, his equal in power, sharing in his glory.... The Spirit ... enlightens all so they may comprehend God.[1]

THE PREVIOUS CHAPTER DEVELOPED A CONCEPTUAL LIMIT THAT THEOLogy must take note of when talking about the light of God. This limit included the thought that theology will not situate what it has to say about divine light by way of linguistic deception, but rather it will take its lead from God's radiant form as *light in himself*. Because theological concepts must be situated with reference to God, a "contingent" notion of divine light can therefore only be replaced by a concept defined by the scriptural indication of the radiant identity of the triune God. Without such a basis, a theological concept of divine light will miss the mark of reflecting upon the way God reveals himself as distinct in three persons. More to the point: if "the mystery of the Trinity is unknown or denied," then the "whole economy of salvation is unknown or denied."[2]

---

1. Basil, *De fide* 1–3 (PPS 47:235–37).
2. Gerard, *Loci theol.* (Tübingen: Georgii Cottae, 1764 [1610]), 3.1.7: "Ignorato vel negate Trinitatis mysterio totus salutis *oeconomia* ignoratur vel negatur."

This second chapter therefore aims to communicate a clarification of this trinitarian trajectory. It proposes a twofold course with regard to a trinitarian theology of divine light. In the first section of the chapter, we will reflect upon the notion that *God is light in himself* is a fitting indicator of God's own radiant identity as Father, Son, and Holy Spirit, which includes the light of the *opera Dei ad intra*, the internal works of God. The second section finds the beginnings of much that is to follow in latter parts of our study by examining the notion that *from himself God shines forth his light*; that is, God's light bound up in his economic, covenantal, external works in which he "shines forth" to human creatures in the darkness of sin and death.[3]

The Light of the Father, the Son, and the Holy Spirit

God's light is the light of the One who has his own radiant identity. And this identity is his uniqueness as the One who exists in this precise manner. As the One who has this radiant identity, God is not an idle god; nor is he merely conceptual furniture in the human apologetic venture of *an sit Deus*. Rather, he is the self-determining One who is beyond the reach of any comparison or class because he "dwells in unapproachable light" (1 Tim 6:16). We therefore come upon the topic of God's triunity with needed restraint:

> Let us use great caution that neither our thoughts nor our speech go beyond the limits to which the Word of God itself extends. For how can the human mind measure off the measureless essence of God according to its own little measure, a mind as yet unable to establish for certain the nature of the sun's body, though men's eyes daily gaze upon it?[4]

When human thought and speech seeks to reflect upon this radiant identity, therefore, it does not seek to "measure off" by ascription, but rather God's triune identity is approached as the "adorable mystery" that is received "by faith and adored with love."[5]

In light of this caution and restraint, we confess that God receives this identity "through and from himself," for it is entirely self-derived.[6] Theo-

---

3. See our explanation of this twofold proposal—namely, *God is light in himself*, and *from himself God shines forth his light*—in the "Introduction" above.

4. Calvin, *Inst.* I.13.21; OS 3:136: "Quomodo enim immensam Dei essentiam ad suum modulum mens humana definiat . . . ?"

5. Turretin, *Inst.* III.q23.1.

6. Ibid., III.q23.4.

logical talk of the divine light, therefore, is not the projection of a creaturely category onto God; it is not the suggestion that there is some quality called "divine light," present everywhere in a contingent manner but found supremely embodied in God. Articulating the concept of God's light "does not declare a relationless excess of God's divinity which . . . must ultimately be, in its burning, a darkness unto people."[7] Nor is such talk merely a synonymous predication of a characteristic placed alongside other incommunicable divine attributes.

This last point is worth emphasizing, due to that fact that some might perceive within Christian talk of God's light a genitive gloss on several divine attributes—namely, aseity, simplicity, or relation.[8] It could therefore be said of this synonymous language that "light" does not (and perhaps ought not) do such work single-handedly in Christian theology. Contrary to this worry we simply state here, as we did in the previous chapter, that light is a theological theme that necessarily *has* to embrace all these concepts—from talk of God's aseity to God's inner co-equality—because the business of this image has to do with attending to the radiant identity of the triune God. Wolf Krötke is instructive on this point, particularly in his insistence that the doctrine of the divine attributes, or "clarities," are to be "understood as clarity of *the trinitartian God*."[9] Thus, the attributes of God are the "relationally rich *doxa*" of the triune God, which are "shown forth according to revelation." In short: "God's clarity is an event in *clarities* which are communicated when God relates himself to a reality outside of himself."[10]

Because Christian talk of light is a conceptual magnification of God's radiant identity, it does not therefore add to this identity nor surpass it, but

---

7. Krötke, *Gottes Klarheiten*, 105: "Die Metapher des Lichtes sagt darum nicht eine relationslose Überhelle der Göttlichkeit Gottes an, die . . . in ihrem Brennen für Menschen letztlich ein Dunkel sein muß."

8. As we noted in our scriptural survey in chapter 1, and as we shall see shortly, the biblical image of "light" encompasses the notion of "life"; and, given various patristic witnesses, "light" is an adequate pointer to the eternal divine *processio* in the Godhead. See, e.g., the forthcoming sub-sections below. Moreover, we find this identification quite magnificently perceived in Barth's insistence that life is light, or, more to the point, that "reconciliation is revelation" (CD IV.3.1:165).

9. Krötke, *Gottes Klarheiten*, 115: "Jede Klarheit Gottes ist als Klarheit *des trinitarischen Gottes* zu verstehen." See Christopher Holmes's clarification that the term "attribute," for Krötke, "is superseded by the term 'clarity', for the latter better indicates the extent to which God's glory—God's relationally rich reality—is communicated in God's concretions" ("God's Attributes as God's Clarities," 59).

10. Ibid., 103: "Gottes Klarheit ist Ereignis in *Klarheiten*, die mitgeteilt werden, wenn Gott sich auf eine Wirklichkeit außerhalb seiner selbst bezieht. Diese Klarheiten ermöglichen sowohl die Gotteserfahrung wie das Reden von Gott."

simply "declares" it as it has already been "declared." In other words, therefore, Christian talk of God's immanent light says at base what Holy Scripture already irrevocably states: "God is light," and says it in such a manner that "God" defines the content of "light," not vice versa.[11] Theological talk about divine light is therefore ascriptive, because such biblical language is "anarthrous and wholly irreversible."[12]

We might once again reiterate a guiding principle for this study: *God is light in himself*. If this holds, then at the beginning of this chapter we must insist that the identity of God is the identity of God the Trinity, distinct in three persons. It is the radiant identity of the God who, as Calvin notes, "proclaims himself as the sole God as to be contemplated in three persons."[13]

Triune Light and Life

"What," we might therefore ask with Barth, "is the more precise meaning ... of God as light in himself?"[14] First of all, we might answer that, according to scriptural witness, God's light is God's life.[15] Because "God *dwells* in unapproachable light," it is thus life precisely as God's life *in se*. This life is the relations of Father, Son, and Holy Spirit. Therefore, light is not a property anterior to God's triune life, but rather describes the absolutely original character of the relations that are God's life. The inner luminosity of the triune God is his reality in the personal *opera Dei ad intra*. These actions are personal relations, that is, modes of existence in which each person of the Trinity is identified in terms of relations to the two other persons. To be more precise: God's light is the radiant plentitude that he is in himself as Father, Son, and Holy Spirit. To speak of God's light is, therefore, an

---

11. Although we may not agree with much of Bultmann's existential exegesis of 1 John 1:5, he nevertheless makes an insightful observation by stating: "the reverse [i.e., 'light is God'] cannot be true." Yet prior to this statement he makes a critical error by commenting that the tautology "God is light" tells us nothing about the identity or essence of God (see *Johannine Epistles*, 16).

12. Davidson, "Divine Light," 62.

13. Calvin, *Inst*. I.13.2; OS 3:109: "... nam ita se praedicat unicam esse, ut distincte in tribus personis considerandum proponat."

14. Barth, CD II.1:643, 646; KD II.1:728–29.

15. The instances of this comparison are many in Scripture, from the creation narratives and wisdom literature (cf. Gen 1:3–5; Ps 36:9) to the mission of the Son pronounced in the NT. Concerning the latter, we find here, again, the NT instance of "life" and "light" in the prologue to the Gospel of John.

undertaking to exhibit a gloss of the Johannine statements: "God is light, and in him is no darkness at all" and "In him was life" (1 John 1:5; John 1:4).

Thus, God the Father, God the Son, and God the Holy Spirit is full of light in himself. And this light is "a dynamic Light," says Sonderegger, which "is altogether alive, personal, and intelligible."[16] Calvin further comments that God's incomprehensible nature dwells in this dynamic and inaccessible light.[17] God's incomprehensible nature is therefore the "expression of his majesty,"[18] which is not "confined to letters or syllables," because "his name is set before us as an image, as it were, so far as God reveals himself to us, and is known by his own characteristic marks themselves, just as men are each by his own name."[19]

Perhaps expanding on these thoughts from Calvin and Sonderegger: since God's light is his "characteristic mark" of his internal glory, and since it represents the dynamic, personal aliveness as the One he is, the image of light does not, therefore, signify some absence of power in God.[20] Rather, as our guiding principle states, *God is light in himself.* That is, God's light figures his manifold triune life, which is "a unity in essence," clarifies Aquinas, "because . . . the persons are co-equals [having] one majesty and essence."[21] The concern of a trinitarian theology of God's light is therefore to specify the particular light that is proper to God in which the relations between the divine persons is seen as God's undivided light. But we must stress that these relations do not somehow emanate from the undivided light, as secondary realities buttressed by a simple divine essence, for God the Father, Son, and Holy Spirit are "coequals [having] one majesty and essence." If such relations did emanate secondarily from this undivided light, it would be, as Aquinas warns, a "further medium" in which the "relationships would be multiplied to infinity."[22] Rather, "God is light primordially in the infinite liberty and uninhibited intimacy of his triune fellowship with himself."[23]

Yet to this we must quickly add that the concept of light does not reduce to the notion that God originates himself. Such a notion implies

---

16. Sonderegger, *Systematic Theology*, 1:348.
17. Calvin, *Inst.* III.20.40; OS 4:350; cf. I.13.1.
18. Calvin, *Comm. Ps.* 9.10 (CO 31:101; CC 4:120).
19. John Calvin, *Comm. Mosis*, "Ex Exodi" 20.7 (CO 24:560; cf. CC 2:409).
20. We note Denys Turner's recent retrieval of several aspects of medieval mysticism and apophaticism, in which the "God who is beyond" is actually a continual set of negative principles or negations (see *Darkness of God*, 272).
21. See, notably, Aquinas, ST 1a.q42.1: ". . . unius magnitudinis et essentiae."
22. ST 1a.q42.1: ". . . relatio multiplicaretur in infinitum."
23. Davidson, "Divine Light," 63–64.

that the Spinozan darkness of non-being is always lurking as the *ex sola* backcloth to God's radiant existence;[24] that "both darkness and light *together* [are] a divine emanation"; that an "originating light *generating*, and *elaborating* God . . . radiates into the world."[25] Nor is God "the eternal light in which . . . the divine life *becomes* conscious of its eternal beauty."[26] Such concepts are to be forcefully rejected. A trinitarian theology of divine light must be used not to conceive God on the basis of a generic metaphysics of causality—where God is "conditioned for existence and action by another cause"[27]—but rather to indicate the radiant identity of the divine being itself. For "we do not say that God creates, produces or originates Himself," Barth clarifies.

> On the contrary, we say that (as manifest and eternally actual in the relationship of Father, Son and Holy Ghost) He is the One who already has and is in Himself everything which would have to be the object of His creation and causation if He were not He, God. Because He is God, as such He already has and is His own being.[28]

Indeed, if a Spinozan understanding of divine light is accentuated too forcefully, it can suppress the features of the *opera Dei ad intra* on the grounds that such a notion appears to posit God as the "self-caused Cause" of ontological

---

24. We refer here to Benedict Spinoza's thoughts in his *Ethica*, 235–66. Several propositions are problematic: "By that which is self-caused, I mean that of which the essence involves existence, or that of which the nature is only conceivable as existent" (*Per causam sui intelligo id cujus essential involvit existentiam sive id cujus natura non potest concipi nisi existens*) (1.d1); and: "[T]he existence of substance must arise solely from its own nature, which is nothing else but its essence" (*quare ejus etiam existentia ex sola ejus natura sequi debet, quae proinde nihil aliud est quam ejus essentia*) (*Propositio* 11). For Spinoza, then, *est causa per se* can only be applied to God, which, in turn, is identical with *aeternus* (cf. 1.*ps*8.19).

25. Vaux, "Light and Sight," 6–7 (emphasis mine).

26. Moltmann, *Trinity and the Kingdom*, 176.

27. Spinoza, *Ethica* 1.*p*28.*dem*.: "causa . . . determinetur ad existendum et operandum."

28. Barth, CD II.1:306; KD II.1:344: ". . . daß er (wie es in dem Verhältnis des Vaters, des Sohnes und des Heiligen Geistes offenbar und in Ewigkeit wirklich ist) der ist, der in sich selber Alles schon hat und ist, was als sein Sein Gegenstand seines Schaffens, Hervorbringens, Verursachens sein müßte, wenn er eben nicht Er, wenn er nicht Gott wäre, der als solcher sein eigenes Sein immer schon hat und ist." Cf. Barth's amendment to the notion of *causa sui* as being a matter of God's self-realization if (and only if) this means that God is in no need of origination (ibid.).

monism, which the image of light aims at striking from the conception of the divine.[29]

In response, Anselm offers several clarifying thoughts as we approach the *opera Dei ad intra*:

> In what sense, then, are we to understand that [God] exists through himself and from himself, if he neither made himself, nor provided matter for himself, nor in any way helped himself to be what he was not already? It seems that perhaps this can be understood only in the same sense in which it is said that light shines, or is shining, through itself and from itself. For "light" and "to shine" and "shining" are related to each other in just the same way as "essence" and "to be" and "being."[30]

Anselm's question and answer provide a groundwork for furthering our discussion, particularly centered on the language of the divine generation and divine light. As we said in chapter 1: any "contingent" or "corresponding" approach to the notion of light when joined to the Trinity is to be rejected and instead a clarification is registered between the distinction of a "mutual light" in the immanent, common divine essence and "ingenerate light" properly associated to the Father, Son, and Holy Spirit in their own mode of subsisting.

The Light of the opera Dei ad intra

Pro-Nicene trinitarian theology once again offers us a particularly helpful dogmatic gloss on the topic of the inner relations of God precisely by its appeal to the biblical image of light. In doing so, it establishes a distinction between the light shared by all three persons by virtue of their sharing in the divine essence ("mutual light") and the light which is the personal property of the Father in his manner, the Son in his manner, and the Holy Spirit in his manner ("ingenerate light"). Gregory Nazianzen suggests such a formula in his comments on the Gospel of John:

> "He was the true light that enlightens every man coming into the world"—yes, the Father. "He was the true light that enlightens every man coming into the world"—yes, the Son. "He was the true light that enlightens every man coming into the

---

29. This is essentially what Spinoza means when he defines God as "an absolutely infinite being, that is, substance consisting of infinite attributes, each of which expresses eternal and infinite essence" (see, *Ethica* 1.d6).

30. Anselm, *Monologium* 6 (PL 158:152–53): "lux, lucere, lucens . . . essentia, esse, ens." Cf. *Monologion and Proslogion*, 17–18.

world"—yes, the Comforter. . . . [H]e was he was he was. There are three predicates—light and light and light. But the light is one, God is One. This is the meaning of David's prophetic vision: "In your light we shall see light." We receive the Son's light from the Father's light in the light of the Spirit . . . it is the plain and simple explanation of the Trinity.[31]

Gregory's "plain and simple explanation" is expounded by the particularly potent language of *homoousion* found in the logic of Athanasius:

> He [the Son] is the Same as God. For the radiance also is light, not second to the sun, nor a different light, nor from participation of it, but a whole and proper offspring of it. . . . [T]he Godhead of the Son is the Father's; whence also it is indivisible; and thus there is one God and none other but He.[32]

Thus, light, according to Athanasius and Gregory, is the lively and eternal relation of the Father and Son. "This example of the light means," Gregory of Nyssa concurs, "that the Son is to be conceived of inseparably with the Father."[33] And if "all that the Father has the Son has also, except the being unbegotten," then "all that the Son has the Spirit has also, except the generation."[34] The Holy Spirit's way of being is, therefore, co-eternal with the Father and the Son, in which he throws his eternal light upon the Father in the Son and upon the Son in the Father.

Consequently, all that the Father is can be seen in the Son and the Holy Spirit, and all that the Son and the Holy Spirit are in the Father, for they "shine forth" and are "sent and given."[35] Thus, the Father, accordingly, is light not only due to essence but also as a property of his own person; the Son is light not only due to essence but also as a property of his own person and mission; and, the Spirit is light not only due to essence but also as a property of his own person and mission. That is, they are "divided without division . . . they are united in division," says Gregory. "And when I speak of God you must be illumined at once by one flash of light and by three. Three in individualities or hypostases."[36] This highlights the guiding proposal

---

31. Gregory Nazianzen, *Or.* 31.3 (PG 36:136; PPS 8:118). See also Beeley's thoughts on this oration in *Gregory of Nazianzus*, 197–98; and McGuckin, "'Perceiving Light from Light in Light,'" 7–32.

32. Athanasius, *c. Ar.* 3.13 (PG 26:348; NPNF 4:395). See also Heron, "*Homoousios* with the Father," 58–87.

33. Gregory of Nyssa, *Letters* 35.7c–d (in Silvas [trans.], *Gregory of Nyssa*, 258).

34. Gregory Nazianzen *Or.* 41.9 (PG 36:441; NPNF 7:382).

35. See Athanasius, *Ad. Ser.* 1.20.5 (PG 26:577; PPS 43:85).

36. Gregory Nazianzen, *Or.* 39.11 (PG 36:348–49; NPNF 7:355).

we mentioned above, namely, that *God is light in himself*; and this radiant identity includes the mutuality of the Father's giving light to the Son and the Holy Spirit, who in their turn have light in themselves. We may again phrase this in pro-Nicene terms: all three persons are "mutual light" by virtue of their common divine essence, and each person is "ingenerate light" according to their one divine substance subsisting in three modes.[37]

At first sight, however, this distinction appears to disrupt a reading of divine light in terms of the personal relations that make up the Holy Trinity, precisely because it differentiates between a threefold "mutual light" and an "ingenerate light" proper to each person. This might be deemed to focus too much on some kind of Plotinian subordinationism or emanationism in which the "Light becomes dimmer the further it is from its Source."[38] For instance, if the Father's "ingenerate light" becomes definitive of the divine nature, then the personal properties *ad intra* of the filiation of the Son and the spiration of the Spirit may easily seem secondary to paternity. And when this happens, light becomes linked with a common divine essence *behind* the relations of the divine life. "And if someone says that this light is an independent reality, separate from the *nature* of Him Whom it signifies, of Whom it is only a symbol," Palamas says in highlighting our worry, "then let him show where and of what kind this reality is, which is shown by experience to be unapproachable.... So it is obvious and clearly demonstrated that this light is neither an independent reality, nor something alien to the divinity."[39] It is Moltmann, however, who posits a problematic reality behind God in the divine act of creation:

> Every stage in the creation process contains within itself the tension between the light flooding back into God and the light that breaks forth from him. In other words, every act outwards is preceded by an act inwards which makes the "outwards" possible.[40]

---

37. Cf. again, the later Constantinopolitan additions to the Nicene Creed: "We believe ... in one Lord Jesus Christ, the only-begotten Son of God, begotten from the Father before all time, Light from Light, true God from true God, begotten not created, of the same essence as the Father.... And in the Holy Spirit, the Lord and life-giver, Who proceeds from the Father, Who is worshiped and glorified together with the Father and Son" (in Leith [ed.], *Creeds of the Church*, 33).

38. On Plotinus's use of this term in regards to the doctrine of creation, see Gunton, *Triune Creator*, 35. See also Tanner's worry about this in "Perceived Properties of Light," 125.

39. Palamas, *Triads* 3.1.12, 17.

40. Moltmann, *Trinity and the Kingdom*, 110.

This withdrawal into such a principle of light is not necessary, however, and can be amended by appealing to the perichoretic character of the divine persons in the *opera Dei ad intra*, the free and glorious *opera Dei personalia*.[41]

Therefore, we might say that God's light is his radiant existence as the Father, the "ingenerate" one who is eternally the Father of the Son and the one from whom the Holy Spirit proceeds; God's light is his radiant existence as the Son, who is the "only-begotten" of the Father and who, with the Father, spirates the Holy Spirit; and God's light is his radiant existence as the Holy Spirit, who proceeds from the Father and the Son. The light of God is the "antecedently transcendent" *opera ad intra*.[42] This notion of *opera Dei ad intra*, the *Leiden Synopisis* clarifies, "is to be understood . . . as referring to an activity internal to God[;] . . . that is, the way God acts in his being so that, turned back on himself, he establishes a real relationship through the sharing of the divine essence."[43] Yet we must quickly add that the *how* of these "personal works" is, in Barth's estimation, "beyond the totally questionable truth of our own thoughts and words."[44] So, once again, we come to the matter of the eternal *opera Dei ad intra* by first confessing ignorance, lest we "go mad . . . for prying into God's secrets."[45]

Still, without spelling out the *how* of the inner works of God, we might go on to affirm that the light of God is not merely the property of being unbegotten, begotten, or the one who proceeds; rather, it is the radiant aliveness of the Father *a nemine*, the Son *a Patre*, and the Spirit *ab utroque*. Giving an account of God's light is thus to speak of the eternal movement of his existing as Father, Son, and Holy Spirit. This radiant movement is therefore founded by the fact that the three distinct eternal persons mutually exist in each other, in which their personal characteristics can be perceived.

What can be said of the properties of each person and of their relations must not propose, as some suggest, a society of fundamentally "distinct centers of self-consciousness, each with its own proper intellect, will, and action," which is thus bound into a unified whole, just as (analogously) the mythical beast "Cerberus has three brains and therefore three distinct states

---

41. The *opera Dei personalia*, the personal works of God, are stated here to distinguish the begetting of the Son and spirating of the Spirit from the *opera Dei essentialia*, the essential works of God.

42. See Barth's reflections on the notion of the eternal, "antecedent" begottenness of the Son, particularly in the creedal formulation of "Wir glauben an Jesus Christus als an den vom Vater vor aller Zeit Gezeugten" (KD I.1:447–52; cf. CD I.1:426–29).

43. Doctorum et Professorum in Academia Leidensi, et al., *Synopsis*, 9.10.

44. Barth, CD I.1:475; KD I.1:498.

45. Gregory Nazianzen, *Or.* 31.8 (PG 36:141; PPS 8:122).

of consciousness."⁴⁶ God's "mutual light" is not the product of his immanent relations, whatever this odd example of Cerberus might imply.⁴⁷ Still less is it a matter of a divine mathematical equation, where the sum of the relations equals the "unity of the collective."⁴⁸ Rather, the person of the Father, the person of the Son, and the person of the Holy Spirit may be identified by properties that distinguish each person and so are incommunicable. That is, the properties of each triune person simply specify what each divine person is in relation to the other persons—*relationes personales*—showing both the particular diversity and the particular unity within the being of the One God.⁴⁹

In pursuing such notions we do not seek to drive a wedge between the unity and triunity of the divine essence; the light of the Son and the Holy Spirit that they have as partakers in the One divine essence is not a quarantined instance from their personal properties as the one who is eternally generated and the one who eternally spirated. Moreover, it entails that we allow that the relations of the Godhead are not subordinate and that they are mutually perichoretic.⁵⁰ The Father is, according to his person, light only as he stands in relation to the Son and the Holy Spirit; his "very hypostasis . . . shines forth" in the Son and the Holy Spirit.⁵¹ The Father's light is not anterior to the act and relation of begetting and spirating. Yet this does not mean, as Calvin warns, that the relation of Father and Son and Holy Spirit is reversible, namely, that "the Father is the Son, and the Holy Spirit the Father, without rank, without distinction."⁵² Rather, it implies that the relation is mutual because the terms "Father, Son, and Spirit . . . imply a real distinction."⁵³

Above all, we need to grasp that God's light is his existence in these personal relations. God is light in himself in the mutuality of paternity ("that which it comes about that the Father is not made, not begotten"), filiation ("that which the Son receives and has in himself his whole and complete essence from the Father"), and spiration ("that by which the Holy Spirit

---

46. Moreland and Craig, "The Trinity," 30, 41.

47. Moreland and Craig eventually compare this with a view that "God is soul," and thus can contain "parts" of consciousness, will, and so forth (ibid., 41).

48. Swinburne, *Christian God*, 181.

49. See Athanasius, *c. Ar.* 2.62 (PG 26:280).

50. On the "inexpressible circuminsession" of the persons of the Trinity, see Turretin, *Inst.* III.q23.13–15.

51. Calvin, *Inst.* I.13.2; OS 3:109.

52. Ibid., I.13.4; OS 3:113.

53. Ibid., I.13.17; OS 3:131.

from eternity receives is the same complete essence from the Father and the Son").⁵⁴ Thus: *God is light in himself.*

But a necessary caution arises once again regarding our thoughts and speech about this immanent light of God. The *opera ad intra* are matters for thought in view of God's form *ad extra*. Yet the importance of the economy in the order of the intellect should not be misconstrued for the significantly different claim that "God actualizes himself in the world by his coming into it," or that the only substantial distinctions of God's inner trinitarian life are those "self-actualized" in "his acts in salvation history."⁵⁵ God's triunity is not merely "manifested and experienced in the history of salvation,"⁵⁶ nor is it strictly a matter of "what He is in relation to the world which He created."⁵⁷ On the contrary, Calvin clarifies, the economic eventually "has no effect on the unity of [God's] essence."⁵⁸ Yet the opposite distinction between "economic" and "absolute" must not be "pressed in such a way," Webster likewise warns, "that the 'absolute' acquires greater weight than the 'economic' in determining the *essentia dei*." Thus, in an account of the *opera Dei ad intra*, "theology does not seek to fall into a bifurcation of the *essentia dei* and God's revealed will and activity."⁵⁹

What therefore takes place in the *opera Dei ad extra*, the external works of God, is not a history in which God, as it were, "eternally and functionally subordinates himself,"⁶⁰ but rather a history occasioned by the divine

---

54. Bucanus, *Inst.* 3.12: "Paternitas proprietatem est incommunicabilis primae personae trinitatis, qua fit ut pater . . . non factus, non genitus, sed gignens ab aeterno filium. . . . generatio, sive filiation . . . qua filius accipit et in se habet totam et integram suam essentiam a patre. . . . Processio . . . qua spiritus sanctus, ab aeterno eandem illam et integram essentiam a patre et filio accipit et inse totam habet."

55. Pannenberg, *Systematic Theology*, 1:333, 392.

56. Moltmann, *Trinity and the Kingdom*, 158. See Moltmann's further thought that God's "eternal perichoresis" as Father, Son, and Spirit is seen perceived in "their opening of themselves for the reception and unification of the whole creation," and that the "economic Trinity" is somehow "perfected" and "completed" at an eschatological horizon, and thereafter "raised and transcended in the immanent Trinity" (ibid., 157, 161).

57. Brunner, *Dogmatics*, 1:247. More precisely, Brunner states that the "divine attributes . . . all point back to God's Nature, but they express this Nature of God *in relation to different aspects of the created world*" (emphasis mine). The terminus of the doctrine of the divine nature, according to Brunner, is thus "to reflect upon the basis of the Biblical revelation in relation to certain definite aspects of the created world" (ibid.).

58. Calvin, *Inst.* I.13.6; OS 3:116.

59. Webster, "Immensity and Ubiquity of God," 93.

60. This thought, usually ascribed to the eternal and functional subordination of the Son in the Godhead, is influential in some current American evangelical theology.

radiance external to creation, on the basis of which God shines forth into human time from beyond. Though there is no "before and after"[61] in God's eternal relations, there nevertheless is really a history of God among human creatures, seminally found in the mission of the Son as "the true light" of the world; but this takes place only because of God's light *in se*. In other words: the external works of the Trinity are undivided, that is, the *opera ad intra* of God ground his *opera ad extra*. The Son is therefore "of" the world, but he is this because he has been "sent into the world as light" (John 12:46) and is "the radiance of the glory of God" (Heb 1:3); the Holy Spirit is "with" believers, dwelling in them and illuminating them, only because he is "given" to them (John 14:16).[62] Being sent and being given "reflect." And in following this line of "reflection," we come to see that a discerned presence of God the Son and God the Holy Spirit in the world is the *opera divinitatis ad extra* of the eternal *opera trinitatis ad intra* within the radiant being of God.[63]

Several Outcomes

Before continuing on to examine the "reflection" of the internal works in the external works of God's saving acts, let us offer several outcomes of the notion that *God is light in himself*.

We began by restating that a trinitarian theology of divine light is a conceptual articulation of the radiant identity of the triune God. God is thus present to himself in the radiance of his triune being, and in this radiance he has no need of an external source of illumination: "God is and exists absolutely from himself and through himself."[64] But the light that is proper to him *in se* includes the repetition of his presence to a dark reality *ad extra*; only by a gnosticizing origin is God "the cause driven beyond itself to its cause."[65] Thus, as we shall soon see, the sphere of God's "mutual light," the

---

See, e.g., Grudem, *Systematic Theology*, 248–52; Kovach and Schemm, Jr., "A Defense of the Doctrine of the Eternal Subordination of the Son," 461–76; and Ware, *Father, Son, and Holy Spirit*, 21. See the various studies in Jowers and House (eds.), *New Evangelical Subordinationism?*

61. Calvin, *Inst.* I.13.8; OS 3:118. Cf. Calvin's statement that we cannot ascribe to God any "name which means that something new has happened to God in himself [*aliquid novum in seipso accidisse*]" (ibid.).

62. The *opera communia* of the *emanationes* of the Son and the Holy Spirit are examined in chapter 3.

63. This is Bucanus's language in his *Inst.* 3.14.

64. Polanus, *Synt. theol.* II.5: "Deus a se et per se absolute est et existit."

65. Cf. Paul Tillich's thoughts on comparative causality in the being of God (*Systematic Theology*, 1:196); and see also the notion of *Grundaxiom* from Rahner

immanent communion that he is as the Father who is unbegotten, the Son who is begotten, and the Holy Spirit who proceeds from both, is not an enclosed instance of radiance. This aliveness of the relations does not end at the internal works of God, the *opera Dei ad intra*. In its entirety, it is a light- and life-giving movement; God shines forth and meets those in darkness as their savior and communion- and covenant-creator. That is, God's radiant life includes his revelatory external works—though in these external works he "remains at the same time superior to them."[66]

One outcome of this is that, because God the Trinity is the mediator of his own radiant presence, he does not come before the human mind by the categorical result of human reflection in the "order of knowing";[67] nor is God called into the human creature's consideration of the mystery of "*theologia* in time, space, history, and personality."[68] That is, God's light is not found in that which it seeks to illumine—the object of God's shining does not "co-belong in equal measure with the source of light."[69] Rather, God's light is found in the source itself, in the luminous being of God. The light of God is therefore an outline of the identity of the One who beckons human creatures into his radiant presence.

Another outcome of the proposal that *God is light in himself* is what we have thus far proposed in the course of our study: the doctrine of the Trinity is the basis for any account of the light of God.[70] Without a functioning doctrine of the being and action of the triune persons in their unity—that is, the *opera Dei ad intra* and the *opera Dei ad extra*—a trinitarian theology of divine light will reduce to semantic duplicity. It will misread both the character of God's mutual and ingenerate light and the manner of his relation to the world; God's light *in se* will most naturally be thought of as causal will, and his works towards human creatures will be relegated to some remote cause, wholly unconcerned with the logic of the gospel.

We therefore append another principle to our former one: *from himself God shines forth his light*. That is, a trinitarian account of God's light will be concerned to specify the communion that God has in his own inner

(*Foundations of Christian Faith*).

66. Barth, CD II.1:260; KD II.1:291.

67. Gerrish, *Christian Faith*, 304. Gerrish is arguing, with Schleiermacher, that the doctrine of the Trinity, as a "product of reflection on revelation," ought to be discussed at the end of dogmatics, that is, after the "history of redemption and its sequel in the beginnings of the church have been told" (ibid.).

68. LaCugna, *God For Us*, 223.

69. Pickstock, "What Shines Between," 118.

70. See our conclusion to chapter 1.

luminosity and which he covenantally establishes with his human creatures. As Father, Son, and Holy Spirit, God graciously shines forth from the light of his own eternal personal relations. We therefore continue in our second section with a sketch of God's loving, radiant, and gracious turn *ad extra* to human creatures.

God's Shining Forth

This final section is concerned with what Krötke's says about God's light, namely, that it is "an event of complete clarity, that is, of full transparency in itself which is therefore able to give a clarifying share in itself."[71] In other words, God's light indicates God's triune shining forth into the economy in his relational and covenant-creating turn towards his human creatures in the darkness of sin and death. Therefore, we keep before us our latter proposal of a trinitarian theology of divine light: *from himself God shines forth his light.*

Light-in-relation

God's light—that radiance with which he wills and establishes himself—includes his shining forth to creatures. "To speak of the light of God," then, "is to speak of a personal action and mode of relation, the free self-disposing of the Lord of all things includes his energy or impetus of his self-revelation."[72] Talk of God's light is therefore talk of God's "mode of relation" to us as a repetition of his triune identity. Thus, if the term "light" signifies relation rather than some quality, then God is specifically revealed to human creatures in his gracious shining forth. "He is the radiance of light that reaches all other beings and permeates them," says Barth. Thus, "He is not separated from them by any distance, but changes such distance into proximity."[73]

If he is the "radiance of light" in himself, then how does the language of light further distinguish the particular aspect of the unified identity of the triune God's external works and ways? We might answer by saying that God's light not only signifies the radiant identity which the triune God is in himself, but also his proximate acts towards the lives of human creatures.

---

71. Krötke, *Gottes Klarheiten*, 108.

72. Webster, "On the Clarity of Scripture," in *Confessing God*, 40. Webster's remarks are found within the notion that "Holy Scripture is clear because God is light." With Webster's help, we resume the topic of *claritas Scripturae* in chapter 5.

73. Barth, CD II.1:646; KD II.1:729.

God's light in the economy is therefore what we might term a *light-in-relation*. God's light is a light known in shining forth, exhibited in the works of God, namely communion between himself and those whom he illuminates. It is not a matter of self-enclosed radiance. Rather, it is something closer to what Edwards indicates: if God is indeed light *in se*, then "this infinite fountain of light should, diffusing its excellent fullness, pour forth light all around."[74] This *light-in-relation* is simply an articulation of the same reality: the "fountain of light" indeed "pours forth light all around." For if God's relation to us were merely subordinate to his "mutual light," then God's essence would remain utterly beyond us, forever "light inaccessible," forever hidden, forever the *Deus absconditus*; and if God's relation to us were not radiant and bright, that relation would no longer be one in which God shows us the light of his presence.

We might posit here a further condition for making theological sense of God's light: the avoidance of polarizing God's light *in se* and his shining forth *ad extra*. That is, there is no "dramatic entrance and exit"[75] in the works of God, because "as they are indivisible, so indivisibly work."[76] In brief: the divine distance (*God is light in himself*) and the divine approach (*from himself God shines forth his light*) are one movement in God's being and act. Thus, the light manifest in the external works of the triune God is manifest as relation, as a relation between the persons of the Trinity and the human creatures whom God summons "out of darkness into his marvelous light" (1 Pet 2:9). And though God's light stresses his utter transcendence in his internal works, it nevertheless draws attention to God's external works as the One who elects, reconciles, and illuminates his human creatures.

As we examined above, *God is light in himself*; so here, therefore: *from himself God shines forth his light*. In all that God does he is radiant; thus, all God's ways are a "lamp" and a "light" (Prov 6:23), as all his ways are the implementation of his omnipotence. "As the living God is the source of light," Barth clarifies, "His light is omnipotent, and so omnipresent light."[77] Light therefore permeates all of the works of the Father, Son, and Holy Spirit; it is what Gregory calls the "outleaping of Their brightness."[78] The triune God is therefore known in his turning to human creatures, his shining forth, and to

---

74. Edwards, "Dissertation I" (WJE 8:433).

75. Barth, CD I.1:374. Barth concludes that such a division would be "pagan mythology."

76. See Augustine, *Trin.* 1.4 (PL 42:824): "Sicut inseparabiles sunt, ita inseparabiliter operantur."

77. Barth, CD II.1:646; KD II.1:729: "Und so ist sein Licht allmächtiges und also allgegenwärtiges Licht."

78. Gregory Nazianzen, *Or.* 40.5 (PG 36:364; NPNF 7:361).

speak of God's light is to speak on the basis of his radiant self-revealing and saving presence in the midst of human creatures. The decisive consequence of this for how we think about the light of God is, therefore, that the idea of God's light is a *light-in-relation*. That is to say, what it expresses is the origin and relation in which God stands to his creation; it states the temporal "emanations" of God shining forth from his internal works.[79]

In underlining the relational character of God's triune light we are not, however, subjectivizing this concept, translating it into a way of talking about human contemplation of God. To say that would be to fall into the trap that seems to have caught some: the doctrine of the Trinity is not the result of the "soft underbelly" of creaturely experience and contemplation.[80] Nor is this a matter of what Symeon the New Theologian "saw" in his third-person accounts of the contemplation of divine light:

> Suddenly a profuse flood of light appeared above him and filled the whole room.... He was wholly united to non-material light, so much so that it seemed to him that he himself had been transformed into light.[81]

In such tendencies, the character of God becomes the way of describing religious understandings of the divine; if permitted to do so, God's own being becomes a vacuum that we then have to fill with ideas of our own making.

Over against this, talk of God's light preeminently indicates God's radiant being as Father, Son, and Holy Spirit, as we examined in the first section of this chapter. But because it indicates the triune being of God, it is squarely a matter of Christian confession; that is, it speaks not of God absconded from human creatures, but rather of God's presence as the One who shines forth to human creatures in love and grace. God's light is made

---

79. The term *emanationes* here refers to the begetting and spiration of the Son and the Spirit, which implicitly refers to the three *hypostases* of the Trinity. *Emanationes* does not refer to the Plotinian "emanationist" position in which God impersonally "flows forth" or "diffuses" into the economy from the divine *hén*. This notion ultimately becomes anti-trinitarian in nature.

80. See the recent work by Coakley, *God, Sexuality, and the Self*, 190–93; and Coakley's earlier article, "Can God be Experienced as Trinity?" 11–23, regarding the "ineluctably tri-faceted" feature of religious experience. This is not to say that Coakley's *God, Sexuality, and the Self*, is not a very important addition to the discussion of trinitarian theology, particularly on the masculine pronouns ascribed to God. Indeed, Coakley's recent volume is at lengths to respectfully distance her conclusions from several feminist interpretations (see esp. ibid., 336–39). Refer also to the insightful discussion from Kathryn Green-McCreight regarding select feminist interpretations in *Feminist Reconstructions of Christian Doctrine*, 112–7.

81. Symeon the New Theologian, *Catechesis* 22 (*Philokalia*, 4:18).

known to human creatures in the way in which, as Father, Son, and Holy Spirit, God enters into relation with them. This *light-in-relation*—this shining forth in which God in utter freedom does indeed direct himself towards his creation—is the place where God manifests himself to human creatures, and so the place where his being is understood. It is, as Barth notes, a matter of God's freedom, "wholly inward to the creature and at the same time as Himself wholly outward: *totus intra et totus extra*."[82] God is who he is in his works, and his works are his shining forth himself to human creatures *ad extra* as the One who elects, reconciles, and illuminates.

The Light of the Covenant

Yet the history of theology proves that it is perilously easy to think of God's light strictly as a mode of God's otherness, mystery, or transcendence; that is, as "transcendent darkness" or a "darkness brighter than light," which often implies the reverse of relationality, as concerned not with *Deus revelatus*, but with *Deus absconditus*.[83] But to follow that road is to misread much of biblical testimony. The light of God is not to be marked as a *tertium quid* that distances God from creatures; rather, God is light precisely as the One who in glory "reaches all other beings and permeates them."[84] He is the One who "out of the brightness of his presence" (2 Sam 22:13) promises the "everlasting light" (Isa 60:20) that has "come into the world" (John 3:19). Accordingly, God's light is not merely to be connected with his distance but equally with his approach. Put another way: God's "unapproachable light" (1 Tim 6:16) is not different from or other than the freedom in which God is the "light for all people" (John 1:4).

Because it is essential to maintain that God's light is a *light-in-relation*, it is therefore inseparable from the fact that God is a covenant God: *from himself God shines forth his light*. God is not only "the glory of Israel," but also the "light for revelation to the Gentiles" (Luke 2:32). That is, God is light specifically in his gathering a people to be his own, in being present with them. The various declarations in Isaiah, for instance, do not figure God's presence as light merely as God's utter difference, but rather as that which is known in God's covenant-creating work: "The people who walked

---

82. Barth, *CD* II.1:315; cf. KD II.1:354: "Gott ist frei, der Kreatur ganz innerlich und zugleich als Er selbst ganz äußerlich zu sein: totus intra et totus extra."

83. See Pseudo-Dionysius, *Myst. theol.* 1.1–3. Regarding a denial of a human experience of God, and perhaps some corrections concerning the perceived "negation" of experience in mystical theology, see Turner, *Darkness of God*, 252–73.

84. Barth, *CD* II.1:646.

in darkness have seen a great light; those who dwelt in a land of deep darkness, on them has light shone" (9:2).[85] The same notion is picked up in the apostle Paul's testimony before Agrippa:

> To this day I have had help from God, and so I stand here, testifying to both small and great, saying nothing but what the prophets and Moses said would take place: that the Messiah must suffer, and that, by being the first to rise from the dead, he would proclaim light both to our people and to the Gentiles. (Acts 26:22-23)

Commenting on this passage from Acts, Bock notes: "God becomes the occasion for . . . the Jews and the gentiles to enter into divine promise and life (light)."[86] That is, God's shining forth cannot be isolated from God's call and election of a people, from his own kerygmatic message to them. "The creator God has shone 'in our hearts,'" Wright remarks, "in other words, the act is that which brings people into the new covenant."[87]

This indestructible bond between God's shining forth and his "bringing people into the new covenant" is crucial, because it expresses how light is not merely an impersonal or contingent concept, but a relational one, the foundation of the loving relation of the radiant God to his human creatures sitting in the darkness of sin and death. Thus, it "scarcely needs to be said that this divine radiance by which all things are illumined is no impersonal state of affairs," says Webster. Rather: "It is the presence of God the revealer."[88] And this presence, the "purest light which most men cannot approach

---

85. Of course, we bear in mind that there is a particular context associated with these (and other) occurrences in Isaiah: "I will take you by the hand and keep you; I will give you as a covenant for the people, a light for the nations, to open the eyes that are blind, to bring out the prisoners from the dungeon, from the prison those who sit in darkness" (42:6-7); "I will turn the darkness before them into light, the rough places into level ground. These are the things I do, and I do not forsake them" (42:16); "Let him who walks in darkness and has no light trust in the name of the Lord and rely on his God" (50:10); "for a law will go out from me, and I will set my justice for a light to the peoples" (51:4). Cf. the notion of God's *Shekinah* which rests with his people: Gen. 9:17; Ex. 40:35; Ps. 37:3.

86. Bock, "Scripture and Realisation of God's Promise," 42. Cf. Keener's note on the echo of resurrection in this passage (*Acts*, 4:3533).

87. Wright, *Climax of the Covenant*, 189. Wright is commenting here on Paul's connective themes of "light/glory" and "mirror" in 2 Cor 3:3, 4:6.

88. Webster, "On the Clarity of Holy Scripture," 40.

unto," is a saving presence;[89] for in God's "shining with a far brighter light," he "becomes the God and salvation of the sinner."[90]

Therefore the quickening of God's light as "a light to the peoples" (Isa 51:4) makes sense only in the realm of a salvation that that *light-in-relation* establishes. And so God's utter separation from the wickedness of darkness is to be understood within the scope of God's dealings with human creatures in darkness. Light is not the opposite of relation—it is not, again, a *coincidentia oppositorum* in which God strictly resides in "mystical darkness" and is "utterly unknowable."[91] Rather, God as the radiant One is the One who does not simply remain in estrangement but has "come into the world as light," to "purify for himself a people for his own possession," so that they "may not remain in darkness" (John 12:46; Titus 2:14).

As the radiant One who has light in himself, God passes judgment on darkness and sin and negates it, thus "dispelling creaturely darkness by the sheer potency of his inner splendor."[92] Yet God does this not from afar, but in the *emanationes* of the Son and the Holy Spirit. That is, God's "dispelling creaturely darkness" is effected in his triune acts of communion with human creatures, in which the "Father of lights" pardons by taking upon himself the situation of the blinded creature, exposing himself to our darkness, and only in that way "calling us out of darkness into his marvelous light." God's hostility to sin and darkness—that event in which "Divine energy of an exquisite order is deployed"[93]—is the union of his judgment and his grace, namely, the *one moment* of "the darkness passing away and the true light already shining" (1 John 2:8).

But it is just at this point that a theology of divine light must resist restricting the scope of God's relation to the world, and thus identifying God with only one manner of relation. Such a restriction misplaces the doctrine of the Trinity, namely that God, the One who has *light in himself* and *from himself shines forth his light*, is merged beneath the question of whether or not God's light *in se* can be regarded as the absolute ground of his historical theophany: When is "the glory of the Lord shone around them" (Luke 2:9) the "eternal light" of the glory of Father, Son, and Holy Spirit? That is, some might ask, may not the sharp distinction between uncreated light and created light once again mount a challenge to the gospel's instruction to look

---

89. Gregory Nazianzen, *Or.* 2.76 (NPNF 7:220).

90. Witsius, *De Oeconomia Foederum*, 2.1.3.

91. See Pseudo-Dionysius, *Myst. theol.* 1 (PG 3:1000). For more on Denys's use of darkness and light, see Louth, *Denys the Areopagite*, esp. 99–110.

92. Davidson, "Divine Light," 65.

93. Ibid., 66.

for the gospel's God in temporal appearance? Perhaps the shining forth of God's radiant presence depletes God's inner light. We find a related set of reflections from T. F. Torrance:

> God is Light, uncreated light, and it is in the light of that invisible, uncreated Light that the created lights of the world are visible. Thus, we understand the rationalities of nature, or what I have called its *contingent intelligibility*, in the light of the uncreated Rationality of God. *You understand created light in the light of uncreated Light.* It is because God's Light is constant that we believe in the ultimate stability and reliability of the universe he has *correlated to his Light*.[94]

Following Torrance, Mackenzie offers a similar series of thoughts, stating that within

> any consideration of light is to be a threefold consideration: the created light on which nature depends as the ground of its intelligibility and existence; the light of intelligibility which enlightens and informs the mind which is closely related to physical light; and the uncreated Light which is God himself who, by created light, has bestowed on creation a rationality which *corresponds* in its created dimension to the uncreated Rationality which he is as uncreated Light.[95]

Without recasting our conclusions to chapter 1 regarding contingent notions of "created light" and "uncreated light," we simply say of Torrance and Mackenzie that they are here raising several uncertainties, namely, understanding the uncreated light (or "Rationality") of God with regards to contingent light (or "corresponding" intelligibility). The response to these thoughts are, however, found in the opposite direction: it is precisely because God is not accountable to contingent creation and created light—because he is light in himself apart from creation, the "wholly gracious affirmation

---

94. Torrance, *Ground and Grammar of Theology*, 129 (emphasis mine). Of course, anyone acquainted with Torrance's theology will recognize that this is not necessarily his accepted view. For instance, he states elsewhere: "While it is in his Light that we see light, the very splendor of God's Light finally hides him from us. In the mystery of his self-revelation God reserves the innermost secret of his eternal Being as God, into which . . . we cannot intrude" (*Christian Doctrine of God*, 81). On the supposed inconsistencies in Torrance's thought, see Molnar, "Natural Theology Revisited," 53–83.

95. Mackenzie, *'Obscurism' of Light*, 3 (emphasis mine). It is worth noting that Mackenzie's peculiar word, "obscurism," is defined as "the tantalizing mystery of light . . . elusive of our attempts to analyse it" (ix). Several misgivings aside, Mackenzie does a service to the reader in his thoughts on Robert Grosseteste's *De Luce* (ch. 3) and his summary of Gregory Nazianzen's pairing of the image of light with baptism (ch. 10).

of his freedom to be himself as and with himself"[96]—that his commitment to history can be a *light-in-relation*. Thus, there are no realities beyond God that provide the circumstance for the perfecting of God's *light-in-relation*. "The [created] light is not needed as a likeness in which the essence of God may be seen," relays Aquinas.[97] In our terms set above, once again: the internal works of God are shined forth externally in the temporal missions of the Son and the Holy Spirit into the creaturely realm. Yet this does not entail that human creatures or "contingent intelligibility" somehow co-found God by their "correlated light," but simply that the relations of origin between the persons of the Trinity are the "unapproachable light," and the radiant source of the creaturely economy.

Thus, over against the misconstruals quoted above, the dogmatic *locus* for speaking about creatures and historical "contingent intelligibility" is found in the light that God antecedently is in his covenant purposes, namely, in the history of the covenant and in the *emanationes* of the Son and the Holy Spirit. This is a history that saves "apart from any consideration of merit," says Calvin. For God "kept it stored away among his treasures until the time came when he could reveal it by the fact that he determines nothing in vain."[98] It is, therefore, an event grounded in the eternal divine determination; and this determination shines forth *ex pacto* within God's own radiant identity as Father, Son, and Holy Spirit.

The notion of an eternal pact sounds a doctrinal note for us here; namely, that creaturely existence is grounded by "the fact that God determines nothing in vain," which is founded on the light of the covenant. Thus, the divine determination for the salvation of creatures in their existence reflects the inner radiance of the Father who sends and the Son who agrees to be the *sponsor* of the Father's will. This pact is "an eternall transaction and compact between *Iehovah* and the second Person the *Son of God*," Samuel

---

96. Wood, "Maker of Heaven and Earth," 386.

97. Aquinas, ST 1a.q12.5ad2: "Ad secundum dicendum quod lumen istud non requiritur ad videndum Dei essential quasi similitude in qua Deus videatur." Aquinas does add, however, that created light is "not the medium *in* which God is seen, but the means *by* which he is seen" (ibid.), to which must be added his earlier statement, namely that "light" is the "intelligible form" of understanding that is given to the creaturely mind *ex divina gratia* (1a.q12.5*resp*). For an overview of Aquinas's use of light in the *Summa* and elsewhere, see the perceptive study by Whidden III, *Christ the Light*, esp. ch. 3.

98. Calvin, *Comm. Tim. II* 1.9 (CO 52:353; cf. CC 21:195–96): "Dedit ergo quod, nullo merito provocatus, nondum natis assignavit: ac in thesauris suis habuit repositum, donec re ipsa patefaceret nihil se frustra statuere."

Rutherford clarifies. Thus, the Son "gave personall consent that he should be the Undertaker, and no other."[99] Edwards continues this thought:

> The persons of the Trinity were as it were confederated in a design and a covenant of redemption, in which covenant the Father appointed the Son and the Son had undertaken their work, and all things to be accomplished in their work were stipulated and agreed.[100]

The nature of this *pactum*, says Turretin further, is found in "the will of the Father giving his Son as a *lytrōtēn* (Redeemer and head of his mystical body) and the will of the Son offering himself as a sponser for his members to work out that redemption."[101] In short: "there is a compact between the Father and the Son, which is the foundation of our salvation."[102]

Of course by sounding this note regarding a divine "confederated" undertaking of the *pactum salutis*, we must also admit that the notion has difficulties, particularly in its Reformed federal key.[103] Barth, for instance, famously called this doctrine "mythology, for which there is no place in a right understanding of the doctrine of the Trinity."[104] Yet against several readings of his seemingly abrasive statement,[105] it appears that Barth's thoughts are concerned more with bringing *pactum* to its doctrinal terminus; that is, Barth is concerned with what the *pactum salutis* seems to be aiming at, namely, divinity *in abstracto*. Evidently, therefore, it is not a plan to reconcile two attributes of God that are estranged from each other; rather, in Barth's estimation, it is a pact that foreordains the particular form God's mercy will take in the *Heilsgeschichte*. Barth seems more cautious, then, in adopting the Reformed federal notion of *pactum* generally; and we would do well to note, with Berkouwer, that Barth does not merely erase the

---

99. Rutherford, *Covenant of Life Opened*, II.7 (emphasis original). Rutherford continues with a meditation on the "eternall transaction," particularly regarding the "consent" of the Son: "[T]he person designated was the Son only, this lot eternally . . . fell upon him who was . . . *the Lamb of God for-ordained before the foundation of the world* (1 Pet 1:20)" (ibid.; emphasis original).

100. Edwards, *Work of Redemption* (WJE 9:118).

101. Turretin, *Inst.* XII.q2.13: "Pactum Patris et Filii continent voluntatem Patris Filium dantis ut . . . Redemptorem." For an insightful study of Turretin's thoughts on the covenant of grace and predestination, see Beach, *Christ and the Covenant*, esp. 331–7.

102. Witsius, *De Oeconomia Foederum* 2.2.2.

103. For more on the various origins of *pactum salutis*, see Muller, "Toward the Pactum Salutis," 11–65; and *Post-Reformation Reformed Dogmatics*, 4:265–66.

104. Barth, CD IV.1:65.

105. See, notably, Muller, *Christ and the Decree*, 154.

pactum, but rather styles his doctrine of election after his own notion of the doctrine of the *pactum salutis*.[106]

Such worries aside, our aim in this sounding is rather narrow: the *pactum* between the Father and the Son simply reflects their eternal personal properties of "mutual light" and "ingenerate light."[107] Yet at the same time the *pactum salutis* is not, to take Barth's lead, a point at which some vague notion arises in the dark background to the Godhead *in abstracto*; rather, the *pactum* derives from the *modus agenda*, the order of work, in the radiant identity of the triune God which accords with his eternal decree to shine forth into the creaturely economy.[108] God shines forth in loving grace by making a determination concerning human creatures. And so the divine *pactum* and the shining forth towards human creatures are therefore indivisible; the aim of the counsel of God is human creatures in the darkened realm of sin and suffering and death. Thus, the *pactum salutis* is the light of the covenant of grace: the Son with whom the Father covenants is "the head of the church, the body of which he is the Savior" (Eph 5:23). The *pactum salutis*, then, is essential to God's dealings with human creatures.

The Gathering Light and the Scattering Light

Talk of the light of God therefore traces the relation of God to the world *ex pacto*, a covenantal relation in which we can discern the full sweep of the drama of God's works in the acts of "sending," "giving," and "coming"—from the *opera Dei ad intra* and their external execution in the divine *emanationes*—in which the eternal God shines forth to human creatures as *light-in-relation*. Above all, the doctrine of the Trinity thwarts contingent accounts of God's light—contingent in the sense of being established apart from attention to his having *light in himself*. We therefore echo Krötke's important nuance with regards to the divine distance and divine approach: "The triune God meets us *out of the immanence of his Godhead* in unreserved loving, turning to, and welcoming."[109]

---

106. Berkouwer, *Divine Election*, esp. 164–67.

107. Review our thoughts on the *opera Dei ad intra* above; namely, that all three persons are "mutual light" by virtue of their common divine essence, and each person is "ingenerate light" regarding their *emanationes*.

108. These are Rutherford's terms in *Covenant of Life Opened*, II.7.

109. Krötke, *Gottes Klarheiten*, 169 (emphasis mine): ". . . daß uns der trinitarische Gott aus der Immanenz seines Gottseins heraus in vorbehaltlosem, liebenden Zuwenden und Empfangen begegnet."

Thus, God the Father is the one who elects from all eternity the gathering of human creatures as "children of light" (Eph 5:8); God the Son is the one who accomplishes this reconciliation of human creatures by being the "great light," the *sponsor* rescuing human creatures from "dwelling in darkness" and the "region of the shadow of death" (Matt 4:16); God the Holy Spirit is the one who is the terminus of that "calling out of darkness" by illuminating human creatures, and calling them "into the marvelous light" of communion with God. The character of divine light in its relational manner therefore highlights the God who elects, reconciles, and illuminates. In effect, what the doctrine of the Trinity does in this setting is express how God's light is known in his covenant-establishing work. God's light is exactly that which is made known in his love, in his coming to the help of his people, in his shining forth, in his scattering of their darkness, in his illuminating action of communion.

From himself God shines forth his light: this is what we might label as the light that "gathers" (*synagō*)—light in its electing, reconciling, and illuminating feature. Yet as we move to conclude this chapter, we find within this setting the need to consider what can be labeled as the light that "scatters" (*skorpizō*), that is, light as a power that removes darkness and destroys sin.[110] God's light is the undeflected determination that his will for human creatures will not be overcome by darkness. "God really does shine forth, dispelling creaturely darkness by the sheer potency of his inner splendor."[111] As the radiant One, the triune God labors to insure that the destiny of the human creature—that is, being "called out of darkness into God's marvelous light"—will be attained, and sin will not be allowed to restrain the human creature in darkness. God's light is thus joined to his determination that the human creature will reach its destiny. Part of that determination is the opposition of God's light to that which is darkness, "his commitment to scatter the absurdity of the darkness."[112] The darkness is that which has been rejected by God; it is the creature's "shutting their eyes to the light of God in which is formed the prideful barrier to the light";[113] it is, therefore, the

---

110. The notions of "gathering" and "scattering" are evident in the OT and the NT. Regarding the former OT notion, one would naturally think of the various events of exile and diaspora (e.g., 2 Kgs 17:6; Ezek 1–3; see further, Fleming, *Legacy of Israel*, esp. ch. 19). Yet here we are using "gathering" and "scattering" in the sense found in Jesus' sayings recorded in Luke 11:23: "Whoever is not with me is against me, and whoever does not gather with me scatters."

111. Davidson, "Divine Light," 65.

112. Ibid.

113. Tanner, *Christ the Key*, 134.

reason why "people loved the darkness rather than the light because their works were evil" (John 3:19).

Yet as we turn in chapter 3 to a more precise investigation of this "gathering" and "scattering" aspect of God's light in the *emanationes* of the Son and the Holy Spirit, we must be mindful not to bracket this into the only feature of the external works of God. To do that would be to make this into the typically antiquine reading of light as merely the dualistic principle standing in opposition to darkness.[114] Such a hermeneutic fails to see the true end of this "scattering" aspect of God's light, namely as the history of *light-in-relation*. In that history, God's light shows itself in the eternal will of the Father for the human creature, which is expressed in the Son's work of bearing sin, and brought to us in the Holy Spirit's illuminative work in the reconciled. And it is by that history that the human mind is to be illumined and, like Saul on the road to Damascus, "led by the hand" before the radiant presence of God. God's "scattering" light is the destructive power of God's "gathering" light; it is the light of the triune God who must "scatter" everything that thwarts the human creature's life with God. God's light scatters the darkness because it attacks and is opposed to the human creature's destiny. And the end of the scattering of darkness is the human creature's illumination, that is, being gathered into the light of communion with God.

Conclusion

The theological impact of our motif of light is felt precisely in these last statements concerning the "gathering" and "scattering" aspect of God's light. God's light is his "commitment to scatter the absurdity of darkness" and his pact to "bind himself to [the] world in spite of everything."[115] This was the meaning behind our two proposals: *God is light in himself*, and *from himself God shines forth his light*. We now turn to a more precise description of the triune God's loving and illuminating work in his shining forth to the world.

---

114. Of many examples, see the recent study by McCarter, Jr., "Dualism in Antiquity," 19–35. McCarter states that the (first) creation account of Genesis 1 is an ancient Near Eastern instance of a "clearly *eschatological* form of dualism" in its use of a "series of creative separations into binary pairs: light and dark, the super-celestial and sub-celestial waters, the gathered waters and dry land" (ibid., 28–9).

115. Davidson, "Divine Light," 65.

3

The Light of the Gospel

God's Radiant Event of Love

> God is rather the radiant event of love itself. And so . . . he is the event in that he, as the one who loves and separates himself from his beloved, not only loves himself but . . . loves another one and thus is and remains himself.[1]

OUR PRECEDING CHAPTER ESTABLISHED THE NOTION THAT GOD'S LIGHT IS his radiant identity: the radiant One in his threefold luminous being. Thus, as we proposed above, *God is light in himself*. In the totality of the three persons in One divine essence; in the coessentiality and consubstantiality of the three persons; in their proper identities and acts as the one who is unbegotten, the one who is begotten, and the one who proceeds; in their loving acts as the One who *from himself shines forth his light*—God is the radiant One.

An understanding of God's light is therefore ingredient within God's loving, covenantal resolve for communion with his human creatures. Yet an inconsistency looms if the idea of God's utter difference (what we have thus far deemed the *opera ad intra* of God's light) is rejected in favor of love.[2] But a trinitarian theology of divine light must propose that "light"

---

1. Jüngel, *Gott als Geheimnis der Welt*, 448-9: "Gott ist vielmehr das ausstrahlende Geschehen der Liebe selbst. Er ist es . . . indem er, als der von sich selbst, sondern—inmitten noch so großer Selbstbezogenheit immer noch selbstloser—einen ganz anderen liebt und so er selbst ist und bleibt."

2. In so many words, Jüngel reacts to a Feuerbachian worry which sees the statement "God is love" as generally interpreted "im Sinne einer ontologischen Differenz von Gott und Liebe interpretiert, so daß die Liebe durchaus 'zurück- und herabgesezt' wird durch einen dann allerdings 'dunkeln Hintergrund: Gott'" (ibid., 432). In

and "love" are to be seen as joined terms, which both serve as mutual pointers to the radiant work of the triune God, particularly in the divine personal relations: the Father's sending of the Son and, in turn, the Holy Spirit being spirated by both the Father and the Son.

If, indeed as we have thus far proposed, God is *light in himself* as Father, Son, and Holy Spirit, and if it is identical with the particular radiant being which God is, then the light that God is in himself is manifest and active in God's external works of the gospel. In this third chapter, we will deal specifically with this loving and merciful movement of God *ad extra*: first, with the electing work of the Father; second, with the coming of the true light into the world, Jesus Christ; and finally, with the illuminating work of the Holy Spirit. It is to these works of the "radiant event" of divine love that we must now attend.

Election as the Radiant Event of Love

As a point of entry, we might begin by commenting on the structure of the apostle Paul's thinking in Colossians 1:12–14:

> The Father . . . has qualified you to share in the inheritance of the saints in light. He has delivered us from the domain of darkness and transferred us to the kingdom of his beloved Son, in whom we have redemption, the forgiveness of sins." (ESV)

With regards to these statements, we first say that God's "radiant event of love" is active as election.[3] The work of election is a work of God's light because it is a work that "has delivered us," namely, a work in which a human creature has been "qualified" and "transferred" from residing in the "domain of darkness" to have "redemption, the forgiveness of sins," and inclusion in the "kingdom of his beloved Son." The work of election is therefore the eternal work of the God who is light; it is the work in which God has a purposeful aim of his shining forth, namely, to those dwelling in the domain of darkness. And because God is light in himself, even in his eternal decree and pact, he therefore seeks to gather the creaturely "circumference"

---

handling this worry, Jüngel—along with Barth—takes the statement "God is love," and its converse "love is God," as being permissible only if it is filled out by the triune identity of the predicate itself.

3. We must keep before us in this section the fact that God's election is not merely collapsed into a historical instance in the economy. Rather, election is placed squarely in the realm of the covenant, particularly the notion of the *pactum salutis*. See our thoughts in the previous chapter.

of his own radiance in election.⁴ Consequently, election prompts the human creature to "give thanks" to the Father (Col 1:12), because the creaturely "circumference" is qualified to have its existence by "the superabundance of love operating the production of such a creature."⁵

The human creature, qualified and transferred by God, is not merely qualified in and transferred to a monotonous existence. Rather, the human creature is qualified to a lively destiny in communion with God. It is therefore God's determination that "His light should not be unseen, nor His glory without witness, nor His goodness unenjoyed," but rather that the end of the human creature is to be a "partaker of the good things in God . . . framed of such a kind as to be adapted to the participation of such good"; in other words, to have "fellowship with the light."⁶ Thus, the *causa impulsiva* of the will of the God who is light is that we should be God's "saints in light"; his qualifying has as its aim human creatures being "delivered" and "transferred" as saints into the kingdom of his beloved Son.

As God's light is active in this qualifying, delivering, and transferring manner, then God's work of shining forth is at its heart a work "impelled by the love of his glory."⁷ For God "so loved the world" that the he gave the "true light of the world" (John 1:9; 3:16); and in this action there is at work the grace that is given to human creatures in "his beloved Son," in whom they have "redemption, the forgiveness of sins." Just as God's light *in himself* cannot be understood without the notion that *from himself God shines forth his light*, so also God's light cannot be understood without attending to its loving magnification in the external works that establish the human creature by transferring it from the domain of darkness to the kingdom of the beloved Son. Election as the "radiant event of love" is therefore the external work of the eternal will of the Father—indeed: "The Father . . . has qualified

---

4. By "circumference" here we echo Barth's use of the term: "Jesus Christ [is] the illuminating center of which they [i.e., those belonging to God, "His own"] form the circumference saved and illuminated by him." However, we must keep in mind Barth's warning regarding this notion: "The center cannot become the circumference nor the circumference the center" (CD IV.3.1:278–79); cf. KD IV.3:321–2: ". . . die errettende und nun auch erleuchtende Mitte, in welcher sie den durch ihn erretteten und nun auch erhellten Umkreis bilden."

5. Gregory of Nyssa, *Or.* 5 (PG 45:21; NPNF 5:478).

6. Ibid.

7. Heidegger, *Corp. theol.* 5.29: "Ad eligendum quosdam Deum in universum impulit *amor gloriae suae,* cuius stupendo hoc opera divitias palam demonstrare et ex quo laudem gloriae gratiae suae praeparare voluit."

you" (Col 1:12).[8] As the Father, God determines that his loving work is luminous; it is a divine qualification that there should be "saints in light."[9]

The "Radiant Event of Love" and the "Domain of Darkness"

God's light is therefore the "radiant event of love" because it is known in his shining forth *ad extra* that delivers creatures from the domain of darkness and transfers them into the kingdom of his beloved Son. This means that God does not shine forth his light in some abstract manner, particularly in a "more fundamental way" through creaturely "materials."[10] Rather, God upholds the human creature to whom he gives light; yet the creaturely "circumference" of God's radiant life is not docile repose. That is, the Johannine "walking in the light" which corresponds to "as he himself is in the light" summons the human creature to act in a manner chosen by the Father's will for "fellowship with himself" (cf. 1 John 1:7). It is in this way that God loves the human creature, determining that the human creature should have life and light. "For God is Life and Light, and those who are in God's hand are in life and light."[11]

---

8. The seventeenth-century Protestant dogmaticians were particularly concerned with holding this point. Whereas the *causa electionis princeps* is the triune God, *electio* is nevertheless seen as particularly belonging to the Father himself. Thus, e.g., "the Father's election is simply called election [*electio Dei Patris electio*]" (Heidegger, *Corp. theol.* 5.28). Still, the *electio* of the Father, the *sponsio* of the Son, and the *obsignatio* of the Spirit does not divide the movement in the divine election, but is rather, for the Protestant Orthodox divines, a reiteration that "The principal cause of election is—God" (Bucanus, *Inst.* 26.16). Further from John Owen: "The eternal love of God towards his elect is nothing but his purpose, good pleasure, and pure act of his will, whereby he determines to do such and such things for them in his own time and way" (*Death of Death* [*Works*, 10:276]).

9. This "divine qualification" for the creature in the work of election is highlighted by Calvin: although God's will is "summa causa" and is "hidden with him," nevertheless his "righteousness and his rule" are inseparable by the act of his loving election. See Calvin's admittedly scathing letter in *Calumniae nebulonis de occulta Providentia Dei cum responsione* (CO 9:288); "A Brief Reply," in *Theological Treatises*, 335.

10. See David Brown's insistence that "human inventiveness" allows for the divine presence to manifest itself by transcending human "materials in a more fundamental way" in his "Darkness and Light," esp. 181. We might offer Barth's image as a reply: the creaturely "circumference" of the "illuminating center" of God's reconciling action in Jesus Christ is never *this* center but always and ever remains the circumference of this illuminating presence and work (cf. CD IV.3.1:278–9; KD IV.3:321–2). See our thoughts in the forthcoming sub-section.

11. John Damascene, *Exp. Fidei* 4.15 (PG 94:1164; NPNF 9:87).

This "radiant event of love"—this election of the human creature—is therefore the scattering of the darkness of death.[12] The domain of darkness is that which has forsaken the will of God—the "outer darkness" (Matt 8:12; 22:3; 25:30). Specifically, it is the history in which the human creature seeks to establish itself and rejects the radiant will of God. Yet this rejection of God's light is a threat to the human creature, which can only be what it is destined to be in communion with the God who is light. In revolt against the divine determination, the human creature refuses to acknowledge God's radiant presence as "alone good by nature."[13] Thus, the creature falls into sin and darkness: "the enemy of souls, the primary cause of death, the adversary of virtue."[14]

Sin is thus the human rejection of God's summons to communion, an exchange of "the truth about God for a lie" (Rom 1:25). It is the disobedience in which the human creature "boasts" that it can exist in a way other than that founded by God's will, and thus "curse and renounce the Lord" (Ps 10:3). By "despising the Holy One of Israel," the human creature paradoxically opposes itself, becoming "utterly estranged" by sitting in "darkness and in gloom" (Isa 1:4; Ps 107:10). The light shines, then, revealing the terror of sin to the creature sitting in the domain of darkness.[15] "And this is the judgment, that the light has come into the world, and people loved darkness rather than light because their deeds were evil. For all who do evil hate the light and do not come to the light, so that their deeds may not be exposed" (John 3:19–20).

Darkness is therefore the unavoidable environment in which the human creature finds itself; it is the place where, according to Athanasius, the human creature chases after its own selfish pleasure.

---

12. See our conclusions in chapter 2. Our use of "darkness" to denote the creaturely condition is, of course, principally derived from scriptural instances (e.g., Ps 18:28; John 1:4–9; 12:35, 46; Rom 13:12; 2 Cor 4:6; Eph 5:8, 6:12; Col 1:13; 1 Pet 2:9). However, we must add a caution that these scriptural instances are but one facet in the grand linguistic scheme of the doctrine of the fall and subsequent ruin of human creatures: *pollutio spiritualis* and *difformitas naturae*. Henry Blocher is right to address the "seductiveness" of certain metaphors when approaching the topic of sin, in which there arises the "danger of losing sight of the metaphorical distance" (Blocher, *Original Sin*, 110–11). Thus, we keep in mind that our use of "darkness" here and throughout the study is a descriptor (an apt one) of *pollutio spiritualis* and *difformitas naturae* that accompanies the creature's life without the radiant, gracious presence of God.

13. Aquinas, ST 1a.q6.3*resp*.

14. Basil, *Hexaemeron* 2.4 (PG 29b:35; NPNF 8:61).

15. See T. F. Torrance's insightful article regarding the "paradoxical" nature of God's light as both illuminating and blinding those in the darkness in "Immortality and Light," 147–61.

> For as if a man, when the sun is shining, and the whole earth illumined by his light, were to shut fast his eyes and imagine darkness where no darkness exists, and then walk wandering as if in darkness, often falling and going down steep places, thinking it was dark and not light, for, imagining that he sees, he does not see at all; so, too, the soul of man, shutting fast her eyes, by which she is able to see God, has imagined evil for herself, and moving therein, knows not that, thinking she is doing something, she is doing nothing. For she is imagining what is not, nor is she abiding in her original nature; but what she is is evidently the product of her own disorder. For she is made to see God, and to be enlightened by Him; but of her own accord in God's stead she has sought corruptible things and darkness.[16]

How does God help and guard the human creature from "falling and going down steep places?" In what way does God act to save the human creature from the judgment and terror that is brought about by rejecting the will of God?

The triune God himself moves between the human creature and its darkness, thereby halting its defiance of the divine determination. To this darkness, the light of God stands in conflict with an adversary; yet when God shines forth, there can be no possibility that this adversary on the part of the human creature will somehow comprise a real threat to the eternal will of God, for "even the darkness is not dark to you" (Ps 139:12). God's election is wholly original and cannot be repelled by anything the human does to escape it. This means that the eternal decree triumphs over the darkness of the human creature. The Father's will cannot be defeated by the human creature's fall into sin; his will is utterly resplendent, and it is unaffected by any opponent. In the overthrow of darkness, God is once again "the highest and first cause of all things because nothing happens except from his command and permission."[17]

In his eternal "command and permission" for communion, the Father wills reconciliation; thus, God's light is seen in the will of the Father for the human creature that is demonstrated in the Son's work of reconciliation, and shined forth to us by the Holy Spirit's illumination of the reconciled. Only within the terms of that luminous course can God's light be understood for what it is—the "radiant event" of God's love for the human creature in the domain of darkness, a love which wills that the human creature be enlivened

---

16. Athanasius, *c. Gen.* 7.3–5 (PG 25:5; NPNF 4:7).

17. Calvin, *Inst.* I.16.8; OS 3:199: "Dei voluntatem, summam esse probat et primam omnium causam, quia nihil nisi ex iussu eius vel permissione accidit."

and rescued from its "roving state."[18] It is therefore a radiant love that indeed scatters barriers to the human creature's entering into communion with the triune God. In his "radiant event of love" God has ordained us to be his "children of light" and therefore "saints in light." The Psalmist rejoices thus:

> Oh give thanks to the Lord, for he is good, for his steadfast love endures forever!
> Let the redeemed of the Lord say so, those he redeemed from trouble
> and gathered in from the lands, from the east and from the west, from the north and from the south. . . .
> Some sat in darkness and in gloom, prisoners in misery and in irons,
> for they had rebelled against the words of God, and spurned the counsel of the Most High. . . .
> Then they cried to the Lord in their trouble, and he saved them from their distress;
> he brought them out of darkness and gloom, and broke their bonds asunder.
> Let them thank the Lord for his steadfast love, for his wondrous works to humankind (Ps 107:1–3, 10–15).

The radiant One is therefore the One whose "steadfast love endures forever," and whose "wondrous works" include breaking the bonds of darkness so that our destiny comes to pass. What frail human creatures cannot do God himself seeks to remove, to the utter astonishment of the captive human creature in "darkness and gloom." And in this way God accomplishes his will by protecting the human creature, that is, by "gathering," "delivering," "saving," and "loving" his human creature. Indeed, it is fitting that we are implored to "thank the Lord for his steadfast love / for his wondrous works to humankind."

The Reconciling Light

We see that God's "radiant event of love" is active "from the east and from the west / from the north and from the south" (Ps 107:3). It is at work in the course of divine love in which God shines upon humans, bringing them out of "darkness and gloom." God's radiant love stands between the human creature and the threat of darkness, delivering it from this darkness and so breaking its "bonds asunder." This divine love *ad extra*, the economy of God's luminous works, is willed by God the Father, grounded in the eternal

---

18. Athanasius, *c. Gen.* 23.5 (PG 25: 48; *NPNF* 4:16).

decree of election. Moreover, it is a divine course with a comprehensive aim, namely, assembling God's acts towards humans as the "circumference" of his radiance. Yet at the center of this wide-ranging course of divine acts lies a particular covenant history, the history of Israel, and—further up and further in—the history of Jesus Christ, the Son of God, *the* "illuminating center" of reconciliation, in whom God's will overcomes the darkness and in whom, therefore, "the eternal light ... cannot be vanquished or extinguished."[19]

In this overcoming of sin and darkness by the Son of God is found the essential logic of our entire study thus far: in the gospel is found the effective declaration that the domain of darkness, the reign of sin, the shadow of death, is scattered and triumphed over by God himself. "Your light has come, and the glory of the Lord has risen upon you.... [T]he Lord will arise upon you, and his glory will appear over you" (Isa 60:1–2.). The promise of this coming light, God's loving purpose for communion, is accomplished in Jesus Christ. In Jesus Christ there takes place the decisive reconciliation of the human creature that God the Father wills. In him the "light of life" appeared on earth and revealed "the plan of the mystery hidden for ages" (John 8:12; Eph 3:9). Thus, a more precise account of God's scattering of darkness must be appended to this chapter in terms of the movement of the being and act of God the Son who takes on flesh.

"The Word Lighted Down"

In the Son of God there is *"a movement of his being."*[20] This divine movement means a self-presentation grounded *ex pacto divina*, in the basis of the divine covenant, in fulfillment of God's radiant love turned towards the darkened world of human creatures. This radiant movement of the Son and his agreement to this movement entails a self-emptying, a taking upon himself the creature's "form of a servant" by being "born in human likeness"

---

19. Barth, CD IV.3.1:278, 167. The perceptive reader will note that the thoughts here and throughout our present section are influenced heavily by Barth's "Jesus is Victor" paragraph in *CD* IV.3.1, §69.3. A guiding statement for what we are arguing for here might be found in Barth's words: "[A]s a doctrine of Jesus Christ the true light ... Christology is a narration of His history, and specifically the shining of His light, the real speaking of the covenant, the revelation of reconciliation" (ibid.,166).

20. This is part of Webster's first thesis in his "Prolegomena to Christology," in *Confessing God*, 134 (emphasis original). Like Barth's third cycle of the doctrine of reconciliation (*CD* IV.3.1, esp. §69.1–3), Webster's chapter is helpful for our current section. For instance: "*Antecedently present in his effulgent majesty as the eternal Son of God, Jesus Christ is known by virtue of the movement of his being in which as Lord and reconciler he freely gives himself to be known by us, and not otherwise*" (ibid.,131; emphasis original).

(Phil 2:7). "The Word became flesh and lived among us" (John 1:14); that is, "the Word lighted down . . . and appeared as a man" among human creatures in the domain of darkness.[21] The Son of God thus entered into the creaturely world in a new way, "condescending towards us in his love for human beings."[22] And though the Word is "not obscured by the darkness,"[23] human creatures nevertheless "do not know him" and do not wish to "receive him" (1 John 1:6; John 1:10–11). Though the "Word shone and spread its light in their midst," Luther says, creatures still "despised it and remained in darkness."[24]

This means that the Son came to hostile territory, that he "lighted down" into the very heart of the conflict between the light of God and the darkness of human creatures. Yet in this meeting of the true light and the domain of darkness, "We do not have the equilibrium of opposing forces," clarifies Barth, "as though darkness had a claim and power finally to maintain itself against light, as though its antithesis and challenge to light, its restricting of it, rested on an eternal and lasting order."[25] The God who is light does not abandon his human creature in the darkness, but comes to the human creature in the incarnate Son. And the end of the incarnate Son's movement is to restore communion between God and human creatures sitting in the domain of darkness. Thus, the specific pathway of this movement is one along which God overcomes the creature's opposition. Reconciliation is therefore the place where human opposition is overcome in the Son's person and work: the Word made flesh, the light of the world. The presence of this Son is his presence as the true light of the world. And it is a radiant presence, because in his presence he is and acts as one who has in himself the very "clarities" of God, condescending towards creatures in utter freedom and "concretion."[26] Thus, we are unable to bear the "immediate approach of the Divine Being; but through him, as incarnate," says Owen,

---

21. Athanasius, *Inc.* 43 (NPNF 4:60; cf. PG 25:173; PPS 44b:96).

22. Ibid., 8 (PG 25:109; PPS 44b:57).

23. Gregory of Nyssa, *c. Eun.* 4.1 (NPNF 5:154).

24. Luther, *Johannis* 1.9 (WA 46:564.30–32): ". . . das Wort hat durch seine Predigt unter sie geleuchtet und geschienen, habens aber veracht und sind im finsternis blieben."

25. Barth, *CD* IV.3.1:168. Barth's point here is that the "power of light" (i.e., the Word of revelation) must be seen as coming into darkness with "dynamic teleology," that is, with a superiority that has "not so far attained its goal but is still wrestling towards it, being opposed by the power of darkness" (ibid.).

26. Krötke, *Gottes Klarheiten*, 114: "Jede Klarheit Gottes ist im Gleichnis des Menschseins Jesu in menschlicher Konkretion auszusagen."

"are all things communicated unto us, in a way suited unto our reception and comprehension."[27]

God's eternal will—which is his determination to shine forth to us "in a way suited unto our reception and comprehension"—is not set aside when he comes to human creatures and enters into their darkness. On the contrary, as God takes "pity upon our weakness," his resolve to "hold us all the closer" abounds all the more.[28] It abounds in the fact God's Word is light. And this Word, against the defiant human creature and its dark domain, becomes flesh. And as he shines forth to creatures—as he "enlightens those trapped in the darkness of ignorance"[29]—the true light does not become something creatures can handle; the true light is not "summoned by the conditions of darkness that it reaches, as some divine reflex to the self-chosen murk of contingency."[30] Rather, the true light shines with limitless and uncontainable radiance. His presence, therefore, has the character of a present "true light . . . already shining" (1 John 2:8); it is the presence of "the one who is visible, who makes himself visible";[31] it is the presence of God, who would have "remained hidden afar off," Calvin reminds us, "if Christ's splendor had not beamed upon us."[32] Thus, this presence is the presence of "the radiance of the glory of God and the exact imprint of his nature" (Heb 1:3 ESV); it is the particular "light of the knowledge of the glory of God" (2 Cor 4:6).[33]

27. Owen, *Christologia* (*Works*, 1:16).
28. Athanasius, *Inc.* 8 (*PG* 25:109; *PPS* 44b:57).
29. Basil, *Sp. sanc.* 8.19 (*PG* 32:102; *PPS* 42:48).
30. Davidson, "Divine Light," 65.
31. Barth, *CD* IV.3.1:44.
32. Calvin, *Inst.* III.2.1; *OS* 4:8.

33. As we noted in chapter 1, these particular scriptural passages were of paramount importance for the pro-Nicene logic of *homoousios*. Taken with Calvin's statement above (*Inst.* III.2.1), we may briefly recall an ancient debate in the church, namely against Eunomianism. Gregory of Nyssa (and Basil before him) battled Eunomius's statement, "so great is the divergence between Light and Light," and its attendant implications for Christology, namely, "the difference between the generate and the ingenerate is not merely one of greater or less intensity, but that they are diametrically opposed as regards their meaning" (cf. *c. Eun.* 12.2). Thus, as Gregory explains, Eunomius's confusion with the image of light in regards to the Nicene confession

> inferred by logical consequence from [Eunomius's] premises that, as the difference between the light of the Father and that of the Son corresponds to ingeneracy and generation, we must necessarily suppose in the Son is not a diminution of light, but a complete alienation from light. . . . [S]o, if the same distinction is to be preserved between the Light of the Father and that conceived as existing in the Son, it will be

Thus, by the Word who has "lighted down," the absolute darkness of sin has been wholly mastered by the reality that the "light shines in the darkness, and the darkness has not overcome it" (John 1:5). This act of shining is entirely undefeated by the darkness, by the power of Satan, which it overthrows, scatters, and completely destroys.[34] And this is because the incarnate Son is not merely a facet or reflection of God's glory; still less is he simply the Baptist's "witness to the light" (John 1:8).[35] The incarnate Son is neither merely an instance of the "creaturely light of the uncreated Light," nor is Jesus Christ the bare "humanity of uncreated Light."[36] Rather, he is the true light *of* and *for* the world. To receive him is to behold God's radiance and self-revelation, namely, to see in him the glory of God, which is the "glory as of a father's only son" (John 1:14). For Jesus Christ—shining into darkness, facing human hostility, rejected by his own—is the ultimate fulfillment of the petition: "Let the light of your face shine upon us, O Lord!" (Ps 4:6), and he is the one in whom there takes place the execution of the determination of God, namely "fellowship with one another," that is, "fellowship with him" (1 John 1:6, 7).[37]

> logically concluded that the Son is not henceforth to be conceived as Light (ibid).

Gregory, however, explains how the "light unapproachable" of the Father and the "true light" of the Son may be congruent:

> For Paul says, "*dwelling in* light unapproachable." But there is a great difference between *being* oneself something and *being in* something. For he who said, "dwelling in light unapproachable," did not, by the word "dwelling," indicate God Himself, but that which surrounds Him, which in our view is equivalent to the Gospel phrase which tells us that the Father is in the Son. For the Son is true Light, and the truth is unapproachable by falsehood; so then the Son is Light unapproachable in which the Father dwells, or in Whom the Father is (ibid).

34. Cf. Paul's recitation of Jesus' words in Acts 26:18.

35. At first glance, we might be persuaded to note that the patristic use of the analogies "sun–ray–radiance" (e.g., Tertullian, *Apol.* 21; Ambrose, *De fide* 4.9) or "fire and light" (e.g., John Damascene, *Exp. Fidei* 1.8) may do a disservice here. However, as we noted above in chapter 1, what the fathers were after is precisely the point we are making here: the Son is not a facet or "witness" to the light of the Father, but is in fact the light itself, that is, *homousios*. Thus, we affirm that the Son is "never in any way separate from Him, but ever is in Him" (John Damascene, *Exp. Fidei* 1.8 [PG 94:795; NPNF 9:8]).

36. Mackenzie, '*Obscurism' of Light*, 118–19.

37. The fellowship "with one another" and "with him" can be seen as mutual notions, particularly in this first chapter of First Letter of John. See Bultmann's insights on this in *Johannine Epistles*, 19–20.

The Light of and for the World

In the incarnation of the Son is therefore found the one who has "illumined the inhabited world and has been made manifest bodily to it."[38] In this inhabitation, God's light is at work as mercy, as *free* mercy in his *free* presence.[39] The Son has thus become "our intermediary," says Calvin. "Hence, he calls himself 'the light of the world.'"[40] The Son of God, the light *of* and *for* the world, comes to the aid of the sinful human creature, the prisoner in darkness and a captive in the shadow of death. But in the inhabitation of God the Son is found the guarantee that the "Light dawns in the darkness for the upright; he is gracious, merciful, and righteous" (Ps 112:4 ESV). As the exact imprint of God's glory, his shining forth *to* the darkness is entirely for the deliverance of creatures, "in spite of our absurd opposition to it."[41] Yet to what end? That is, how does Jesus Christ, in his solidarity with "human nature which has sinned" thereafter "pay the penalty of sin," and yet at the same time, in his own radiance as the divine Son of God, "bear the burden of the wrath of God in his humanity?"[42] More precisely: How does this light *of* and *for* the world remain the true light in the darkness of his atoning death?

We begin by saying that the Son of God takes to himself ruined human nature, making its darkness his own, though it was not his own and though it was absolutely hostile to him. And though he has a "shining innocence," he nevertheless is "burdened with another's sin," that is, with human transgressions.[43] In this is his light *of* and *for* the world: "the Light of the world penetrates into our darkness, even the fearful darkness of death . . . he destroys death and brings life and immortality to light through the Gospel."[44] He, the radiance of the Father, sharing the "mutual light" of the Godhead, takes upon himself the darkness, guilt, and alienation of the sinful human creature. His divine light is not in conflict with this assumption of the burden of the creature; he does not have to negate the "mutual light" to

---

38. Athanasius, *Inc.* 40 (PG 25:163; PPS 44b:92).

39. Davidson, "Divine Light," 65.

40. Calvin, *Inst.* III.2.1; OS 4:7. Cf. Arnold Huijgen's insights regarding Calvin's use of the image of light and his doctrine of "divine accommodation" and epistemology in *Divine Accommodation*, 268–70.

41. Davidson, "Salvation's Destiny," 156.

42. Ursinus, *Catechesis*, qq.16–7.

43. Calvin, *Inst.* II.16.5; OS 3:489: "relucente innocentia."

44. Torrance, "Immortality and Light," 159.

come to the creature's aid; he is not "extinguished by the darkness."[45] On the contrary, the "true Light shone in our darkness, [and] was not itself overshadowed with that darkness, but illumined the gloom with itself."[46] That is, "God displays his essential glory by demonstrating that . . . he graciously wills to share his life with creatures . . . and that carrying it through means tabernacling among us, in ultimately exquisite lowliness."[47] His taking the part of the creaturely gloom and "exquisite lowliness" is the enactment of his light, precisely because in doing so he restores communion by summoning the human creature into God's light.

Thus, we may affirm that God's light in the *opera ad intra* is made known *ad extra* not in leaving the human creature as a prisoner in the shadow of death, but in the supreme act of love, in which he takes the human creature's penalty upon himself. "Seeing that our humanity was in darkness," Gregory of Nyssa reiterates, "he who shone in our darkened nature dispersed the ray of his divinity through our whole compound . . . and so accommodated our entire humanity to his own light . . . which he himself is."[48] It is only the Son of God who may therefore pronounce: "I have come as light into the world, so that whoever believes in me should not remain in darkness" (John 12:46). In making the human creature's condemnation his own in the person of the Son, God arrests the creaturely plunge into darkness, holding creaturely existence in relation to himself. Without ceasing to be the light *of* and *for* the world—that is, without relinquishing his divine sonship—the Son continues the Father's "radiant event of love" for communion, entering into the darkened state of human creatures, taking "for himself a body that is not foreign to our own," and accommodating the condition to himself.[49]

The same one who is the "radiance of the glory of God" is the one who "had offered for all time a single sacrifice for sins" (Heb 1:3; 10:12). With this contrast we find an exchange: what the unrighteous deserve, the righteous one receives, "the righteous for the unrighteous" (1 Pet 3:18); what the godless deserve, the "Christ" receives (Rom 5:6); what those sitting in the darkness deserve, the "great light" receives (Matt 4:16); and, thus, the condemnation due to creaturely "weakness of flesh" is placed upon the eternal Son "in the likeness of sinful flesh" (Rom 8:3). More pointedly: he was "made sin" (2 Cor 5:21) and therefore "bore our sins in his body on the

---

45. Ibid.

46. Gregory of Nyssa, *Letters* 17.14 (in Silvas, *Gregory Nyssa*, 127; cf. NPNF 5:543).

47. Davidson, "Salvation's Destiny," 156.

48. Gregory of Nyssa, *Letters* 17.15 (in Silvas, *Gregory Nyssa*, 127–28).

49. Cf. Athanasius, *Inc.* 8 (PG 25:109; PPS 44b:57).

cross" (1 Pet 2:24); he is "put to death in the flesh" for human sins (1 Pet 3:18); and he thus became to God a "curse for us" by "hanging on a tree" (Gal 3:13). By this exchange, the Son of God has "made us sons of God with him," says Calvin.

> By his descent to earth he has prepared our ascent to heaven; by taking on himself our mortality he has bestowed on us his own immortality; by taking on himself our weakness he has made us strong with his strength; by receiving our poverty into himself he has transferred to us his riches; by taking upon himself the burden of the iniquities with which we are weighed down, he has clothed us with his righteousness.[50]

Therefore, the blessing of the human creature determined by the Father is achieved specifically in the fact that Jesus Christ, the light *of* and *for* the world, who "knew no sin," becomes the sin-bearer in his "decent to the earth." He bears human sin, and so bears God's wrath against human sin and ignorance by his obedience. Therefore:

> When the darkness of God's judgment surrounds him who in his humiliation called himself the Light of the world, then it is this light which breaks through this darkness. Then the meaning of his life and death becomes manifest, because "he that followeth me shall not walk in the darkness, but shall have the light of life" (John 8:12).[51]

He thus accomplishes this reconciliation "in one body" through the "hostile" event of the cross, surrounded by the darkness of Calvary, without any diminution of his divine light. Though "darkness covered the land" where the cross stood (Matt 27:45), though there was present at Calvary the "power of darkness" (Luke 22:53), the Son of God was able, in the outworking of the "radiant event of love," to enter into the terror of the shadow of death and bear, in the same light, the judgment of divine wrath on the cross. And though there was a "subjection to the power of darkness" in the Son's *poena damni*, it was nevertheless a *subjection* to this power, to this "tasting and realization of the divine wrath," and never fully an "enslavement" to this "power of darkness."[52] It is thus paradoxical that, even in his humiliation and death, even in the darkness of Calvary, Jesus Christ reveals himself supremely as the radiant one in "the offering of his own body."[53] And be-

50. Calvin, *Inst.* IV.17.2; CO 2:1003.
51. Berkouwer, *Work of Christ*, 180.
52. Voetius, *Selectarum II*, 9.167.
53. Athanasius, *Inc.* 10 (PG 25:113; PPS 44b:59).

cause he is God himself, the true light *of* and *for* the world, he could subject himself to the "consuming fire" (Heb 12:29) of God against the power of darkness. God's wrath had to be revealed against the darkness and sin of human creatures, against the power of darkness and the power of Satan. But only God could bear his own wrath upon this darkness; only the light *of* and *for* the world could scatter this power; only God's free mercy was capable of bearing the pain and prospect of destruction to which the human creature existing in open rebellion to him was due; only God could "crush, scatter, and break the whole force" of darkness;[54] and only God's radiant love was strong enough to be committed to, yet not reduced nor imprisoned by, this outer darkness. Indeed:

> Who can plumb the fearful depth of what took place in the passion of Christ, when God incarnate cried out in desperate anguish in his struggle with the powers of darkness made obdurate by his own righteous judgement against them? The Cross tells us that God is not a God who holds himself aloof from mankind in its self inflicted agony of guilt and violence and ontological pain, but has come into the midst of all that we are in our state of perdition in order to bring healing and reconciliation and renewal.[55]

This movement of the Son of God, who has "come into the midst of all that we are," happened in order that there should be no more condemnation for human creatures (Rom 8:1), no more sitting in darkness, so that those who are subject to the Law should be ransomed (Gal 4:5), delivered from the curse of the Law (Gal 3:13), forgiven their debts (Col 2:14), healed by his wounds (1 Pet 2:24), redeemed from all lawlessness (Titus 2:14), destined for salvation (1 Thess 5:9), delivered from the domain of darkness (Col 1:13), and given the promise of resurrection (Rom 6:5). "This he did in his love for human beings," says Athanasius getting to the soteriological heart of the matter,

> so that, on the one hand, with all dying in him the law concerning corruption in human beings might be undone . . . and, on the other hand, that as human beings had turned towards corruption he might turn them again to incorruptibility and give them life through death. For Christ has come, and . . . he illumines absolutely all with his light.[56]

---

54. Calvin, *Inst.* II.16.6; OS 3:490.
55. Torrance, "Immortality and Light," 154.
56. Athanasius, *Inc.* 8, 40 (PPS 44b:57, 93; cf. PG 25:109, 163).

Therefore, "He Himself... is the Victory," says Barth, "the light which is not overwhelmed by darkness, but before which darkness must yield until itself is overwhelmed.... He shines out to the world around."[57] The luminous, victorious work of the Son has significance, therefore, only within the work of God's "radiant event of love," which is to shine upon the human creature through the "light of life."

The Light of Life

The *terminus ad quem* of the Son's temporal movement is not the cross and the tomb. To end here would neglect the fact that the shadow of death "no longer has dominion over him," because "Christ was raised from the dead by the glory of the Father" (Rom 6:4, 9). That is, there is terminus to Jesus' temporal movement, notably captured in Athanasius's statement: "not tolerating his temple, the body, to remain [dead] for long . . . on the third day he immediately raised it up, bearing the incorruptibility and impassibility of the body as trophies and victory over death."[58]

However, contrary accounts of the exaltation of Christ are often found in modern Christology, notably in Tillich's distilling the events of Good Friday and Easter Sunday into separate, mythic categories: "The character of this event [Good Friday] remains in darkness, even in the poetical rationalization of the Easter Story."[59] Over against this, we might side with Barth in speaking of the "one-sidedness" of the events of the cross, resurrection, and ascension.[60] And by "one-sidedness," we do not infer a collapse of the Easter light into the darkness of Good Friday—as, perhaps, Balthasar's work at times implies[61]—but rather that the "inner meaning" of this dark event

---

57. Barth, CD IV.3.1:173.
58. Athanasius, *Inc.* 26 (PG 25:141; PPS 44b:77).
59. Tillich, *Systematic Theology*, 2:154.
60. Cf. Barth, CD I.1:180–81; KD I.1:188.

61. See, e.g., Hans Urs von Balthasar's theology of Holy Saturday which includes the notion that, by the *descensus*, "Hell belongs to Christ, and Christ in rising with the knowledge of Hell can communicate that knowledge to us also" (*Mysterium Paschale*, 176). More precisely, in his *The Glory of the Lord* Balthasar sees implicit in the "momentum of the Father's will" for the Son's *kenosis* leading directly from the cross to "the burial of his body and the going of his dead soul to the other dead" (*Glory of the Lord* 7:229). Or, more acutely still, Balthasar sees that the "whole structure of [the Son's] being and his time is built upon . . . his kenosis," which, by his death and descent to hell, the "whole superstructure of the Incarnation" is subsequently removed. That is, the Son's obedience to empty himself and go to the farthest region of Hades reveals the "basis of the entire event of the Incarnation" and the "eternal will of the Son within the Trinity" (ibid., 231). By offering these quotations we are not seeking to discount the

on the cross is given its "proper weight" in the discrete, subsequent event of the resurrection.[62] Of course, this "one-sidedness" is due to the fact that the cross and resurrection of Jesus Christ are held together not by a symbolic understanding, as Tillich would have it,[63] nor by "some metaphysical background"[64] of our own conceptual making, but rather by the particular history of the one whose "eyes are like a flame of fire, and on his head are many diadems, and he has a name written that no one knows but himself," by the radiant one who is "clothed in a robe dipped in blood, and the name by which he is called is The Word of God" (Rev 19:2–3). We continue to speak, therefore, of the light *of* and *for* the world not only by the history of the crucified one, but of that continued presence of Jesus Christ as the radiantly risen and ascended one. And if we are to speak responsibly of God's "radiant event of love" in the movement of Jesus Christ, then we must also speak of the resurrection, ascension, and session of the Son of God.

In sketching this further movement of the Son, let us therefore take a cue from what has thus far been an essential (albeit implicit) text from Barth:

> We begin with the statement that he, Jesus Christ, *lives* [and] as Jesus Christ lives, he also shines out, not with an alien light which falls upon him from without and illumines him, but with his own light proceeding from himself.[65]

Thus, the first-century confession that "this Jesus God raised up" (Acts 2:32) is a witness to the basic reality that this living one is "both Lord and Messiah" (Acts 2:36). As the living Lord and Messiah, Jesus is "alive forever and ever" (Rev 1:18). His being "raised up" is thus the witness to the fact that "in him is the light of life," that he has this lively light "proceeding from himself." His luminous life, therefore, is derived from nothing other than his partaking in the one divine essence. Jesus' risen life is his triumphant divine light, and his resurrection is the declaration that his own light proceeds

---

importance of Balthasar's work; rather, we highlight the instances where he appears to make the event of Holy Saturday the *ultima ratio* through which the events of Good Friday and Easter Sunday *must* be interpreted.

62. This notion is Jüngel's in "Vom Tod des lebendigen Gottes," 121–2. Jüngel goes on to affirm that Good Friday and Easter Day are "two sides of one and the same mystery."

63. Cf. the various statements from Tillich, e.g.: "This Cross, whatever the historical circumstances may have been, is a symbol based on a fact" (*Systematic Theology*, 2:154; cf. ibid., 155–65).

64. Jüngel, *Gottes Sein ist im Werdern*, 6.

65. Barth, CD IV.3.1:39, 46; KD IV.3:41.

from himself. It was the "rising of the Sun of Righteousness alone," relays Owen "that dispelled the darkness that was on the earth, the thick darkness that was on the people."[66]

From his being raised up, the entire movement *ad extra* of the Son is to be seen as the light of eternal life. His earthly ministry was the "Light that has come into the world" (John 3:19) from the eternal foundation that "In him was life," and, at his resurrection, the witness and proclamation that this "life was the light of all people" (John 1:4). Consequently, the resurrection is part of the same free and radiant divine movement of the Son's joyful agreement to undertake the will of the Father *ex pacto*; and this movement is the actuality of God's "lively light" as the one who has life in himself.[67] Exhibiting in this way the lively light of the Son, his being raised up is his state of exaltation, his victory and triumph over darkness and death, his life *totus gloriosus*.[68]

The stages of the state of exaltation—resurrection, ascension, and session at the right hand of the Father—together found the declaration of the reign of Christ. Risen from the dead, he is the one who rules, perforating "any natural sequence of worldly cause and effect," absolutely transcending all limitations.[69] The stages of exaltation are not, of course, to be seen as the Son's attaining a "status that is not his antecedently,"[70] but rather the instance of the conclusive pronouncement of his essential lively radiance, "glowing with brightness and glory heavenly and divine."[71] The resurrection of Christ, the *primus gradus exaltatio*, is the public display of the secret power of light *of* and *for* the world, "the proof by which that dead man was proved to be God's Son and was justified."[72] In the resurrection, the eternal identity of Jesus Christ is sustained and his enemies in the darkness are led "as a host of captives in his train" (Ps 68:18; cf. Eph 4:8). The resurrection of Christ reveals the reality that until now has been partially hidden, namely the Son's being "the radiance of the glory of God and the exact imprint of his nature" (Heb 1:3). Therefore, "God raised him up," and consequently "the darkness is passing away and the true light is already shining" (Acts 2:24; 1 John 2:8): true light, because Jesus Christ is the one who is the "exact imprint" of God's

66. Owen, *Christologia* (*Works*, 1:93).
67. See Heidegger, *Corp. theol.* 4.51.
68. Bucanus, *Inst.* 26.18.
69. Davidson, "Salvation's Destiny," 165.
70. Ibid., 166.
71. Polanus, *Synt. theol.* II.6.22.
72. Coccejus, *Summa*, 42.15: "1) argumentum, quo elle homo mortuus demonstratus est Filius Dei esse, et iustificatus est."

nature. The radiantly risen one is therefore exalted "far above all things" (cf. Eph 1:21; Col 1:17); he is the one "raised up to the highest ineffable glory."[73] Thus, the continued and unhindered "shining out" with "his own light proceeding from himself" is the work of this one.

To know the radiantly risen one "is to know the coming and indeed the continuous and unequivocal victory of light over darkness which cannot be arrested by any resisting element in man, by any devil."[74] His reign as the exalted "Lord and Christ" is therefore located in the "heavenly kingdom" (2 Tim 4:18) in which he is free from limitation. Thus, the second stage of exaltation, ascension, follows resurrection because, as the radiant one shares in the eternal light of God, his existence post-Easter involves a transcendent local withdrawal from and over the creaturely realm. At this point there is manifest the fact that "the Word did not suffer loss in taking a body in order that he should seek to receive grace."[75]

But the exaltation of the radiantly risen one, the fact that he is the "light of life," does not negate his being near to us. In other words, though the radiantly risen and ascended one's presence is no longer in bodily fashion, he nevertheless freely binds himself to those to whom he presents himself in the power of his Holy Spirit. Thus, the radiantly risen one is not present by "any precarious power or power of created nature," but spiritually present, by virtue of his personal divine will, by virtue of his further exaltation of session at the right hand of the Father.[76] Thus, the "nature of that presence which the Lord promises to his followers ought to be understood spiritually," Calvin comments on Matthew 28:20:

> Since he can assist us by the grace of his Spirit, as if he stretched out his hand from heaven. For he who, in respect of his body, is at a great distance from us, not only diffuses the efficacy of his Spirit through the whole world, but actually dwells in us. . . . Christ *was taken up into heaven*, not to enjoy blessed rest at a distance from us, but to govern the world for the salvation of all believers.[77]

---

73. Polanus, *Synt. theol.* II.6.22.

74. Barth, CD IV.3.1:266; KD IV.3:306: "Ihn selbst erkennen, heißt den kommenden endgültigen und damit auch den jetzt schon fortschreitenden, von keinem Widersetzlichen im Menschen, von keinem Teufel aufzuhaltenden, den unzweideutigen Sieg des Lichtes über die Finsternis erkennen."

75. Athanasius, *c. Ar.* 1.42 (PG 26:97; NPNF 4:123).

76. Bucanus, *Inst.* 26.3-4: "Non ulla precaria aut naturae creatae."

77. Calvin, *Comm. harm. ev.*, Matt 28:20 (CO 45:824; CC 17:390, 393).

In his reign, the radiant one shines forth in communicative nearness to human creatures sitting in the domain of darkness; this radiantly risen one sets himself in relation to human creatures and sheds abroad the "light of the knowledge of the glory of God" (2 Cor 4:6). Thus, the Son's communicative action is in "no need of supplement. . . . It declares itself as reality. It displays itself. It proclaims itself."[78] And the state of exaltation of Jesus Christ is therefore part of the positive definition of God's being *light in himself* and *shining forth his light*. God is light in this manner. Jesus Christ, exalted in all things, is *the* fundamental reality, for his action "displays itself" and "proclaims itself." He is this, of course, in the personal relation to the Father and to the Holy Spirit, because "the holy and blessed Trinity is indivisible and united in itself," says Athanasius. Thus:

> When the Father is mentioned, with him is both his Word and the Spirit who is in the Son. If the Son is named, the Father is in the Son, and the Spirit is not external to the Word. For there is *one grace* from the Father which is perfected through the Son in the Holy Spirit.[79]

To speak of the resurrection of Christ is therefore to speak of the cause of the resurrection in the will of the Father who raises the Son from the dead (cf. John 17:24), and so to speak of the "Spirit of him who raised Jesus from the dead" (Rom 8:11) in whom the "*one grace* from the Father [is] fulfilled through the Son and in the Holy Spirit" that shines forth on creation.

This "one grace" which shines forth to human creatures in the work of the triune God is, Barth reminds us, "distinguished . . . from human capacity," and is instead characterized as "light which shines out of the darkness and back into the darkness of the crucifixion of Jesus Christ back into the darkness of our own lives."[80] This "one grace," extending from the resurrection, is the power of the exalted one, in session at the right hand of the Father, and it is the "power which shines into the darkness of our life, by which we are made bright even in the midst of darkness because we are as it were revealed to ourselves as those who belong to this exalted and true man."[81] As this risen one, the radiant power of the exalted Son is that light from which all other lights receive their luminosity; more precisely, in him creatures receive the overflow of the light and love of God.[82] The radiantly

---

78. Barth, CD IV.3.1:7.
79. Athanasius, *Ad. Ser.* 1.14.6 (PG 26:564; PPS 43:75; emphasis mine).
80. Barth, CD IV.2:310.
81. Ibid.
82. Gregory of Nyssa, *De perf. Christ.* (PG 46:264). Cf. Williams, *Resurrection*,

risen Christ, therefore, "does not need to receive light from without, from men, the world, or the faith community."[83] Rather, the resurrection of Christ is that divine act in which there is manifest the eternal light of God in the Son, who is the ground of all things that exist. Creaturely existence is therefore being faced by the shining of the "light of the knowledge of the glory of God in the face of Jesus Christ" (2 Cor 4:6). It is in this gracious encounter that human creatures are properly "illumined and moved by him."[84]

Thus, by the state of exaltation—the "great sign of the love of God" in which God has reconciled us with himself, in which is made manifest the scattering of darkness by his light[85]—it has become possible that in Jesus Christ "we have redemption through his blood, the forgiveness of our trespasses, according to the riches of his grace" (Eph 1:7). By his blood Jesus Christ has justified human creatures (cf. Rom 5:9; Heb 1:3), by his resurrection death and darkness are scattered (cf. 1 Cor 15:54; John 1:5), and by his ascension and session salvation is offered, access to the "throne of Grace" is granted, and light is given to human creatures (Heb 4:16; John 1:9). Jesus Christ has thus procured for human creatures the freedom to live in the light in the Lord (cf. Eph 5:8).

But this becoming light by Christ is a gift, that is, it is always "in the Lord." Thus, the creaturely standing is a standing *in God*, who "puts the other, as it were, in the place of himself; and regards the good done to him as done to himself. So far love is a binding force, since it aggregates another to ourselves, and refers his good to our own."[86] That is, in the person of his

---

esp. ch. 3.

83. Barth, CD IV.3.1:46; KD IV.3:49. Given Barth's comment, the undertaking in which belief in the resurrection is bracketed from the reality of the risen Christ misinterprets the object of faith, which is the Son of God himself in his self-radiating reality. Often times, the work of N. T. Wright seems to be lacking such precision. For instance, Wright is of the persuasion that we approach Christology as a "portrait of Jesus as he was in his lifetime" before we embark on the "evidence before us" for the resurrection (*Jesus and the Victory of God*, 614). Or, perhaps more recently, Wright states that Jesus' ministerial statements and the event of the resurrection "*joined up with the expectation of yhwh's return on the one hand and the spirit of God on the other to generate a fresh reading of the messianic texts which enabled a full christological awareness to dawn on the disciples*" (*Paul and the Faithfulness of God* 2.3, 692–93; emphasis original). There is a long history of such an approach to Christology and the resurrection itself. For a good treatment of this, at least in light of NT scholarship, see Barclay, "The Resurrection," 13–30.

84. Athanasius, *Inc.* 42 (PPS 44b:94).

85. John Chrysostom, *Hom.* II, 1 Tim 1:8–10 (NPNF 13:479).

86. Aquinas, ST 1a.q20.1ad.3.

Son, the God who is light scatters sin and darkness in order that a chosen people will meet with his grace, love, and mercy.

> But you are a chosen race, a royal priesthood, a holy nation, God's own people, in order that you may proclaim the mighty acts of him who called you out of darkness into his marvelous light. (1 Pet 2:9)

That is God's "radiant event of love." God "called you out of darkness," entering the situation of human ruin in love and grace. He did this in order to bring the human creature out of darkness to its proper glory in God's "marvelous light." In doing so, he has rescued the human creature from its own domain of darkness. And by the Holy Spirit, God has gathered a people marked above all by proclaiming or praising the "excellencies" of the loving God who has given the "light of life" through the radiantly risen one.

The Illuminating Spirit

Combined with the work of the radiantly risen Son rescuing human creatures from the domain of darkness, and his state of exaltation, stands a further movement of God in the illumination and restoration of human creatures to communion with God. The Holy Spirit is the agent of those divine acts through which creatures reach their intended destiny. The Holy Spirit gives the light of life, acting in and shining upon the human creature in such a way that there occurs the terminus of the Father's loving will. "We receive the Son's light through the Father's light in the light of the Spirit."[87] In this movement, which is a gift, the Holy Spirit makes actual in the human creature the blessing for which it has been qualified in God's "radiant event of love." That gift is communion between the *God who is light in himself* and his "saints in light."

Yet an adequate description of this renewed relationship that the human creature participates in must contain an account of the doctrine of the church, as well as an account of the doctrine of illumination. However, before embarking on this narrower course—which chapters 4 and 5 will address—we may offer here, in our examination of the "radiant event of love," a brief sketch on the work of the Holy Spirit in establishing human communion with God in relation to several further matters.

---

87. Gregory Nazianzen, *Or.* 31.3 (PG 36:136; PPS 23:118).

The Radiant Identity of the Holy Spirit

First, in reiterating this divine determination for the human creature, we must again affirm the identity of the third person of the Trinity.[88] As with the work of the Father and the Son, the work of the Spirit is the radiant work of God. The Holy Spirit is light because he is intrinsic to God's "mutual light" and not merely an external divine force, for "unless a thing be light itself, how can it display the gracious gift of light?"[89] That is, God is the "Threefold light" and so the Holy Spirit is light.[90] The Holy Spirit is within the luminous sphere of divinity, and only as such is he the light-giver. In his shining in and upon the human creature, the Holy Spirit is no mere immanent principle. Rather, the Spirit is coeternal with the Father and the Son "because of the power of eternity," and the Spirit's work is inseparable from the works of Father and Son "because of the unity of brightness."[91] As the "radiant event" of the Father's will is the *fons actionis* of reconciliation, and as the "radiant event" of the Son's work is the *medium actionis* in his triumphing over darkness, so also the "radiant event" of the Holy Spirit's work is the *terminus actionis* of what has been willed by the Father and achieved by the Son.

Thus, the same Spirit whose illuminating gift restores communion between God and lost human creatures, is the same one that shares in all the properties of the One divine essence: he is in every respect "infinite in power, unlimited in goodness, immeasurable by time or ages."[92] Moreover, the Holy Spirit has his personhood in terms of the divine *hypostaeses*, that is, in the order of the *opera Dei personalia* in which he is spirated by the Father and the Son, and thus has "unity and indivisibility in every work . . . from the Father and the Son."[93] Sharing "a kind of consubstantial communion,"[94] he is entirely separate from creatures, and only so does he shine in them and give himself to them with his own "power from on high" (Luke 24:49)—*to*

---

88. It is refreshing to see Christopher Holmes's retrieval of the notion that "one's pneumatology is only as good as one's wider doctrine of the Trinity" in his recent study, *Holy Spirit*, 213.

89. Gregory of Nyssa, *Sp. sanc.* 22 (NPNF 5:324).

90. Gregory Nazianzen, *Or.* 33.11 (PG 36:228; NPNF 7:332).

91. Ambrose, *De fide* 4.9.108 (PL 16:638): ". . . coaeternus, propter virtuis aeternitatem: inseperabilis, propter claritudinis unitatem."

92. Basil, *Sp. sanc.* 9.22 (PG 32:107; PPS 42:53).

93. Ibid., 16.37 (PG 32:134; PPS 42:70).

94. Augustine, *Trin.* 15.27.50 (PL 42:1007): ". . . communio quaedam consubstantialis."

creatures and not a "spirit made common" *by* creatures.⁹⁵ Basil offers a good reminder worth quoting at length:

> Whoever hears "spirit" cannot impress on his mind a circumscribed nature ... or one at all similar to creation.... Rather, the Spirit perfects others, but himself lacks nothing. He lives, but not because he has been restored to life; rather, he is the source of life. He does not grow in strength gradually, but is complete all at once. He is established in himself and present everywhere. He is the source of holiness, an intellectual light for every rational power's discovery of truth, supplying, so to say, through himself. He is inaccessible in nature, but approachable in goodness.... He is portioned out impassibly and participated in as a whole. He is like a sunbeam whose grace is present to the one who enjoys him as if he were present to such a one alone ... and still he sends out grace that is complete and sufficient for all.⁹⁶

Thus, the Spirit's "complete and sufficient" external works are *his* works as the one who has the divine nature, wherein his "supplying" light to the human creature he nevertheless remains "complete all at once" with the Father and the Son in a "procession of love."⁹⁷

Grace and Participation

Second, as the "sign of sanctification" the Holy Spirit's works are works of grace.⁹⁸ The Holy Spirit is given to creatures—e.g., "I will send" (John 14:26) and "I will pour out" (Acts 2:17)—in fulfillment of the divine will and as an exercise of God's "radiant event of love." Moreover, the mode of the Spirit's illuminative work on and in the reconciled confirms his being the *medium actionis* on and in all human creatures. By the Spirit, God breathes into human creatures the breath of life. Creatures therefore have this "light of life"

---

95. Schleiermacher, *Christian Faith*, §§122–23. See Schleiermacher's insistence that the "common spirit [i.e., the common self-consciousness] is only the Holy Spirit insofar as the activity it induces is a prolongation of Christ's activity" (§122.3). Perhaps more pointedly in Schleiermacher's "first theorem" of §123, we hear that "the Spirit is not something supernatural or mysterious [for] the human would be no more human if we had to conceive it united with a higher nature in one person, so our life and the life of other believers would no longer seem to be humanly interconnected.... Thus, union is realized in the form of a common spirit, [that is,] we share in the Spirit as a common consciousness" (§123.2-3).

96. Basil, *Sp. sanc.* 9.22 (PG 32:107–10; PPS 42:53).

97. Aquinas, *c. Gen.* 4.26.1.

98. Aquinas, ST 1a.q43.7ad6.

in a particular way, by virtue of an external quickening origin, which is the Holy Spirit. This principle is a pure gift, which is proper to the Holy Spirit.[99] But this gift imparted by the Holy Spirit is, indeed, the "light of life," and not merely a relation to another external light. By the Holy Spirit, therefore, the human creature participates in the movement of reconciliation, not as its own cause but as one "called out of darkness into his marvelous light."

Of course, we must quickly qualify what is meant here by the term "participation," as its use in this setting causes confusion. In employing such language, contemporary theology has often turned to the thinking of Calvin—namely, Book 3 of the *Institutio*—as being the classic marker of a Protestant notion of *participatio Christi* or, more precisely, "partakers of the divine nature" (*theias koinōnoi physeōs*, 2 Pet 1:4).[100] Some readers of Calvin correctly argue that *participatio Christi* is accomplished by the Holy Spirit, who "allows true participation in the very life of God—which is the *humanity of Christ*."[101] That is, Calvin seems to appeal to the Holy Spirit as the bond of participation in Christ so that he may advance a union with Christ that preserves the ontological distance between God and human creatures, "acting as a safeguard against substantial participation."[102] And yet the interpretation simultaneously arises that when Calvin speaks of *participatio Christi* it implies a "Trinitarian participation—our adoption."[103] There seems a miscalculation here: if it is the Holy Spirit who enables the human creature "called out of darkness into [God's] marvelous light" to have a spirit of adoption, and yet there remains an ontological distance *realiter* between the Spirit and the human creature, how then can participation or adoption be a trinitarian participation or adoption in the *opera Dei ad intra*? Quite simply, this is not Calvin's primary way of speaking about such concepts. Rather, Calvin's primary way of speaking about adoption or participation is in terms of regeneration and illumination.[104]

---

99. Cf. Aquinas's thought that "Gift" is a proper name given to the Holy Spirit, because it denotes the "proprietas origins Spiritus Sancti, quae est processio" (ST 1a.q38.2ad2).

100. See, e.g., Tamburello, *Union with Christ*; Butin, *Revelation, Redemption, and Response*; Carpenter, "A Question of Union with Christ?" 363–86; and the very capable study of Macaskill, *Union with Christ*, esp. 77–99. See further: Billings, *Calvin, Participation, and the Gift*; and "Union with Christ and the Double Grace," 49–71.

101. Canlis, *Calvin's Ladder*, 145. Cf. Calvin, *Inst.* III.2.7; OS 4:15–6.

102. Ibid.

103. Ibid. See Muller's worry that Canlis's conclusions "create a false picture, indeed, a caricature, both of Calvin's thought and of the theologies of the later Reformed" (*Calvin and the Reformed Tradition*, 242).

104. Indeed, the great Princetonian reader of Calvin's work, B. B. Warfield, states

> God justifies not only by pardoning but by regenerating. . . . Whomever, therefore, God receives into grace, on them he at the same time bestows the spirit of adoption, by whose power he remakes them into his image. But if the brightness of the sun cannot be separated from its heat, shall we therefore say that the earth is warmed by its light, or lighted by its heat? Is there anything more applicable to the present matter than this comparison? The sun, by its heat, quickens and fructifies the earth, by its beams brightens and illumines it.[105]

Thus, Calvin's use of the term "adoption" implies that the human creature "participates" in the relation of the Son to the Father—a relation that, by the Holy Spirit, is characterized by human participation in the unique relation of the Son to the Father only by a *"creaturely version"* and *"replication of the relations,"* as Davidson insightfully states.[106] What human creatures thus participate in are the benefits of that radiant work of the Son, namely, "growing together with Christ," which is the unifying basis of the new life of the human creature, effected by "the power of the Holy Spirit."[107]

From Calvin we might therefore infer that this participation is a *unio-praesentia gratiae tentum*: a union made possible and preserved by grace alone. Of course, this does not mean that by the Holy Spirit human creatures are made into cooperating or supplementary agents alongside God. The human creatures called into the light are therefore "never absorbed or assimilated into God," says Davidson further, they "never *contribute to* God's own endlessly self-maintaining and complete life."[108] It is, after all, a *unio spiritualis*, a spiritual union under the auspices of the Holy Spirit. Thus, being "in the light" does not entail being "the light" itself (cf. Eph 5:8–9). The partnership with God that the Holy Spirit imparts is a commu-

---

that this is "the very hinge of [Calvin's] doctrine" (*Works*, 5:112). More recently, in speaking of the *ordo salutis*, Muller states that, for Calvin, "Regeneration . . . is so closely linked to repentance that the two terms can be taken to indicate two sides of the same divine work." Consequentially, "Repentance . . . is an effect of 'participation in Christ' [and] the second grace, regeneration, follows logically (not temporally) upon the first grace just as participation follows union" (*Calvin and the Reformed Tradition*, 209–10).

105. Calvin, *Inst*. III.11.6; OS 4:187–88.

106. Davidson, "Salvation's Destiny," 174.

107. Calvin, *Inst*. III.11.5; OS 4:186. Cf. Muller: ". . . contra Canlis in particular, union with Christ was not understood [by Calvin and the later Reformed] as a final product of the *ordo salutis* dependent on completion of all steps in the series—rather it was understood and typically explicitly identified as the very basis of the sequence of the application of salvation" (*Calvin and the Reformed Tradition*, 240).

108. Davidson, "Salvation's Destiny," 174.

nion in which the creature is illuminated as *creature*—that is, as a "*creaturely version*" of participation—in which the creature qua creature is called to reflect in its *creaturely* acts the divine act of illumination. Illumination is thus not a matter of *participatio* in God's work but rather of the renewal of the human vocation. And in that is accomplished the "radiant event" of God's love for the human creature.

The Spirit's Loving Illumination

Finally, then, we see that God loves the human creature that he shines forth upon. And so the Holy Spirit's work in the economy of redemption is to impart the light of life. The Spirit maintains human creatures by moving and shining upon them so that their dignity is preserved and destiny achieved. A brief look at what the classical tradition of dogmatics calls the "doctrine of divine illumination" exemplifies this principle in stating how God acts on the human intellect.[109]

We might stay with Calvin and observe his handling of this matter in Book 2 of the *Institutio*—the context, it is important to note, is not a discussion of cognitive acts per se, but a reflection on the fact that human creatures are "utterly blind and stupid in divine matters," in the course of which the regeneration or illumination of the mind by God is treated.[110] The topic from which Calvin begins—the "blindness" of the unregenerate creaturely mind—commences with quoting John 1:4-5, and he goes on to state that this passage "shows that man's soul is so illumined by the brightness of God's light as never to be without some slight flame or at least a

---

109. We will look more closely at this "theory" or "doctrine" of illumination in chapter 5, particularly in connection with theology as the "activity of the illumined human mind."

110. See esp. Calvin, *Inst.* II.2.19-21; OS 3: 261-64: ". . . in rebus divinis caecam prorsus esse et stupidam." Of course, Calvin's "doctrine of illumination" is not limited to this section of the *Institutio*, as Calvin himself would be quick to point out. His early work—particularly his *Catechismus (1538)*—is emphatic in depicting the Holy Spirit as the one who "illumines us with his light" in order that we learn the "goodness we possess in Christ" (ibid. [CO 5:341]). One may also look to his commentaries, namely, his comments on Ps 36:9 (i.e., illumination as "supernatural gift"; CC 5:12), 1 Cor 2:10 (i.e., the "special illumination of the Spirit," CC 20:110), and 2 Cor 3:6 (i.e., illumination as regeneration; CC 20:174). Beyond key scriptural passages, Calvin also admits that the tradition guides his course regarding illumination, particularly Augustine's doctrine of illumination. See Augustine and his idea that the intelligence is illumined "ab eo lumine illo intelligibili perfusa quodam modo et illustrata cernit, non per corporeos oculos" (*De div.* 46.2 [PL 40:31]). For a thorough review of Augustine and his heirs, see Schumacher, *Divine Illumination*, esp. 52-68.

spark of it; but that even with this illumination it does not comprehend God."[111] Calvin's insistence that "even with this illumination it does not comprehend God" is meant to refute the possibility of comprehending God through the *lumen naturae*. The person who depends on the light of nature to discern "spiritual mysteries," Calvin says, "comprehends nothing."[112] Rather, through the "Spirit of regeneration" there is a "special illumination" of the creaturely mind.[113] "Flesh is not capable of such lofty wisdom as to conceive God and is God's, unless it be illuminated by the Spirit of God."[114] The mind is therefore not moved or illumined by another. Rather, as the *interior magister*, the Holy Spirit "by a wonderful and singular power forms our ... minds to understand."[115] The effect of this on the matter of illumination is registered in the subsequent trinitarian statements: "[T]he sun rises upon the earth when God's Word shines upon men; but they do not have its benefit until he who is called the 'Father of lights' (James 1:17) either gives eyes or opens them. For wherever the Spirit does not cast his light, all is darkness."[116]

Spelling this out in these sections, Calvin lays down two principles intended to undermine the assumption that knowledge of God is framed by the natural creaturely mind.[117] First, God—not the human creature—is the one who illumines God's "mysteries"; second, therefore, "God is open only to him whose mind has been made new by the illumination of the Holy Spirit." Yet there is no sense here that illumination of the human mind is compromised by the fact that the Holy Spirit is the one who illumines the human creature. To speak of divine movement is not to eliminate creaturely movement but to say that, as created, it has its "keenness" as a secondary component. We see this in some of Calvin's later comments in the *Institutio* regarding the results of illumination:

> Therefore, as we cannot come to Christ unless we be drawn by the Spirit of God, so when we are drawn we are lifted up in mind

---

111. Calvin, *Inst.* II.2.19. Calvin's emphasis is surely on the latter phrase: "... sed eat amen illuminatione Deum non comprehendere" (OS 3:261).

112. Calvin, *Inst.* II.2.20; OS 3:263: "nempe qui naturae lumine nititur. Ille, inquam, nihil in spiritualibus mysteriis Dei comprehendit."

113. *Inst.*; OS 3:262.

114. *Inst.*, 2.2.19; OS 3:261.

115. *Inst.*, II.2.20; OS 3:263.

116. *Inst.*, II.2.21; OS 3:265: "... quia ubicunque Spiritu suo non resplendent, Omnia tenebris occupatur."

117. For a good study of Calvin on the natural knowledge of God, see Steinmetz, *Calvin in Context*, 23–39.

and heart above our understanding. For the soul, illumined by him, takes on a new keenness, as it were, to contemplate the heavenly mysteries, whose splendor had previously blinded it. And man's understanding, thus beamed by the light of the Holy Spirit, then at last truly begins to taste those things which belong to the Kingdom of God.[118]

Thus, having been "lifted up," "illumined," and "beamed upon" by the Holy Spirit, the human creature is therefore able, through "keenness" as a secondary component, to "contemplate the heavenly mysteries" and "truly begin to taste" the goodness of the kingdom of God. "God works in his elect . . . through his Spirit," Calvin continues, "illuminating their minds and forming their hearts to the love and cultivation of righteousness, he makes them a new creation."[119] In short: God recreates the created intellect and the Spirit who is light "beams upon" its operation, "to the love and cultivation of righteousness" found in communion with God.

But we cannot end our outline of the work of the Holy Spirit here with Calvin; indeed it must extend throughout the remaining parts of our study itself. For the time being, however, we may offer a glimpse of the pathway ahead. In agreement with the illuminating work of the Spirit is his work in the community of "saints in light," that is, the church. By the Spirit is gathered a human "circumference" to the Son's radiant work. Illumination is the regeneration of human created nature, and the restoration of all those powers in which it entails. Most of all, the communion with God that the Holy Spirit enacts in human creatures is a lively, quickened, and radiant movement "in the effectual application of all unto the souls of men—made gloriously conspicious."[120]. The shining of the Holy Spirit upon human creatures thus gives a new intellectual nature, pronouncing Jesus Christ to the gathered saints of the church and illuminating the human mind to learn from his teaching.[121] Thus, by the Holy Spirit, God orders human creatures as a "circumference" of this divine radiance; and by virtue of God's self-radiance in the coming of the Son and the Spirit there takes place a human proclamation.

This proclamation is the creaturely movement as a "circumference" and "reflection" of the divine work of illumination.[122] That is, "the knowledge of God given to man through his illumination," says Barth,

---

118. Calvin, *Inst.*, III.20.40; OS 4:350.
119. *Inst.*, II.5.5; OS 3:303.
120. Owen, *Pneumatologia* (*Works*, 3:23).
121. Again, see chapter 5 for further explication of this point.
122. See our thoughts in chapter 4.

is the claiming not only of his thinking but also of his willing and work, of the whole man, for God. It is his refashioning to be a theatre, witness and instrument of His acts. Its subject and content, which is also its origin, makes it an active knowledge . . . in which man leaves certain old courses and enters and pursues new ones. As the work of God becomes clear to him, its reflection lights up his own heart and self and whole existence through the One whom he may know on the basis of His own self-declaration. Illumination . . . is the *total* alteration of the one whom it befalls.[123]

The "*total* alteration" of creatures happens in God's light, for it is here that they really do see light (cf. Ps 36:9). And this promise of illumination has its fulfillment, therefore, in the gathering of the "saints in light." In this gathering of saints is realized the "refashioning to be a theatre, witness and instrument" of God through the illuminating love of the Spirit of Jesus Christ. This loving "*total* alteration" defines the setting of the church, for it is here that the work of God truly illumines the "heart and self and whole existence through the One whom [we] may know on the basis of His own self-declaration."

Conclusion

With this we complete a sketch of the movement of God's "radiant event of love." In this movement we see that the "radiant event" of God's love for creatures is figured in his shining forth himself into the darkness and sin of the human creature. In doing so, God achieves his determination that creatures should be gathered into his "marvelous light." The divine shining forth takes effect as the act of love in which God elects, reconciles, and illuminates human creatures: determined by the Father, accomplished in the temporal movement of the Son, and brought to its term by the Holy Spirit. The gospel is thus the pronouncement of this glorious work of the triune God. And by this work God builds and preserves a gathering of saints in light whose task includes a cry of praise: "Hail, gladdening Light!" This cry may form a proper doctrinal connection between what has been proposed here in chapter 3 and what is to come in chapters 4 and 5. God is the radiant One in a threefold manner; and he is the One who has eternally willed to gather the church—that "circumference" gathered around the "illuminating center" of the evangel, Christ—his dwelling place. We therefore turn in the

---

123. Barth, CD IV.3.2:510; KD IV.3:586: ". . . totale Veränderung dessen, dem sie widerfährt."

coming chapter to examine God's continued and sustained shining upon the gathering of the saints in light.

4

Pro Ecclesia
The Saints in the Light of God

> You are the light of the world. A city set on a hill cannot be hidden. Nor do people light a lamp and put it under a basket, but on a stand, and it gives light to all in the house. In the same way, let your light shine before others, so that they may see your good works and give glory to your Father who is in heaven. (Matt 5:14–16)

THE FORMER CHAPTER GAVE AN ACCOUNT OF GOD'S LOVING EXTERNAL works in the "radiant event" of the evangel with which he elects, reconciles, and illuminates a human "circumference" in the radiant *emanationes* of the Son and the Holy Spirit. Thus, an account of the light of God in its threefold form is incomplete without attention to this gathered "circumference" of human creatures with whom God is radiantly present. This present chapter is concerned with a description of the church as the gathering of saints in the light of God. It will therefore be concerned with the trinitarian basis of the saints in the light, followed by several intonations on the visible "outshining" marks of the gathered church.

Trinity, Incarnation, and Ecclesiology

We begin, however, by asking *how* the light of God and the light of the church are to be associated. That is, can we merely reduce talk of God's light and work to the light and work of the church? That the doctrine of the Trinity is foundational for talk of ecclesiology has been noted since the earliest theology of the church, particularly in Tertullian's notion that "properly and principally the church is the Spirit himself in whom is the Trinity of the one divinity—Father, Son, and Holy Spirit."[1] This association has found a good deal of renewal in contemporary trinitarian theology, especially in those forms of trinitarian thought which stress that the Trinity is a "society or community of three fully personal and fully divine entities," not only founded by their personal relations, but in their gracious relation to the creaturely gathering of the church.[2] Such insights from modern trinitarianism often champion the relation of the Father, Son, and Holy Spirit as the foundation for the church, and the church is therefore deemed the "political alternative"[3] of the human calling to society, and thus the social extension of reconciliation through its "reproducing on earth the mystery of the unity in diversity" of the essence of God.[4] Perhaps more pointedly: the gathering of "fellow-humans to which we are restored by grace" is a "reflection and extension of God's own life-in-communion."[5]

A rather engaging study regarding these current factors is found in Volf's *After Our Likeness*, where he argues that there are "creaturely correspondences to this mystery of triunity," or, more precisely, that there is an "ecclesial correspondence to the Trinity."[6] Volf therefore seeks to examine

---

1. Tertullian, *De pud.* 21 (PL 2:1024): "Nam et ipsa ecclesia proprie et principaliter ipse est spiritus, in quo est trinitas unius diuinitatis, Pater et Filius et Spiritus sanctus."

2. See Plantinga Jr., "Social Trinity and Tritheism," 27.

3. Hauerwas and Willimon, *Resident Aliens*, 41. Beyond these examples, social trinitarian thought has notably been presented by David Brown ("Trinity, Personhood and Individuality," 21–47), Moltmann (*Trinity and the Kingdom*, viii, 172–73), Volf (*Exclusion and Embrace*; *After Our Likeness*); Zizioulas (*Being and Communion*); and Franke ("God Is Love," 105–19). There are also the more analytic positions from Swinburne (*Christian God*); Forrest ("Divine Fission"); and Moreland and Craig ("Trinity," 21–43). For criticisms, see the particularly insightful studies by Coakley ("'Persons' in the 'Social' Doctrine of the Trinity," 123–44), and Kilby ("Perichoresis and Projection," 432–45).

4. Ware, *Orthodox Church*, 240. There are stronger statements in, say, LaCugna: "*Trinitarian life is also our life*" (*God for Us*, 228; emphasis original).

5. Van den Brink, "Social Trinitarianism," 350. Van den Brink's study makes several bold conclusions—namely, that a "person who reads the New Testament would naturally develop a social account of the economic Trinity" (ibid., 349)—but summarily waffles when he states that we "safely leave" the metaphysical questions of the unity of the *essentia Dei* to "philosophers of religion . . . to come up with proposals that may achieve this" (ibid., 348). Indeed, such a "safety net" allows van den Brink to posit any theological claim of social trinitarianism he sees fit. A similar claim, incidentally, is asserted in the recent dogmatics of Gerrish, *Christian Faith*, 303.

6. Volf, *After Our Likeness*, 192, 194. Volf is essentially arguing that the church, both *particularis* and *universalis*, is an *imago Trinitatis*.

the "correspondences" between the character of the trinitarian persons, on the one hand, and that of ecclesial persons on the other, so as to highlight how the structure of the divine relations structure ecclesial relations.[7] This "structure of divine relations" is described as "a communion in which personhood and sociality are equiprimal," which, in turn, makes the church "a communion corresponding to the Trinity."[8] The result of this relation of the church to the triune life is that those "assembled in the name of Christ can be an . . . ('image') of the Trinity."[9] Volf clarifies this position elsewhere:

> So when I speak about human *imaging* of the Trinity, I mean the human beings receive themselves as created in the image of the Trinity by the power of the Spirit. . . . Because God has made us to reflect God's own triune being, our human tasks are not first of all to *do* as God does—and certainly not to make ourselves as God *is*—but to let ourselves be indwelled by God and to celebrate and proclaim what God has done, is doing and will do.[10]

At the heart of Volf's work is the belief that there is a likeness, correspondence, or "imaging" between the divine nature and the social relations of the nature of the church. For instance, he rightly claims that "the nature of God . . . fundamentally determines the character of the Christian life," yet he fails to show how the being of God is of a fundamentally different order than its human, ecclesial existence.[11] Such appeals to the so-called *imago Trinitatis* suggest that this "image" is a natural predicate of ecclesial existence.

We might place alongside Volf's reflections on Trinity and ecclesiology the closely linked conception of the church as the "extension of the incarnation": the church is the ontological union between Christ and the church. One instance is found in Tillich's notion that the person and work of "the Christ" is resolvable into the "primacy" of the "Spiritual Community."[12] We

---

7. Ibid., 204.
8. Ibid., 213.
9. Ibid., 197.
10. Volf, "Being as God Is," 7.
11. Ibid., 4.

12. Tillich, *Systematic Theology*, 3:149. Cf. "We do not use the word 'church' for the Spiritual Community, because this word has been used, of necessity, in the frame of the ambiguities of religion. At this point we speak instead of that which is able to conquer the ambiguities of religion—the New Being—in anticipation, in central appearance, and in reception." However, Tillich continues, churches may be the "manifest religious self-expression" and the "actualization and the distortion" of the Spiritual Community (ibid., 153–54).

find such affirmations throughout Tillich's thoughts surrounding the identity of "the Christ" and the church, particularly in his foundational comment that "Christ would not be the Christ without those who receive him as the Christ."[13] Thus, the "Spiritual Community" is identical with the "New Being"[14] of Christ in that

> The term "Body of Christ" expresses the unambiguous life created by the divine Presence, in a sense similar to that of the term "Spiritual Community." . . . The Spiritual Community is [therefore] unambiguous; it is New Being, created by the Spiritual Presence. But, although *it is a manifestation of unambiguous life, it is nonetheless fragmentary, as was the manifestation of unambiguous life in the Christ* and in those who expected the Christ. The Spiritual Community is an unambiguous, though fragmentary, creation of the divine Spirit.[15]

The outcome is that Christ is "receptively" or "communally" formed.

Tillich might be a rather severe illustration; but related forms of thought can be found, for instance, in Bonhoeffer, who notably suggests—in the midst of the rising *Nationalsozialismus* of his time[16]—that the *Gemeinde* is the body of the risen Christ as the sole means of his presence and visibility: "The body of the exalted Lord is also a visible body, taking the form of the church-community."[17] Elsewhere he states emphatically that

> Between [Christ's] ascension and his coming again the Church is his form and indeed his only form. . . . The Church is the body of Christ. Here body is not only a symbol. The Church *is* the body of Christ, it does not *signify* the body of Christ. . . . It is a comprehensive and central concept of the mode of existence of the one who is present in his exaltation and humiliation.[18]

A blunt expansion of this thought is found in Gary Badcock: "Jesus Christ the Son of God is not who he is without the church."[19] Badcock of-

---

13. Ibid.

14. "New Being" is defined by Tillich early on in his *Systematic Theology* as "a reality in which the self-estrangement of our existence is overcome, a reality of reconciliation and reunion, of creativity, meaning, and hope" (ibid., 1:49).

15. Ibid., 3:150–53.

16. For an insightful background Bonhoeffer's Christology from his "mittleren periode," see Feil, *Theologie Dietrich Bonhoeffers*, esp. 177–89.

17. Bonhoeffer, *Nachfolge*, (*Werke*, 4:242).

18. Bonhoeffer, *Christ the Center*, 58–59.

19. Badcock, "The Church as 'Sacrament,'" 199.

fers a clarification of this rather involved statement regarding the identity between the church and the risen Christ, namely that "there needs to be a recognition of the primal theological fact that the church is part of the *mystērion*, part of the gospel."[20] Thus, Badcock suggests that the best way to grasp ecclesiology is through "sustained reflection on the theme of the body of Christ, especially in its sacramental dimension."[21] However, several worrisome stations are reached by Badcock's notion. Of note is his insistence that the church is part of the gospel; that "room is made" in the "being of God" for the ecclesial gathering; and that the church as *mystērion* is "theologically primary" and of "first importance."[22]

An idiom from John Webster is worth recording here in response: the "gospel and church exist in a strict irreversible order, one in which the gospel precedes and the church follows."[23] Beyond Badcock's misinterpreting the order of primacy in the life of the church—specifically in its receiving of, what Webster calls, a "unilateral grace"[24]—it is therefore doubtful if the distinction between Christology and ecclesiology is adequately secured by reference to the "sacramental dimension" of the transcendent presence of Christ to his body: much more is required besides the Bonhoefferian reduction of Christ to the "realized" church and sacrament.[25]

---

20. Ibid.

21. Ibid.

22. Ibid.

23. Webster, "On Evangelical Ecclesiology," in *Confessing God*, 154. Cf. ". . . ecclesiology may not become 'first theology' . . . so that it becomes the doctrinal *substratum* of all Christian teaching" (ibid., 155).

24. Ibid., 154.

25. Badcock, "Church as 'Sacrament,'" 200. Cf. Bonhoeffer, *Christ the Center*, 59: "Christ as sacrament is also in the Church and is the Church." Perhaps Jüngel's ordered thoughts are worth noting here. In a swift article, "The Church as Sacrament?" (an ironic title given Badcock's) Jüngel clarifies that a sacrament is "not a completion but rather a visible, concrete form of that representation and presentation of the sacrifice of Christ accomplished *illic et tunc* and already brought to speech in the gospel." When pondering whether or not the church itself is a "sacrament," therefore, Jüngel argues that if the church "celebrates . . . the history of Jesus Christ as the declaration and impartation of God's gracious presence" only then may it be called "not a basic sacrament but rather the great *sacramental sign* which represents Jesus Christ." Jüngel concludes that the "church testifies to the sacramental being of Jesus Christ" through, among many things, "listening to him as God's Word, . . . celebrating him as that Word, . . . and confessing that Jesus Christ died for us" (Jüngel, "Church as Sacrament?" 204, 206, 212–13.).

But this talk of the church as *mystērion* conjures the more straightforward incarnational ecclesiology from Vatican II's *Lumen Gentium*. Here we find the précises of the problem:

> Christ is the Light of nations. Because this is so . . . a light [is] brightly visible on the countenance of the Church. Since the Church is in Christ like a sacrament or as a sign and instrument both of a very closely knit union with God and of the unity of the whole human race, it desires now to unfold more fully to the faithful of the Church and to the whole world its own inner nature and universal mission. . . . [T]hrough [the Church] He communicated truth and grace to all. But, the society structured with hierarchical organs and the Mystical Body of Christ, are not to be considered as two realities, nor are the visible assembly and the spiritual community, . . . rather they form *one complex reality* which coalesces from a divine and a human element. For this reason, by no weak analogy, it is compared to the mystery of the incarnate Word. As the assumed nature inseparably united to Him, serves the divine Word as a living organ of salvation, so, in a similar way, does the visible social structure of the Church serve the Spirit of Christ, who vivifies it, in the building up of the body.[26]

According to *Lumen Gentium*, the church and Christ are "not to be considered as two realities," but rather hypostatically as "one complex reality which coalesces from a divine and a human element." Moreover, the church itself communicates "truth and grace to all." Such reflections, beyond containing a rather problematic view of soteriology, place undue weight on "cooperation" and are problematic for *the* event of the incarnation of the Word, one that is a function of the community that solely functions "in the *Catholic* Church, which is governed by the successor of Peter and by the Bishops in communion with him."[27] Even Balthasar notes that:

> Only the Catholic Church has . . . inner dramatic tension [of Marian and Petrine holiness] and [this] is what makes her the extension ("fullness," "body") of Christ as well as his partner ("Bride") enabling her to participate in Christ's redemptive mission and, undergirding this, in his trinitarian being.[28]

---

26. *Lumen Gentium* 1, 7, 8 (emphasis mine).

27. Ibid., 8 (emphasis mine).

28. Balthasar, *Theo-drama*, 3:358. Balthasar does note—via Barth—that a "scandal of division" in the church should be treated "as we treat our sins and those of others" (ibid., 446).

More could indeed be said here, particularly with reference to the seeming transmission of agency from Christ to the church.[29] Yet it should be noted that there is suspiciously lacking here a robust notion of *theologia crucis*, the theology of the cross. Though *Lumen Gentium* affirms that "through the Cross [the church] arrives at the light which knows no setting," the cross, we might note, is integrated into the church's spirituality and the pious Mariology that results.[30] It is not expounded in terms of *solus Christus*, but rather the "Hegelian" *totus Christus*; and the Eucharistic depiction of the cross is reduced to a symbol of the continued communion in the unity of all believers who form one body in Christ.[31]

Of course, much ink might be spilled in response to this and other aspects of incarnational theology, and the more "social" approaches to trinitarian theology and their consequences for ecclesiology. Yet for our present purposes two preliminary worries might be noted. First, such descriptions of the nature of the church as a "correspondence" to or "extension" of the relatedness of God or the incarnation of the Word lack proper attention to the radiant identity of the triune God. The gracious character of the church, its utter dependence on the grace of God's work, is often bracketed by the implementation of the language of "extension," "correspondence," or "participation." The "Hegelian" or, consequentially, the "Moltmannian" pattern of much modern ecclesiology meets little opposition from those who

---

29. With regards to "identity," even Aquinas, as a great *doctors ecclesiae* of the Roman Catholic Church, is measured in his approach to any reduction of the "body" to that of Christ (or vice versa):

> In metaphorical speech [of the "body of Christ"] *we must not expect a likeness in all respects*; for thus there would be not *likeness but identity*. Accordingly a natural head has not another head because one human body is not part of another; but a metaphorical body, i.e. an ordered multitude, is part of another multitude as the domestic multitude is part of the civil multitude; and hence the father who is head of the domestic multitude has a head above him, i.e. the civil governor. And hence there is no reason why God should not be the Head of Christ, although Christ Himself is Head of the Church. (ST 3a.q8.1ad2, emphasis mine)

30. Cf. *Lumen Gentium* 62: "This maternity of Mary in the order of grace began with the consent which she gave in faith at the Annunciation and which she sustained without wavering beneath the cross, and lasts until the eternal fulfillment of all the elect." An extreme case of this is also seen in Balthasar's thoughts that Mary is seen as a "model and . . . prototype of the Church" (*Theo-drama*, 3:338–39).

31. Cf. *Lumen Gentium* 3: "As often as the sacrifice of the cross in which Christ our Passover was sacrificed, is celebrated on the altar, the work of our redemption is carried on, and, in the sacrament of the eucharistic bread, the unity of all believers who form one body in Christ."

incorporate the doctrine of the church and the doctrine of the Trinity.³² Rather, Turretin is worth considering here: "There is the wildest difference between the mystical union of believers with God and the divine union of the persons of the Trinity."³³

Second, such descriptions of the church's relation to the triune light and life of God or the event of the incarnation reveal deep investments in divine immanence, as notably captured in LaCugna's notion that God's trinitarian life is "the life of communion and indwelling, God in us, we in God, all of us in each other."³⁴ Such immanentist positions often stress the association between the acts of God and the acts of the church, which undoubtedly endangers the free shining forth of God's work. Zizioulas further emphasizes this point when he states: "Ecclesial being is tied to the very being of God."³⁵ Such an ecclesiology places undue weight upon the church as agent, and, likewise, reduces the passivity or receptivity that is at the center of the church as a *creature* of divine light. For if the being of the church is an *exact* image of the mutual light of the divine perichoresis, or if the church is reducible to the radiant event of the incarnation of the Word, then it is precisely in the *shining forth* of the church that the *shining forth* of the triune God finds its actualization.³⁶ In a way, then, this approach to ecclesiology makes the work of the church a participation in the divine acts, rather than a reflection of those acts. In short: the light that "shines in the darkness" of John 1:5—the utter resplendence of the work of the Son, by the Father, terminus in the Spirit—is to some point threatened when the church is deemed to enter into the undertaking of the *opera Dei*. One consequence of this is that the light of the church is no longer utterly external, no longer shining from the outside to the inside, but in some sense infused into the church by the church's *koinonia* with God, so that "the community we share

---

32. See Rowan Williams's note that the Hegelian and Moltmannian trinitarian models are "controlled by the desire to take history seriously, to bridge the gap between a remote eternity and the concrete temporal world; but they end in evasions of the temporal" (*On Christian Theology*, 161). In the very least, I would add that, for Moltmann, this means a collapse not only of the "Father's giving-up the Son" at Calvary, but also the perichoretic identification of the church with the triune life.

33. Turretin, *Inst.* III.q28.13.

34. LaCugna, *God for Us*, 228. Cf. the critique from Molnar, *Divine Freedom*, 128.

35. Zizioulas, *Being as Communion*, 15.

36. We might note a worry with Bonhoeffer's statement that "the Word is also itself Church, in so far as the Church itself is revelation and the Word wishes to have the form of a created body" (*Christ the Center*, 59).

is our shared participation in the perichoretic community of trinitarian persons."[37]

This chapter, however, seeks an alternative definition of the relation between the doctrine of God's light and the doctrine of the light of the church. This is principally due to the fact that it makes what we examined in the previous chapter—namely, election as the "radiant event of love"—essential to the nature of the church. Where the "social" trinitarian and incarnational language of participation, extension, imaging, perichoresis, or correspondence unduly stresses the connection of divine and ecclesial acts, the language of election as the "radiant event of love," on the other hand, focuses on the reality that grace is the ground of the church's existence. The church lives by the eternal gift of the radiantly risen and ascended Christ and the illuminating Holy Spirit, who is the *terminus actionis* of the will of the Father in gathering saints out of darkness into "his marvelous light." In this manner, we shall continually speak of the church's "light" as a circumferential "light," an external "light," a non-controllable "light," a bestowed "light"—in short, a light that the church finds itself *in*, or indeed gathered *around*, through the radiant grace of the triune God.

However, a further caveat must be entered so as not to divide God and church. It is true that the alien character of the church—its utter difference from God—can be so emphasized that the ecclesiology which results is withered, in the sense that it separates God and the human gathering and interprets God as simply a transcendent reality in which the "*distinctiveness of the church of believers*" becomes the "*prerequisite to the meaningfulness of the gospel message*."[38] The bulwark against this hazard, however, is not to erode the difference between God and the human historical reality of the church, that is, to over emphasize ecclesiology. Rather, the most effectual safeguard is to offer a theological account of the nature of the church called into God's light: that is, to manage our thinking as we have thus far sought to do in this study by the light of the gospel. The discipline of the evangel will compel us to say both that the church's light is a visible form of human life and work ("a city on a hill"), and also that the life and work of the church are visible insofar as they have within themselves a primary (albeit dim) "reflection" of the work and word of the God who is light, and that this church "actually shines among men."[39]

---

37. Grenz and Franke, *Beyond Foundationalism*, 179. Add to this statement Moltmann's provocative interpretation of 1 John 4:16 as pertaining to the "perichoretic community between the Trinity and the human community" ("God in the World," 376).

38. Yoder, "A People in the World," 74–5 (emphasis original).

39. Barth, CD IV.3.2:763; KD IV.3:874.

The Trinitarian Basis of the Church's Light

We therefore seek to investigate the notion that the church is *in* the light of God; but it is *in* the light, not by some ontological participation in the divine light, but by its summons by God and in its receiving of the divine benevolence. The church's light is that which it is because of its utter dependence upon God's "miracle of grace," upon the fact that *God is light in himself;* and *from himself God shines forth his light.* In developing this notion we will first discuss the basis for the church's light. That is, we pursue the thought that the light of the church has its basis in the work of the Trinity in electing, reconciling, and illuminating a people to become God's covenant partners and saints in light.

In pursuing this course, we begin by saying that within the realm of human time there exists a gathering of people who comprise the covenant people "in the light." Their corporate life is the mark that there is a human response to being called "out of darkness and into [God's] marvelous light" (1 Pet 2:9); to the divine self-pronouncement—"I am the light of the world" (John 8:12)—there actually corresponds a human reality—"*You* are the light of the world" (Matt 5:14). But the existence of such a reality is not founded in creaturely imaging and correspondence; indeed, from the side of human creatures it is nothing other than complacent rationality, for the realm of human time rests within the domain of darkness, endeavoring to rebel through the "works of darkness" (Rom 13:12), and thus refuse God's summons. Alienated from God, human history is replete with the rebellious enterprise called the "people who loved the darkness" (John 3:19). But part of the gospel proclamation is the claim that there now exists the shocking reality of "children of light" (Eph 5:8; 1 Thess 5:5). There is a form of common human life that can only be described as children or saints "in the light," that is, a people for God's own possession: *congregatio sanctorum*. That such a people in the light exist is a gift of grace, and that this community does not collapse back into the domain of darkness, lies within the saving work of the God who is light—*from himself God shines forth his light.*

Talk of the church's being *in* light is thus based on talk of *the* light of the triune God. He, the radiant One, is the basis of the church's life and of its work. In offering a description of the sum of the church's history and of its work, including its being "a city set on a hill" (Matt 5:14), is therefore to be deployed with language about God. God is not merely the church's *causa remota*; rather, the church *is* because God *is*. "Ecclesial being"—and here we might amend Zizioulas's statement—is a reality *because* of the "very being of God." In other words, the church is the "light of the world" because God is the true light of the world. And therefore the light of the church is a matter of humbly turning to face the works and ways of the radiant triune God.

The Johannine Pattern

Why is the triune God the basis of the church's light? For an answer, we might pause and look at the "trinitarian" explanation of this point in the First Letter of John.[40] There, the light of the church, which results in "walking" and having "fellowship with one another" (1:7), is grounded, first, in the loving, electing work of God the Father. "See what kind of love the Father has given to us, that we should be called children of God; and so we are" (3:1). Considered in the general scope of the first, third, and fourth chapters of the epistle, these assertions can be seen as carrying a twofold pronouncement: that the basis of walking "in the light" of fellowship is election, and that the aim of this election is walking "in the light." If walking "in the light" has an enduring human shape, then that shape is to be located in its creative basis in the loving, electing work of God the Father summarized in a single expression: "that we should be called." But together with this: if there is an election of grace, then it is no mere self-encompassed divine movement, but an effective power in human history, that which has as its aim the illumination of "children of light," bound to God as a reflection of his own proper light, "as he himself is in the light" (1:7). As we put forth in chapter 3, so here: election is God's "radiant event of love."

By this time a significant concern for understanding the church's light begins to materialize. The dynamic of the church's light is found in election and gathering by God. The gathered saints *in* light, those elected by the love of God, owe its origin to a shining forth from outside itself—on account that "his purity shines forth in us"[41]—striking from consideration

---

40. We say "trinitarian" in light of the "proto-trinitarian" teaching perceived in the First Letter of John. Of course, this "proto-trinitarian" teaching is not *necessarily* derived by direct exegesis, but rather as recognizing conceptual patterns and patterns of divine action, namely, patterns of God's redemptive action in the economy as revealed in Holy Scripture. Thus, beyond the passages that follow, we find of particular insight the verbs *echō* and *menō* as found in ch. 2 of the letter. Granted, these verbs are rendered within the particular response of the Christian as *echō* and *menō* the Father and the Son simultaneously by confession and abiding; yet there is a faint anticipation of *homoousios* found in 2:23–24, marked by several continuous expressions: "No one who denies the Son has the Father. Whoever confesses the Son has the Father also. Let what you heard from the beginning abide in you. If what you heard from the beginning abides in you, then you too will abide in the Son and in the Father."

41. Calvin, *Comm. Ioannis ep.* 1.6 (CO 55:304–5; CC 22:164): "si eius puritas in nobis luceat." See Calvin's further remarks: "What God communicates to us is not a

that this power belongs to us but rather that it "has been *given* [and] it is from mere bounty and generosity that God makes us his children."[42] Neither in its foundation nor in its continual work is the gathering of saints in light a self-sufficient and self-generated gathering. Rather, it is a creature of the given and antecedent light of grace. The dynamics of its light is, therefore, in no self-generating way the power of the church. God sets apart the church from the darkness. The church does not separate itself from the darkness, for it has neither the power nor the ability to do so. The church's light is the outcome of the divine determination, "that we have been called," and not of any human acts of quarantining an "illumined" group from the "unillumined." In this manner, the true light of the church is very different from human factionalism. Only God is light (1:5); only God may lovingly elect the "children of light"; only an elect church is a gathering of the illumined. The church's light is thus based on the "radiant event of love" in the Father's election of human creatures.

Moreover, if we might continue our review, the gathered church *in* the light, which is the purpose for election, is based on the reconciling work of the Son of God. Remaining with the First Letter of John, we hear:

> And we have seen and testify that the Father has sent his Son to be the Savior of the world.... [I]ndeed our fellowship is with the Father and with his Son Jesus Christ.... And if we walk in the light, as he is in the light, we have fellowship with one another, and the blood of Jesus his Son cleanses us from all sin (1 John 4:14; 1:3, 7).

The Father's will is effected in his sending of the Son who is the "Savior of the world." If we ask how the will of the Father is undertaken in the Son, the First Letter of John gives us a series of additional notions: the one who is "made manifest to us" (1:2); the one who "came by water and blood" and is testified to by the Holy Spirit (5:6); the one who "laid down his life for us" (3:16); the "propitiation" for "the sins of the world" (2:2); the one who "cleanses us from all sin" and is "faithful and just to forgive us" (1:9); the one in whom the "love of God is perfected" (2:5); the "advocate" (2:1); the one who has "eternal life" (5:12); the one who is the "true God" (5:20); and the one who is the "true light" of the world, as he himself is the victorious light

---

vain fiction (*inane figmentum*); for it is necessary that the power and effect of this fellowship should shine forth in our life; otherwise the possession of the gospel is fallacious" (ibid).

42. Ibid., 3.1: "... datam esse caritatem, significat hoc merae esse liberalitatis, quod nos Deus pro filiis habet. Unde enim tanta nobis dignitas, nisi ex Dei amore?" (CO 55:329; cf. CC 22:203).

"already shining" (2:8; 1:5, 7). Of course, the image of light, particularly in the first two chapters of the Johannine letter, reiterates the totality of Christ's reconciling work: the objective work of Jesus Christ in his death and resurrection, which is the divine act of defeating sin and putting an end to the darkness and pollution of human creatures, namely by the fact that "the darkness is passing away and the true light is already shining."[43] That work, though incomparable and radiant, is nevertheless a work that suggests a human target in the arc of its trajectory: it "is true in him and in you" (1 John 2:8). Thus,

> the church of Christ has lived and will live so long as Christ reigns at the right hand of his Father. It is sustained by his hand; defended by his protection; and is kept safe through his power. For he will surely accomplish what he once promised: that he will be present with his own even to the end of the world.[44]

Finally, we might say that the church's being *in* the light, which is the purpose of election and which is undertaken and accomplished in the reconciling work of the Son, is illuminated and brought to terminus by the Holy Spirit. Again from the First Letter of John: "By this we know that we abide in him and he in us, because he has given us of his Spirit" (1 John 3:24). By "abandoning all her own wisdom" and permitting "herself be taught by the Holy Spirit," the church, gathered and "shone upon," is made into God's dwelling place.[45] The work of the Spirit is to apply the reality that is willed in election and founded in reconciliation: the particular movement of being "called out of darkness" into God's "marvelous light." The Spirit completes the plan of reconciliation (cf. Rom 8:16), whose resolve is that there should be a creaturely existence of "walking in the light, as he himself is in the light," that is, a covenant relationship between himself and human creatures whom he has elected, reconciled, and illuminated by drawing them into a covenantal relation with himself.

Talk of "election," "reconciliation," and "illumination," is calculated: it is not a discourse on mere "imaging," "extension," or "participation." For

---

43. Cf. Marshall's points regarding this in *Epistles of John*, 108–11. See also our conclusions in chapter 3.

44. Calvin, *Inst.* Pref.: "Errors About the Nature of the Church," 6; cf. OS 3:23, *Praefatio*: "Vixit sane Christi Ecclesia, et vivet quandiu Christus regnabit ad dextram Patris: cuius manu sustinetur, cuius praesidio defenditur, cuius virtute suam incolumitatem retinet. Praestabit enim ille indubie quod semel receipt, se affuturum suis usque as consummationem seculi."

45. *Inst.* IV.8.13; CO 2:855. Calvin is here qualifying the argument that *errare non posse ecclesiam in rebus ad salutem necessariis*.

instance, "abide in him and he in us" (1 John 3:24) does not mean ontological union between God and the church, á la Moltmann, Volf, and LaCugna. The mention of "in God, and God in him" is not ontological communion, but the saving divine agency that recreates a relationship between God and his human creatures, anticipated in the church which is a covenantal "people that have such . . . one dwelling in the midst of them."[46] The terminus of the work of the Son, the light *of* and *for* the world, is delivering human creatures from being "in darkness" (1 John 1:9), from alienation. That work of deliverance is turned towards its completion—though not here and now, as it is still a "present darkness" (Eph 6:12)—by the Holy Spirit, who not only enacts a transformed relation to God the Father (cf. Rom 8:15), but also renews "fellowship with one another." Consequently, the terminus of the work of the church's being illumined and renewed is not the work of the church itself. The church is not the "end of the subject because the Holy Spirit becomes the agent of the triune God's knowledge through the church's core practices and teaching," as Reinhard Hütter argues;[47] nor is the Spirit defined as "a dimension of human life" in which the church is to be rendered a place where "*it* gives holiness to the religious communities . . . of which *it* is the invisible Spiritual essence," as Tillich proposes.[48] Rather, as Calvin says in commenting on 1 John 3:24,

> it hence appears that we are God's children, that is, when the Spirit rules and governs our life [and] whatever good works are done by us, *proceed from the grace of the Spirit,* and that *the Spirit is not obtained by our righteousness, but is freely given to us.*[49]

---

46. Edwards, "God Amongst His People" (WJE 19:460).

47. Hütter, "The Knowledge of the Triune God," 26 (emphasis mine).

48. Tillich, *Systematic Theology*, 3:111, 155–56. Tillich's cumbersome language is couched in his discussions regarding the "latency" (i.e., "before") and "manifestation" (i.e., "after") of religious communities, which includes the historical "churches." Of course, Tillich wishes to deny that he is here strictly discussing the classical rhetoric of *ecclesia visibilis* and *ecclesia invisibilis* (cf. ibid., 152–53); rather, he wishes to recast these terms into his notion of latency and manifestation, so that, for instance, the "churches" contain a "state of being partly actual, partly potential" (ibid., 153). As is, Tillich's discussion descends into confusion as he continually states that the Spiritual Community is the agent of action in making the "churches" holy, in overcoming "profanization," "demonization," and the "ambiguous life." A glaring hole in Tillich's account of the divine agency of the triune God is his notorious ascription of speaking "symbolically of God as Spirit" (ibid., 111). The upshot for Tillich: the "Spiritual Community" is the "inner *telos* of the churches" because of the symbolic character of the "Spiritual Presence" of the Spirit, and therefore is *itself* "the source of everything which makes them churches" (ibid., 165).

49. Calvin, *Comm. Ioannis ep.* 3.24 (CO 55:345; CC 22:227, emphasis mine).

Thus, if there exists a covenant gathering of saints in light—if the will of the Father is to call human creatures out of darkness and into his light, if the reconciling work of the Son is realized in human history in a form of common life—then it is because the church exists by the Spirit's free luminous agency, and by the dynamic coming of the Spirit, in the realm of illuminative renewal in which "the Spirit is not obtained by our righteousness, but is freely given to us."

So far, then, we have proposed that the basis of the light of the church is not the power of the church but the saving work of the trinitarian God. The church's light is therefore an *external* light. Because the church is illuminated by the light of grace, and because this grace is a movement of God's "radiant event of love" in his election, then in the case of the church the *nota* of light is not a matter of the attributes of the church. God's light is proper to him, and yet he is "nothing like that light with which we are acquainted."[50] The light of the church, by contrast, is not a natural condition or quality. As with all the titles of the church, the church is what it is as a result of the radiant presence and action of the triune God in building a people into a "spiritual house" (1 Pet 2:5).[51] In other words, "the church is called the light of the world not in competition with Christ, Who is the Light of the world, but on account of *His* unique presence."[52] This reality is, once again, a pronouncement of the ontological imperative for the church found in 1 Peter 2:9–10:

> But you are a chosen race, a royal priesthood, a holy nation, a people for his own possession, that you may proclaim the excellencies of him who called you out of darkness into his marvelous light. Once you were not a people, but now you are God's people; once you had not received mercy, but now you have received mercy.

Here we have the heart of what needs to be said about that nature of the church. The church is what it is "now" by God's gracious and "received" election and love. This requires a rejection of the thought that the work essential to the church is self-generated: "Once you were not a people, but now you are God's people" by virtue of "him who called you out of darkness into his marvelous light." And it entails a "proclamation"[53] of the fact that the

---

50. Irenaeus, *Adv. Hær.* 2.13.4.

51. Regarding the predicate of light ascribed to the church in the context of the NT, see Minear, *Images of the Church*, esp. 127–29.

52. Berkouwer, *Church*, 36.

53. We propose here and throughout that the action of *exangellō* is a sufficient description of the church's action, as found in 1 Pet 2:9–10. Of course, this verb is unique

work essential to the church is God's by his "excellencies," for the church is comprised of "a people of his own possession." There is, therefore, a suitable docility to the nature of the church, for faith—that is, proclamation of, assent and trust in, the gracious shining forth of God—is the central act of the church. From this ontological imperative about the church's constitution there follows a further imperative regarding the action of the light of the church: all the acts of the church must exhibit a proclamation of the "excellencies" of the One who *is light in himself* and *from himself shines forth his light*: the electing Father who reconciles in the Son and renews by the illumination of the Holy Spirit.

Proclaiming and Outshining the "Gladdening Light"

Many of our previous sections were often managed by various reflections from Holy Scripture, particularly the First Letter of John, the First Letter of Peter, and the Letter to the Ephesians. In turning to the "outshining" acts of the gathered saints, however, we might take as a guiding expression a text from third-century Christian worship, that is, the earliest recorded hymn, often entitled *Phōs Hilarón, Lumen Hilare*, or "Hail, Gladdening Light."[54] This "ancient witness," as Basil calls it, is believed to have been sung by the early church at the empty tomb of Christ as a candle burned, symbolizing his resurrection.[55] The hymn—using the translation and arrangement from John Keble—is translated thus:

> Hail, gladdening Light, of his pure glory poured

---

to this passage, yet it bears similarity to the instances of "proclamation" in the NT when ascribed to the church, namely, Paul's use with regards to the Lord's Supper: "For as often as you eat this bread and drink the cup, you proclaim [*kataggelló*] the Lord's death until he comes" (1 Cor 11:26). Beyond the confessional undertones—and the same primitive word as the Pauline instance—the Petrine use of *exangelló* denotes the specific action of "announcing from within" or "announcing out of" the church (cf. the preposition *ex* paired with the verb *angelló*). Thus, "proclamation" in the subsequent pages of our chapter will be synonymous with "recognition," etc. However, "proclamation," in this context, continually harkens back to 1 Peter 2:9–10 and the particular act of faithfully announcing out of the gathered church the "excellencies" of God's calling a people out of darkness into the marvelous light of communion with himself.

54. The hymn was first recorded in the *Didascalia*. See also Davidson, *Birth of the Church*, 286–87; Bradshaw, *Origins of Christian Worship*, 173.

55. Basil deems this hymn to be composed by Athenogenes before his martyrdom "through fire." Basil continues with a bit of background, saying that the hymn was sung at the "lighting of the lamp," when believers "put forth the expression as an ancient one, and no one ever considered them impious when they said, 'we glorify the Father and the Son and the Holy Spirit of God'" (*Sp. sanc.* 73 [PG 32:205; PPS 42:114]).

> Who is the immortal Father, heavenly, blest,
>   Holiest of Holies, Jesus Christ our Lord!
> Now we are at the sun's hour of rest,
>   The lights of evening round us shine,
>   We hymn the Father, Son, and Holy Spirit divine!
> Worthiest art thou at all times to be sung
>   With undefiled tongue,
>   Son of our God, giver of life, alone:
>   Therefore in all the world thy glories, Lord, they own.[56]

The brief hymn comprises three parts: a "hailing" of the Son, who is the "gladdening Light" and the *fons luminis de lumine*;[57] a recitation of the act of hymning the divine Trinity; and a glorification of the saving work of Christ, prescribing that praise be paired with proclamation: "Worthiest art thou at all times to be sung / With undefiled tongue." This undertaking of proclamation is visible as the basic character of the church's light, for, in the act of recognizing the radiant identity of God, the church joins with all those who have been illumined by the divine summons out of darkness and into God's marvelous light, and become the "spiritual house" which is light in its proclamation of this radiant One, the "Father, Son, and Holy Spirit divine!"

To develop our thoughts further, we keep *Phōs Hilarón* before us as we concentrate on three guiding questions: (1) What is it about proclamation that makes it basic to the church's being the "light of the world?" (2) What is it that the church aims at in proclaiming the triune God? (3) In what acts of proclamation is the church's light visible?

The Proclamation of the Church

What is it about proclamation that makes it basic to the church's being the "light of the world?" (Matt 5:14). Proclamation is, as Barth clarifies, the act of *credo*, that is, "simply the act of recognition of the reality of God."[58] It

---

56. Keble's English translation is the standard in the Anglican *Book of Common Prayer*, though the hymn is often titled (in its American equivalent) "O, Gracious Light." See *Book of Common Prayer*, 64.

57. Cf. "Lumen hilare iucunda lux tu gloriae, fons luminis de lumine, beate Iesu caelitus a Patre sancto prodiens. Fulgor diei lucidus solisque lumen occidit, et nos ad horam vesperam te confitemur cantico. Laudamus unicum Deum, Patrem potentem, Filium cum Spiritu Paraclito in Trinitatis gloria. O digne linguis qui piis lauderis omni tempore, Fili Dei, te saecula vitae datorem personent. Amen."

58. Barth, *Credo*, 5; cf. ". . . schlicht den Akt der Anerkennung der den Menschen angehenden Wirklichkeit Gottes in Gestalt bestimmter, aus Gottes Offenbarung

is an act of "recognition" in which the radiant identity and "excellencies" of that which is other than the church is proclaimed. In this recognition, the church simply turns to God's reality, humbly proclaiming its "Amen" to God's radiant way of being:

> For what we proclaim is not ourselves, but Jesus Christ as Lord, with ourselves as your servants for Jesus' sake. For God, who said, "Let light shine out of darkness," has shone in our hearts to give the light of the knowledge of the glory of God in the face of Jesus Christ. (2 Cor 4:5–6)

Proclamation in this sense is not an activity of the church *in abstracto*. Rather, in the totality of its activities, the church exists by the basic structure of proclamation—it is the collective praise in all it is by the fact that it is the creature of God's grace. What the church proclaims, therefore, is "not ourselves" but the One who "has shone in our hearts to give the light of the knowledge of the glory of God in the face of Jesus Christ."

Because of this, the church's being the "light of the world," too, is at its heart a proclamation. The light of the church, as we have seen, is not some inactive property but an event. That event, the history we call the church's light, is a twofold event. The history of the church's light includes as a principal movement the condescension of God who, in his *shining forth his light*, elects, reconciles, and illuminates "the church . . . in splendor" (Eph 5:27). And it includes as a secondary movement the assembly of saints in light, gathered by God's grace, among whom and by whom the equiprimordial light of the Father, Son, and Holy Spirit is proclaimed.[59] The church's light arises as part of this history of grace and proclamation. The church is "in the light" and the "light of the world," namely, as it cries "Hail, gladdening Light!"

This proclamation is commenced, of course, in God himself: "For God, who said, 'Let light shine out of darkness,' has shone in our hearts." The church cannot proclaim unless God opens its mouth, "that it may confess his name."[60] Proclamation is thus generated, not by the church, but by God's disclosure of himself as the radiant One by the "light of knowledge" in revelation, that is, "the eloquence of God's presence and activity, God so act-

---

gewonnener Erkenntnisse." See also Barth's comment that the "Akt des Credo" is the "Akt des Bekenntnisses" (ibid., 7). We might also pair this with John Webster's notion: "*the act of confession is a responsive, not a spontaneous act*" ("Confession and Confessions," in *Confessing God*, 72; emphasis original).

59. See Heidegger, *Corp. theol.* 26.4.

60. Augustine, *Conf.* 5.1: ". . . ut confessitur nomini tuo" (PL 32:706; cf. NPNF 1:79).

ing in relation to creatures that his actions constitute his address of them."[61] Revelation—the "eloquence of God's presence and activity"—is thus shined forth and pronounced salvation; and revelation produces the assembly of saints in light, the gathering of those called out of darkness into the light of communion with the everlasting Father, the eternal Son, and the illuminating Holy Spirit. Only on the basis of this divine "address" and "constitution" is it possible for the people of God to proclaim the ancient expression: "We hymn the Father, Son, and Holy Spirit divine!"

The Radiant Subject of Proclamation

What is it that the church focuses on in proclaiming the triune God? In short: the church in the light proclaims the radiant identity of God. The God who is turned to and proclaimed in this way is the radiant subject of the work of salvation—the eloquent One who, in "his perfect adequacy," is the subject of the "universal pertinence of what he has accomplished *ephapax*."[62] He is the "Father of lights" (Jas 1:17); the true Son who is the true "gladdening Light"; the Holy Spirit, the comforter and illuminator—"Light thrice repeated; but One Light and One God."[63] He is manifest in the divine work of delivering human creatures from the domain of darkness and sin. And the church realizes the object of its being called out of darkness by God when it proclaims this radiant and eloquent work. Consequently, it joins in the creaturely worship that is fitting to God alone:

> Let them praise the name of the Lord,
>   for his name alone is exalted;
>   his majesty is above earth and heaven.
> Bless the Lord, O my soul!
> O Lord my God, you are very great
> You are clothed with splendor and majesty,
>   covering yourself with light as with a garment,
>   stretching out the heavens like a tent. . . .
> Let them praise the name of the Lord,
>   for his name alone is exalted;
>   his majesty is above earth and heaven (Pss 104:1–2; 148:11–13).

These distinct praises form a proclamation: "Bless the Lord O my soul! / O Lord my God. . . . You are clothed with splendor and majesty / covering

---

61. Webster, "Biblical Reasoning," in *Domain of the Word*, 118.
62. Davidson, "Salvation's Destiny," 166.
63. Gregory Nazianzen, *Or.* 31.3 (NPNF 7:318; cf. PPS 23:118).

yourself with light as with a garment. . . . [H]is majesty is above earth and heaven!"

More precisely: the church *in* the light proclaims the Father of radiant majesty. God's majesty as Father is the absolute uniqueness of his being, ways, and works, a radiance that is limitless in scope as he is "the Father almighty."[64] This radiant majesty is not an isolated attribute; it is, rather, a property of the One divine essence which characterizes all that God is.[65] And so God's light, too, is inseparable from his majesty; and this is why the church *in* the light praises the Father of radiant majesty by crying: "You are very great!"

The church *in* the light proclaims the only-begotten Son, "Light of Light," worthy of all praise. *Phōs Hilarón* in its totality is marked by a high Christology, especially in its brief presentation of the Son's matchless saving work, so that over the entire hymn is found emblazoned the words from the final stanza: "Son of our God, giver of life, alone." Here, in the ancient expression of the Trinity as the aim of the church's hymning, the focus is on the person who is present in that work. This one is proclaimed as the true light; in being this, he is appropriately "Worthiest at all times to be sung," for he shares in the "mutual light" of the Godhead, and is rightly the object of the church's praise.

The church *in* the light proclaims the Holy Spirit, the one who illuminates human creatures. The Spirit appears momentarily in the presentation of the church's "hymning" section in the middle stanza of *Phōs Hilarón* (i.e., "We hymn . . ."). Yet this brief mention of the Holy Spirit is vital for the account of redemptive history that *Phōs Hilarón* seeks to hail. For *paraklētos* assembles the idea that the Father and the Son would be a remote cause if not for the fact that as Spirit, God agrees to be near to his saints in light forever:

> And I will ask the Father, and he will give you another Helper, to be with you forever, even the Spirit of truth, whom the world cannot receive, because it neither sees him nor knows him. You know him, for he dwells with you and will be in you. (John 14:16–17)

---

64. On the theological import of this first clause of the Creed, see the recent thoughts of Thiselton, *Systematic Theology*, 75–76.

65. This is Barth's point regarding "glory" as essentially synonymous with "light" when discussing the perfections of God (see CD II.1:646–49). Cf. Davidson's discussion of this in "Divine Light," 54–56; and Ramsey's qualification of this exegetical rendering in *Glory of the Lord*, 23–27.

The Holy Spirit is sent by the Father through the Son in order to instruct the saints (cf. John 15:26). Without the Holy Spirit, the "Hail!" of the church would be aimless; indeed, instead of the "bride of Christ" the church would be the "widow of Christ."[66] God's saving of his people, his shining upon, illuminating, and upholding the saints in light—none of this would be conceivable without the proclamation of the Spirit's divinity, without the *credo* that we hymn the Spirit along with the Father and the Son. "That is to say," Barth says, "the Holy Spirit . . . is in the same manner the eternal Spirit, as the Father is the eternal Father, as the Son is the eternal Son."[67] Failure to proclaim this point is the simultaneous failure to proclaim: "I believe in the Holy Ghost."[68]

Let us now bring these loose ends together with regard to their association to the church's light. The church is the gathering of the saints in light as it faithfully proclaims and praises the radiant identity of the God who is *light in himself*. God's light is God "clothed with splendor and majesty" as Lord and Savior. As he reveals his being *light in himself* and thus *shines forth his light*, he gathers and illumines for himself a people, set apart for his praise and for the work of "proclaiming his excellencies." In this is formed the humble human reflection of the vision in the Apocalypse: "And the city has no need of sun or moon to shine on it, for the glory of God gives it light, and its lamp is the Lamb" (Rev 21:23).

The Visible Outshining of the Light of the Church

Finally: In what acts of proclamation is the church's light visible? Our enquiry into the light of the church has thus far implicitly traced the passage quoted at the beginning of this chapter:

> You are the light of the world. A city set on a hill cannot be hidden. Nor do people light a lamp and put it under a basket, but on a stand, and it gives light to all in the house. In the same way, let your light shine before others, so that they may see your good works and give glory to your Father who is in heaven. (Matt 5:14–16)

What is often exegetically garnered from this passage in the Sermon on the Mount is the notion of *ecclesia visibilis*, the visible church: "let your light

---

66. This is Luther's point in his *Resolutiones* 72 (WA 1:620.8): ". . . habet vidua Christi."

67. Barth, *Credo*, 118.

68. Ibid.

shine before others, so that they may see your good works and give glory to your Father who is in heaven." Initially, therefore, we need to probe the notion of *ecclesia visibilis* and its proper use in this context.[69]

A good deal of contemporary ecclesiology has been deeply committed to *ecclesia visibilis*, that is, to the church's tangible and historical character as an ordered society and sphere of "public existence . . . as 'political' community in time."[70] Its opposite notion, namely *ecclesia invisibilis*, the invisible church, therefore recedes from view, since it seeks to spiritualize the church without objective social form. One effect is that the externality of the church is preeminently emphasized, that is, the historical activity of the church in which the nature of the church is visible is of utmost importance. One instance might be briefly noted.

In *Resident Aliens*, Hauerwas and Willimon claim that the church is "the visible, political enactment of our language of God" and the "visible people of God."[71] They are indeed right to state that the church is the "visible people of God" known in its acts. However, in this "colony of heaven" the distinction between "church" and "world" is unclear. The church and its saints do not withdraw from, transcend, or surpass the world: not geographically, but certainly not in terms of virtue or political organization. The act of crossing the threshold of a church is not an act of stepping up onto higher ground; nor is it a bracing event in which, as Hauerwas and Willimon put it, we "strike hard against something which is an alternative to what the world offers."[72] At stake here, especially for the nature of the church, is the degree to which the church will be oriented inward in its visibility as a "colony of heaven," or the degree to which it will be oriented outward as a light, witnessing beyond itself to the radiant identity of God.

Thus, the *ecclesia visibilis* is not simply a sociopolitical presence that can be examined in an empirical manner. Nor does the *ecclesia visibilis* allow us to speak of the church as the center of "individual" human activity; that is, talk of the individual is not the region in which our talk of ecclesiology and God is to be found.[73] To do so would not only subvert the sense

---

69. Craig Evans, for instance, believes that "implicit in this saying" is that God's people will, through their good deeds, insure that the "city of Jerusalem will indeed shine throughout the world." That is, Evans is more concerned to understand Jesus' saying within the context of which it was spoken. See Evans, *Matthew*, 112.

70. Webster, "Evangelical Ecclesiology," 175. Webster is here seeking to recover the notion of the church's "'spiritual' character of its visible life," i.e., *ecclesia invisibilis* (ibid.).

71. Hauerwas and Willimon, *Resident Aliens*, 82, 171.

72. Ibid., 94.

73. This is not to deny that there is theological legitimacy in talking of individual

that the light of the individual *saint* occurs within the gathering of God's *saints* in light; it would also threaten to collapse the transcendent work of God's shining forth—his election, reconciliation, and illumination of human creatures—into an *ecclesiola* of the individual saint and not the realm of "common illumination," as Edwards calls it.[74] The danger of collapse is perhaps perceived in ecclesiologies that reduce the nature of the church to the sphere of individual moral "actors," "dramaturges," or to being "advisors" to God the "Director." That is, the sphere of the church as the "Theatre of the gospel" is reduced to the realm of the individual.[75]

Rather, the *ecclesia visibilis* is the *visibilis* of the *ecclesia invisibilis*; it is what Barth called the "emergence and outshining of the true Church from the concealment in which it is enveloped by the sinfulness of all human volition."[76] In speaking of this "emergence and outshining," Barth did not aim to deny that the church always has a social form; he simply sought to uphold that the church has its visibility not by virtue of "creating and conferring its [own] reality," but by virtue of the "continuation of the operation of the Holy Spirit."[77] *Ecclesia visibilis* is therefore a "phenomenal" and "spiritual" event.[78] It is the emergence and outshining which can only be

---

deliverance from "sitting in the darkness" and the individual's restoration to the destiny found in the radiant event of the Father's loving work of election, the Son's loving work of reconciliation, and the Holy Spirit's loving work of illumination. We are here concentrating, however, on that event of God gathering a people as a reflection of his radiant identity as Father, Son, and Spirit.

74. Cf. Edwards, *Great Awakening* (WJE 4:177).

75. See, e.g., Vanhoozer, *Drama of Doctrine*; and a further clarification of this theme in his recent *Faith Speaking Understanding*. We must note that Vanhoozer and others are not necessarily concerned with reducing that nature of the church to the image of "drama," yet it might be a consequence of such thought if taken too far in that direction. For instance, a recent perceptive study by Vander Lugt, *Living Theodrama*, perhaps comes close to expressing this worry in speaking about the church as the "theatre company" that exists to "entertain" and "offer a good performance." However, Vander Lugt does state that "the ecclesial company exists to witness not just to entertain"—though this "adept," "believable," and "skillful" act of witness is a "witness to the truth of theodrama," which seems to bring the worry of a reductionist image of the "dramatic" nature of the church to the surface once more (see ibid., 139–41).

76. Barth, CD IV.2:619; KD IV.2:701: ". . . in einem freien Hervortreten und Herausleuchten der wirklichen Kirche aus der Verborgenheit, in die sie durch die Sündigkeit."

77. Ibid.

78. We use this in Webster's manner: "The 'visible' church is the phenomenal church: the church has its form . . . as a human undertaking, and which is present in the history of the world as a social project," which is grounded in the "Holy Spirit's empowerment . . . and therefore through the same Spirit is the church visible"

illustrated by the "freedom of grace; the mighty act of the particular divine mercy" of the presence of the triune God.[79] It cannot be transformed into mere phenomenal form, and it cannot be fully perceived without "faith awakened to this revelation" in the word and work of God.[80]

Barth's reflections raise a concern for talk of the church's being *in* the light of God. The "emergence and outshining" of God's saints in light is visible not merely as something predicated of the church on the basis of its actions; to follow this path would be to transform the notion of light into something which the church itself created—into that which a recent papal encyclical letter calls "the light of the believing subject which is the Church"[81]—and so to oppose the NT occurrence and declaration of "God is light." Rather, visible light is proclaimed of the church (i.e., "You are the light of the world"); and that proclamation is not a recognition of a property which the church has *in se*—namely, that human faith "brightens the interior of the Church"[82]—but rather a recognition of that which it is by virtue of being within the realm of the sovereignty of God. In short, again: the church is *in* the light and not *the* light.

Yet one could argue for a more "participatory" roll of the church given several biblical expressions, namely 1 John 1:7 ("But if we walk in the light, as he himself is in the light, we have fellowship with one another"). However, as Bultmann rightly notes, the phrase "as he is in the light" does not denote an equivalency with the human undertaking to "walk in the light." Rather, the phrase "to be in," Bultmann continues, "characterizes the being of that same person who is said 'to be' light."[83] That is, where some might see the "as" (*hos*) signaling a simultaneity between the work of the church or, perhaps more problematic, between the human creature and God's radiant work, the passage is, if we are correct in our reading, in fact stating something perhaps more in line with the context of the Johannine letter

---

("Evangelical Ecclesiology," 180).

79. Barth, CD IV.2:619.

80. Ibid.

81. Francis I, *Lumen Fedei* (2013) §36. *Lumen Fidei* possess many merits, particularly the anthropological insistence that "our human lights are not dissolved in the immensity of his [God's] light, as a star is engulfed by the dawn, but shine all the more brightly the closer they approach the primordial fire, like a mirror which reflects light" (§35). However, the letter ultimately espouses the view that the "visible light" of the church is found in individual faith and piety (cf. §51). This seems rather backward to our conclusions thus far regarding the *alien* and *external* nature of the church *in* the light.

82. Ibid., §51.

83. See Bultmann, *Johannine Epistles*, 20.

itself. That is: "But if we walk *in* the light and not the darkness—as God is the ground of this walking due to the fact that he is himself *the* light—then we have fellowship not only with our fellow saints in the light but also with God himself through Christ."

In the church's emergence and outshining, therefore, its action is wholly oriented towards the action of the Trinity, in electing, gathering, and illuminating. More precisely, the church's actions, or "visible phenomena," are "indications of the presence of the Spirit who bears Christ to the church and the world and so fulfills the Father's purpose."[84] The church's acts do not complete, extend, or continue God's work, which is his own shining forth, and which alone is properly a matter of his being *light in himself*. The church's acts of outshining have their foundation and their sustaining energy in God; they recognize God's work and attend it with their witness; and, in the "dark riddle" of existence, they reflect the radiant work of the radiant God.[85]

Yet *how* does the church act to outshine and reflect the radiant work of God? How does it "emerge" from the "concealment" of the "sinfulness of all human volition?" It is necessary that we add three brief, concluding points to this section regarding the "visible phenomena," or outshining, of the church *in* the light.

The Listening Church

First, the church's light is outshined as it listens to the gospel; that is, the church is *in* the light as the *ecclesia audiens*, the listening church. Listening to the gospel is always an *opus novum*, and so the church's light is always a process of the church being illuminated as it turns to face the "light of the gospel" by the fact that God himself "brings us to the light of the Gospel," thus giving us ears to hear.[86] Facing the gospel means being confronted with its pronouncement: "the surpassing power belongs to God and not to us" (2 Cor 4:7). In such listening the church is once again confronted with the gospel's declaration that God is the One who shines forth, the One who "has shone in our hearts to give the light of the knowledge of the glory of God in the face of Jesus Christ" (2 Cor 4:6), the One who is renewing his people and undertaking the divine pledge: "the darkness is passing away and the true light is already shining" (1 John 2:8). The message of the gospel is that Jesus

---

84. Webster, "Evangelical Ecclesiology," 182.

85. Barth, *Johannesevangeliums*, 56 (*Gesamtausgabe* II.9). This thought is found within Barth's comments on John 1:5.

86. Barth, CD IV.2:522; KD IV.2:595.

Christ is "the propitiation for our sins, and not for ours only but also for the sins of the whole world" (1 John 2:2); it is the message that this revelation and action is identical with the "advocate . . . Jesus Christ the righteous" (1 John 2:1), the one who laid down his life in order that his people might love as he loved and "walk in the light as he himself is in the light" (1 John 1:7; cf. 2:10).

But to face that message of the gospel as *ecclesia audiens* is already also to face the call of the gospel: the aim of God's work of salvation is human creatures "walking in the light." And this phrase "walking in the light," Edwards clarifies,

> implies not only an enjoying and dwelling in [God's presence], but *living* and *acting* under the influences of it. [This] light of life [is an] animating, quickening light. We read of Christians' walking as children of light (*Ephesians 5:8*), and [there] is doubtless one thing implied in walking as children of light: not only walking in the reception and impression of this [light], but so as it were to shine with the reflection of it (*Matthew 5:16*).[87]

Thus, the church also outshines its light as it faces the gospel's call to walk in this "animating, quickening light." And this call is a lively call, and thus a call to a "living and acting" way under the impress of its light, to "shine with the reflection of it." As a call, therefore, the gospel is the declaration of "walking in the reception and impression" of this light as saints in light; it is, as Calvin says, "to point out the road in which the *children of light* ought to walk."[88] This includes the church facing the pronouncement that corresponds to the "radiant event" of election, namely, to the fact that the "dynamic of being chosen determines the modes of common life and activity in which the church is visible."[89] Thus, the call of the gospel is the lively call of God. And the call of God through the message of the gospel is that the church ought to have as one of its "modes of common life and activity" the especial conduct of walking in the light "before others," not simply to prevent the corruption of the church, but with the aim that others "may see your good works and give glory to your Father who is in heaven" (Matt 5:16).

The church's being "before others" requires that the church remain faithful above all to its own special task of turning to, facing, and listening to the true words promised to it by the call of the gospel. Yet this listening also includes the very real possibility of "true words" issuing *extra muros*

---

87. Edwards, "Of Those Who Walk in The Light" (WJE 25:708).

88. Calvin, *Comm. ep. Eph.* 5.9 (CO 51:217; CC 21:309): ". . . ut viam indicet, qua ambulare filios lucis convenit."

89. Webster, "Evangelical Ecclesiology," 184.

ecclesiae, outside the walls of the church. These "lesser lights,"[90] as Barth famously calls them, are beyond the light of the "circumference" of the church. Yet "in themselves" those truths and lights have "nothing to do with God as Founder and Lord of His covenant."[91] They do, however, in light of the one revelation of God "stand objectively in a supremely direct relationship with the one true Word . . . Jesus Christ, who is their sovereign."[92] In other words, Barth says in another passage, "even though it is perhaps incontestable that there are real lights of life and words of God in this sphere too, He alone is the Word of God even here, and these lights shine only because of the shining of none other light than His."[93] This language is therefore not one of human capacity, but the "capacity of Jesus Christ" which, as it happens, goes beyond the "sphere of the Bible and the Church," because "there is no secular sphere abandoned by him or withdrawn from his control."[94]

Thus, the *ecclesia audiens* must "eavesdrop on the world at large" not only to hear the true voice of the gospel, but the voice of secular words that may or may not confront the church with a summons to faith and to repentance.[95] These words from the "others," before whom the church must outshine its light with responsible "living and acting," are not a louder call in competition with that of the gospel. Rather, the "lesser lights," the call of the "others," are simply the agreement with the gospel *extra muros ecclesiae*. And if this is indeed the case, says Barth, then "we may confidently believe that the latter are true words, and thus be ready for obedience, in the direction indicated, not to the words as such, but to the word of scripture illuminated and made more pressing by them."[96] These "lesser lights" are not alongside the "one great Light" in Jesus Christ; nor do these "lesser lights" represent some essentially different content or truth that would then need to be reconciled with the "one great Light" by means of some overarching

---

90. Barth's notion of "Lichterlehre" has provoked the question of whether he is saying something more than the first sections of the *Dogmatics* allows. For this view, see Berkhof, "Barths Lichterlehre," esp. 36, 48. However, Jüngel is quick to rebut this claim by stating that, beyond several historical errors, one cannot maintain "daß Barth 'seine Ansichten in diesen Fragen' mit KD IV/3 vorgetragenen Entwurf 'grundlegend geändert' habe [regarding the *notitia dei naturalis*]" (*Gottes Sein ist im Werden*, 22, n.26).

91. Barth, CD IV.3.1:151.

92. Ibid., 125. Note that Barth says these words are "laid upon their lips" by the true Word (ibid.).

93. Ibid., 96.

94. Ibid., 118–19.

95. Ibid., 117.

96. Ibid., 125.

argument from nature. Rather, these lights sound out in a variety of forms the single truth already present in the self-sufficient and unique form of the "great Light," Jesus Christ.[97] And if the church is to be the church that listens, according to Barth, it must listen to such words if, and only if, they repeat the call of the gospel.[98]

The summons of the gospel—and perhaps the summons to the gospel by secular words in proximity to the one light of Christ—is thus a summons to obedience; it is a call, says Barth further, "to our own free action as the men we are." Barth continues:

> Hence the saying of Jesus to His disciples in Mt. 5:16f.: "Let your light so shine before men that they may see your good works, and glorify your Father which is in heaven." But the fact that they have or are this light—"ye are the light of the world," "a city that is set on a hill," the candle which is not "put under a bushel, but on a candlestick—is not something that they have snatched or resolved of themselves, but something that they have become in virtue of His calling.[99]

The call of the evangel to walk in the light—the "something" that the church has "in virtue of His calling"—directs the church outwards, away from sinful rebellion and towards life in the light of God's love for those "sitting in the darkness," to those who may or may not be speaking "true words." Thus, "because they have been rescued from the darkness by God's mercy," the church is allowed to let its "light shine before others."[100] For if "walking as children of light" means the emancipation of the church for the truth of "the gospel of the glory of Christ"—that is, the fact that the "works of darkness" have been exposed by the light of Christ (cf. Eph 5:13–14)—then "shining before others" is the free obedience in which the church acknowledges another's cause and makes it its own.

---

97. For an insightful study of these themes, see Ensminger, *Karl Barth's Theology*, esp. 30–40. Ensminger's study as a whole seeks to clarify Barth's work against some religio-historical backcloth. Of note for our purposes is Ensminger's thoughts on the *Lichterlehre*: "For the Christian community . . . Barth encourages openness to other lights—yet these will only be recognized as such after encountering the Light that is the one source of light" (ibid., 30).

98. This is the qualifier for these "true words" according to Barth. He does acknowledge, moreover, that there are words that "derive not from the light which lightens the darkness but from the darkness itself, so that they can be regarded as untrue words" (CD IV.3.1:126).

99. Barth, CD IV.2: 593; *KD* IV.2: 671.

100. Calvin, *Comm. ep. Eph.* 5.8: ". . . quia ex tenebris erepti sint Dei misericordia" (CO 51:217; cf. CC 21:309).

Thus, as the church is the *ecclesia audiens,* the "other" is no longer seen as a hazard, even though they "dwell amidst the darkness," because the church faces the "light of the gospel."[101] This outshining of the church in its "walking" is a counterpoint to the "horrible blindness" wrought by darkness.[102] And this means that, according to Calvin,

> believers must walk in the light because they are "children of light." This is done, when they do not live according to their own will, but devote themselves entirely to the obedience of God—when they undertake nothing but by his command. Besides, such obedience is testified by its *fruits of the light.* Such as *goodness, righteousness, and truth.*[103]

Undertaking "nothing but by his command" includes walking in the light, obediently bearing the "fruits of the light" for which the church has been set apart. How, then, is the church *in* the light? It is so by *ecclesia audiens,* that is, by attention to the call of the gospel and obediently walking in the light.

The Witnessing Church

Second, and on a related note, the church's light is outshined as it bears witness to the world in darkness. "Let your light shine before others . . . that you may proclaim the excellencies of him who called you out of darkness into his marvelous light" (Matt 5:16; 1 Pet 2:9). The origin of the church's light, as we have seen, is entirely external; the consequences of this are that, first, it is manifest as listening to the gospel's call. Likewise, the goal of the church's light, its derivative outshining, lies beyond itself. Webster is instructive here:

> The church points to the prevenient perfection of the triune God. It witnesses to God the Father's omnipotently effective purpose which in Jesus Christ has broken through the realm of deceit and opposition, which is now supremely real and limitlessly active in his risen presence, and which is unleashed with converting power in the Spirit of Christ. Of all this, the church is the attestation.[104]

---

101. Ibid., 5.11 (CO 51:217; CC 21:310).
102. Ibid., 5.8: "horrendam caecitatem" (CO 51:217).
103. Ibid., 5.10 (CC 21:310; cf. CO 51:217).
104. Webster, "Evangelical Ecclesiology," 186; cf. : "the church simply *points.* . . . Yet this does not mean a reduction of the church to pure passivity. . . . Attestation is human *activity* bent to the service of God" (ibid., 185–86).

The supreme end of the church *in* the light is the hymning of the radiant triune God; but its intermediate goal is bearing witness to the "most beautiful and glorious object" of God's radiant work in Jesus Christ.¹⁰⁵ As the gathering of the saints in light, the church proclaims or attests the excellencies of the Father's mighty purpose in Jesus Christ, and its being illumined by the Spirit.

In an important sense, the dynamic of light includes not only a withdrawal "out of darkness" but also a sending "into darkness." The light of the saints is not a mere self-illumination, so to speak; if it were, then it would all too quickly become mere factional hostility towards a world held captive in "a hellish night of darkness."¹⁰⁶ Such withdrawal is dubious, not least because it tends to assume that the line between being "in darkness" and being "called into the light" corresponds with the line between the "church" and the "world." It is also because theories of withdrawal almost inevitably transfer the divine movement of the "radiant event" of election into social exclusivity, and so make the church's light into a "pure" sphere over against the dark domain of the world, namely into a superior "island of one culture in the middle of another,"¹⁰⁷ or into those "inside the circle" piously looking at those "outside the circle."¹⁰⁸ Rather, the church

> will be noticeable to others outside, shining for them and usable towards them in the service of divine vocation as "children of God . . . in the midst of a crooked and perverse nation, among whom ye shine as lights . . . of the world." . . . The light which is not set on a candlestick but under a bushel could not be bright, nor could the seed which is not sown in the field of the world but left to itself remain alive. The peace of God experienced in the community and by its members could only be a false peace *if limited to this circle and enjoyed only within it.*¹⁰⁹

It is precisely this transposition of light into a "false peace" that leads to the wrong kind of visibility. Authentic visible ecclesial light has a quite different character. Being "noticeable to others outside" and "called out of

---

105. Edwards, "Christ, the Light of the Word," 546.
106. Ibid., 538.
107. Hauerwas and Willimon, *Resident Aliens*, 12.
108. This is Schleiermacher's point in his Pietistic rendering of election entailing those moving from the outer circle to the inner circle in *Christian Faith*, §§114, 120.
109. Barth, CD IV/3.2:510, 764 (emphasis mine); KD IV.3:586. Cf.: "Es könnte der in der Gemeinde und von ihren Gliedern erfahrene und erlebte Friede Gottes, auf ihren Kreis beschränkt und nur in ihm genossen, nur ein fauler Friede sei" (KD IV.3:874).

the world, . . . the community is genuinely called into it," Barth continues. "And the reality of its calling out depends upon there being no gap between it and the calling into which ineluctably follows, upon the separation from and the turning to the world taking place in a single movement."[110] There is, unquestionably, a radical, manifold gathering, a "calling out" and a "turning to," that effects the church's withdrawal and which gathers its members into a company of "saints" and "children" of light. And that withdrawal is visible as "self-denial," the church's refusal to return to the darkness, by which, as the apostle Paul reminds us, "at one time" each saint was held captive (Eph 5:8). Ecclesial light is therefore visible as witness, as good works that are transparent to and declare the wonderful deeds of the God who is light in himself. In doing so, its visibility is like John the Baptist: though "He was not the light," he came "to bear witness about the light" (John 1:8).

Yet it must be added here that such witness is met precisely in the church's obedient response to its commission from Christ: "All authority in heaven and on earth has been given to me. Therefore go and make disciples of all nations, baptizing them in the name of the Father and of the Son and of the Holy Spirit, and teaching them to obey everything I have commanded you" (Matt 28:18-20). More precisely, the church fulfills its witness and summons to "make disciples of all nations" as its saints acknowledge the triune God in the "illuminative" act of baptism.[111] The church is therefore in the light of God, not because it has already attained the state of being perfect, but because through the "radiant event" of God's election, reconciliation, and illumination of human creatures, the church is judged, crucified, buried, and raised to new life in the One who alone has "all authority." Therefore the nature of the church's sacramental witness is one in which the church, says Jüngel, lets "God perform his work—this and this alone is the function of the church's action."[112] Agency in the "illuminative" act of baptism is not ecclesial, therefore, but rather found in God's "work that has already been accomplished."[113] Baptism is entirely an acknowledgement that "the fruit and efficacy of baptism proceed from God the Father adopting us through his Son, and, after having cleansed us from the filth of the flesh through the

---

110. Ibid., 764.

111. "Illumination" (*photismos*; *illuminatio*) is a common title ascribed to baptism by various early fathers. See, e.g, Clement, *Instr.* 1.6.26.1-2; *Misc.* 1.5; Hilary *Ps. 118* 3.9; John Chrysostom, *Hom. ep. Rom.* 10; *Hom. Act.* 20; Tertullian, *De bapt.* 6; Basil, *Sp. sanc.* 15.35; and Gregory Nazianzen, esp. *Or.* 39. For a thorough study of this topic, and the early theological undertones associated with baptism, see Ferguson, *Baptism in the Early Church*, 108-9.

112. Jüngel, "Church as Sacrament?" 203.

113. Ibid., 204.

Spirit, restoring us anew to righteousness."[114] Thus, central to the church's outshining is God's triune work of regeneration signified in baptism. And the church concerns itself with the new creature of God: that event in which the human creature's destiny is established even as the human creature is "put to death" and "made alive" in Christ. "For baptism is the cross," says John Chrysostom. "What the cross and burial is to Christ, Baptism is to us, even if not in the same respects. . . . For if we shared in [Christ's] death and burial, much more will we share in resurrection and life."[115]

The church is concerned, therefore, with that regeneration bestowed by the "kindling, warm, and fiery" Spirit in which true human being is to be found as God "cleanses and illuminates the man."[116] Baptism is called "illumination" because it is a witness to the world that "in the name of Jesus Christ, who was crucified under Pontius Pilate, and in the name of the Holy Ghost, who through the prophets foretold all things about Jesus, he who is illuminated is washed."[117] And in following patristic catechesis further, the rationale for this sacrament of baptism is that the saints will not be ignorant, but rather, by being "illuminated by this splendor of the soul" through the Holy Spirit they are thus given a myriad of blessings, namely:

> aid to our weakness, the renunciation of the flesh, . . . the fellowship of the Word, the improvement of the creature, the overwhelming of sin, the participation of light, the dissolution of darkness, . . . the carriage to God, the dying with Christ, the perfecting of the mind, the bulwark of faith, the key of the Kingdom of heaven, the change of life, the removal of slavery, the loosing of chains, the remodeling of the whole man. Why should I go into further detail? Illumination is the greatest and most magnificent of the Gifts of God.[118]

In this "magnificent" gift of baptism is found both "a pledge of eternal life before God" and "an outward sign of faith before men."[119] It is this

---

114. Calvin, *Comm. harm. ev.*, Matt 28.19 (CO 45:824; CC 17:387): ". . . baptismi efficaciam fructumque manare, quod Deus pater in filio suo nos adoptat, et per spiritum a carnis nostrae sordibus purgatos reformat in iustitiam."

115. John Chrysostom, *Hom. ep. Rom.* 10, 6.3–4 (PG 60:482; NPNF 11:405).

116. Gregory of Nyssa, *On the Baptism of Christ* (NPNF 5:520, 522).

117. Justin Martyr, *Apol.* 60 (PG 6:417; ANF 1:183). This is one of the earliest uses of "illumination" as a title for baptism in Christian theology.

118. Gregory Nazianzen, *Or.* 40.3 (PG 36:361; NPNF 7:360). Regarding these points from Gregory, see Mackenzie, *'Obscurism' of Light*, 143–66; and Beely, *Gregory Nazianzus*, 65–89.

119. Calvin, *Comm. har. ev.*, Matt 28.19 (CO 45:822; CC 17:385).

"outward sign" in which we find the particular outshining of the church. For after the *ablutio* of the saint, "it is not possible for the light of a Christian to be hid; not possible for a lamp so conspicuous as that to be concealed."[120] To the world in the darkness, therefore, this act reveals the covenant that "contains a type of death and of life" in the renewing "pledge of life" from the Holy Spirit.[121] Through this pledge of regenerating illumination, the church bears "witness to the light."

The Praying and Praising Church

Third, and final, the light of the church outshines in its prayer that "the city has no need of sun or moon to shine on it, for the glory of God is its light, and its lamp is the Lamb" (Rev 21:23). If the essence of ecclesial light is the proclamation of the radiant identity of the triune God, then the primordial act in which light is outshined is the church's prayer that God's light is the true and saving light, namely, the light *of* and *for* the world. That prayer is not, we must note, a prayer that the church somehow works to establish the light of God. On the contrary: it is a prayer that God *himself*, as the true light, "gives it light," by the "lamp of the Lamb"; it is a prayer that the saints in light "may be burning and shining lights, stars in the right hand of Christ, full of light, set to enlighten the world and the church of God."[122]

Moreover, in praying this prayer, the church *in* the Lamb's light points back to the saving acts of Jesus Christ. It is the proclamation that "in the new covenant, everything that is termed light remains firmly set, without the possibility of being removed."[123] The prayer of the church, its cry that in this matter God will take up its own cause and "give his light," is thus rooted in the Lamb of God. And so as it prays this prayer, the church outshines its light, namely, its proclamation of the radiant identity of God in his radiant deeds. And this is a prayer that its "gates will never be shut by day" (Rev 21:25). That is, to God's shining forth and outshining there corresponds the church's "shining forth" or "outshining" in its "*proclaiming* . . . the *magnalia*, the mighty acts of the One 'who hath called you out of darkness into his marvelous light.'"[124]

But preceding all these acts of outshining—namely, obediently listening to the summons of the gospel, bearing witness to the light of God, and

---

120. Chrysostom, *Hom. Act.* 20, 9.10–12 (PG 60:131–32; NPNF 11:134)
121. Basil, *Sp. sanc.* 15.35 (PPS 42:67).
122. Edwards, "Sons of Oil, Heavenly Lights" (WJE 25:270).
123. Balthasar, *Glory of the Lord* 7:86.
124. Barth, CD IV.3.2:510; KD IV.3:586.

praying that God's light is the true light *of* and *for* the world—will once again be the church's outshining of praise. At the end of his commentary on the Psalms, Calvin clarifies this point:

> If we would have our minds kindled, then, to enlarge in this religious service [of praise], let us meditate upon God's power and greatness, which will speedily dispel all such insensibility [to his presence]. Though our minds can never take in this immensity, the mere taste of it will affect us . . . that we may worship God with constant sacrifices of praise, until being gathered into the kingdom of heaven, we sing with elect angels an eternal hallelujah.[125]

Praise is the church's protestation against "all such insensibility" to the radiant presence of God; it is the rejection of the human creature's former rebellion against God as the light of life; it is the human "struggle to voice" speech to God as being "something irreducibly other than itself";[126] it is the act in which, having their "minds kindled," humans engage in recognizing God's "power and greatness" as they enlarge their "religious service" to one another and to the world. In sum, therefore: the church outshines its light as it continuously worships God and recognizes his radiant identity with "an eternal hallelujah."

Conclusion

We might draw these reflections to a close with what Barth had to say regarding the goal of the church:

> [The church] cannot be an end in itself. It has it for God, who is so very much for us men that He will not have it otherwise than that before He has finished speaking His last Word some, and even many, should already be for Him. And it has it for the world in order that as a provisional representation of the justification which has taken place in Jesus Christ it may be the sign which is set up in it, which is given to it, which summons it, in order that it may be to it a shining light—a feeble and defective but still a shining light—until the dawning of the great light which will be the end of all time and therefore of this end-time.[127]

---

125. Calvin, *Comm. Ps.* 150.6 (CO 32:442; CC 7:320–21).

126. Williams, *On Christian Theology*, 9.

127. Barth, CD IV.1:739; cf. KD IV.1:826: ". . . klein, mangelhaft und bescheiden scheinende, aber scheinende—Licht zu sein, bis das große Licht anbrechen wird, das das Ende aller Zeit und so auch dieser Endzeit sein wird."

With this in mind, we therefore repeat the basis from which the church and its saints shine in the world, though it may be a "feeble and defective but still a shining light," as found in one of our guiding biblical passages:

> But you are a chosen race, a royal priesthood, a holy nation, a people for his own possession, that you may proclaim the excellencies of him who called you out of darkness into his marvelous light. Once you were not a people, but now you are God's people; once you had not received mercy, but now you have received mercy. (1 Pet 2:9–10)

In sum, *Phōs Hilarón*:

> Hail, gladdening Light, of his pure glory poured
>   Who is the immortal Father, heavenly, blest,
>   Holiest of Holies, Jesus Christ our Lord!
> Now we are at the sun's hour of rest,
>   The lights of evening round us shine,
>   We hymn the Father, Son, and Holy Spirit divine!
> Worthiest art thou at all times to be sung
>   With undefiled tongue,
>   Son of our God, giver of life, alone:
>   Therefore in all the world thy glories, Lord, they own.

5

The Illumined Mind

Theology in the Presence of the Radiant One

> Being informed and informing others by Holy Scripture . . . let us draw near to theological questions, setting at the head the Father, the Son, and the Holy Spirit, of whom we speak; that the Father may show us his will, and the Son may offer a helping hand, and the Holy Spirit may inspire us; or rather that illumination may come upon us from the One light of God, One in diversity, diverse in unity, wherein is a wonder.[1]

THE LIGHT OF GOD, OUR STUDY HAS ARGUED, IS A WAY OF TALKING OF THE identity of the triune God, and so, as we have seen, God's light characterizes his radiant existence as Father, Son, and Holy Spirit. The triune God's radiant identity is enacted in the works of election, reconciliation, and illumination, in the work of salvation in which God is determinatively, savingly, and graciously present to his people. God's light is thus a *light-in-relation*: it expresses both "an inner-trinitarian relation" as well as God's dealings with the creatures he has made and seeks to redeem.[2] This is the sense of God's unending act of shining forth upon human creatures for their renewal and restoration. Light shined forth to human creatures is not possessed light, but derived light; and the primary mark of the saints *in* light, the church *in* light, is thus its external orientation, its "walking in the light," its ordering towards God as its source and the object of its continual praise. In short, we have up to this point been reflecting on a twofold proposal: *God is light in himself*,

---

1. Gregory Nazianzen, *Or.* 28.1 (PG 36:26–7; PPS 23:37).

2. Krötke, *Gottes Klarheiten*, 84: "Eigenschaft ebenfalls eine innertrinitarische Beziehung mit zur Sprache bringen müßte."

and *from himself God shines forth his light*. That is, the One who is light is the radiant One in our midst.

Our thoughts on the declaration that "God is light" have therefore been from the standpoint of Christian theology. Situated among God's saints in light, theology directs the church's devotion to and consideration of the "light of the gospel." With this final chapter we move to address the topic of theology as a result of the confession that "God is light." Yet before starting we must keep in mind that the answer to this question is found within the complex topography of the wider doctrinal landscape thus far examined, namely, within the doctrines of God and of the church. Therefore, this chapter shall be concerned with what bearing the radiant reality of the triune God might have on the tasks of theology as an activity of the "illumined mind."

The Illumined Mind

The context for the human task of theology is God's rescue of the human mind out of the darkness of ignorance into the light of communion. As "God is Light, perfect, intellectual, and intelligible Light," says Sonderegger, so "this Personal Light shines in the darkness, the darkness of creaturely time and striving to know."[3] The human mind, therefore, must be "enlightened in order that you may know the hope to which he has called you, the riches of his glorious inheritance in his holy people" (Eph 1:18). Theology, knowing the hope of the Christian call, can therefore only occur if it is founded on the mind's illumination by the radiant presence of the One who alone has *light in himself*.

Yet since the advent of what might loosely be called "modern" thought, the mind or *ratio* has typically been considered a *scientia naturalis*, a natural knowledge, of human ontology. For instance, Immanuel Kant's memorable answer to "What is the Enlightenment?" displays the spirit of the rise of modernity. The "Enlightenment," he relays, is the daring to use understanding "without being guided by another. *Sapere aude*! Have the courage to use your own understanding! is therefore the motto of the Enlightenment."[4] Thus, for Kant, human cognition "is itself the legislation for nature, i.e.,

---

3. Sonderegger, *Systematic Theology*, 1:348–49.

4. Kant, "Was ist Aufklärung?" 169 (*Werke* 4): "Selbstverschuldet ist diese Unmündigkeit, wenn die Ursache derselben nicht am Mangel des Verstandes, sondern der Entschließung und des Mutes liegt, sich seiner ohne Leitung eines andern zu bedienen. Sapere aude! Habe Mut, dich deines eigenen Verstandes zu bedienen! ist also der Wahlspruch der Aufklärung."

without understanding there would not be any nature at all."[5] Echoing Kant's pronouncements, modernity often views human cognition as a natural law, which is able to determine what human creatures ought to do and ought not to do. The intellect is therefore its own authorization and magistrate; that is, the mind's "causes and effects, are fastened to [the human creature's] throne"; and the human mind is, moreover, "the standard of right and wrong." Living for the "Good," according to contemporary trends in virtue epistemology, is therefore conditioned purely by the inherent "value," "reliability," or "*intentional* relation" of human cognition and its ends.[6] And having "epistemic certainty" derives not from the work of an external, divine source, but the *a priori* condition of the human intellect, namely "a *reasonable belief* to the effect that the activity characteristic of this virtue is a reliable way of achieving one's epistemic goals."[7] The "possibility of natural innate knowledge" is therefore aprioristically possible, whether this derives from the mind's conformity to the natural law or from the randomness of "natural selection or some other evolutionary mechanism."[8]

Whatever the case, such notions of human cognition from modern culture are, according to Christian confession, deeply flawed.[9] They are

---

5. Kant, *Critique of Pure Reason*, A126. Kant's modern epistemological program is, of course, set within its own context, namely as a reaction, on the one hand, to the so-called "outmoded" Aristotelianism of medieval cosmology, and, on the other hand, to Cartesian dualism. The former was seminally found in Aquinas, who noted that the "rule and measure of human acts is the reason" (ST 1a2ae.q90.1*resp.*). Yet Aquinas qualified this with the notion that *sacra doctrina*, based on revelation, could attain knowledge of God when God aids creaturely reason (cf. ST 1a.q1.6*resp.*); that is, knowledge of God was qualified as a revelatory event. The latter, Cartesian, approach entailed prior knowledge of God. Thus, Descartes's famous *cogito, ergo sum* summarily marked the advent of an epistemology that held knowledge of God over against human self-knowledge; namely, knowledge of God served as the requisite ground for creaturely cognition (see Descartes, *Meditationes*, esp. *meditatio* IV). Against these approaches, Kant saw "knowledge" as arising through the function of what is called "the categories of understanding" and the data received through the senses. And in founding the limits of creaturely reason in this way, Kant brought an end to the idea that the objective ground of the world—that is, God—could be known, for we have no sense data for God. God could only be postulated and not known; human consciousness thus became the starting point, "without being guided by another" (see idem.).

6. Baehr, *Inquiring Mind*, 137 (emphasis original).

7. Ibid., 126 (emphasis original).

8. Lackey, "Why we don't deserve credit," 358.

9. For more on the historic theological reaction to the Enlightenment's emphasis of *lex naturalis*, see Olson, *Journey of Modern Theology*, esp. 44–71. See also the impressive surveys from Dorrien, *Kantian Reason and Hegelian Spirit*; and Frame, *Western Philosophy and Theology*, 214–50.

flawed simply because they do not set the human mind within the realm of redemption. They are flawed because they do not apprehend that the intellectual adoration of God is possible only as human reason is humbled by the fact that it is not its own author. The modern claim that human reason is "the legislator for nature,"[10] or *scientia naturalis*, therefore posits the utterly perilous position of reason as "original or self-founding after the manner of the uncreated divine reason."[11] And if the human mind is the capacity for rational independence and originality, then the mind's reliance on the Holy Spirit—namely, the mind's ultimate destiny in God—is rejected, for the human mind does not need to be "illuminated" and rescued from the darkness of ignorance and sin and death.

Yet contrary to Kant's disapproval of such "dogmatism," we must summarily depart from this modern venture because the proclamation of the gospel compels us to confess that human creatures, including the mind, have been blinded to the "light of the gospel of the glory of Christ" within the history of human sin and redemption.

Theories of Illumination

In further reflecting upon this last statement—namely, that human creatures, including the mind, have been blinded to the "light of the gospel"—we might find an instructive outworking of the classical understanding of the theory of divine illumination.[12] In saying this, however, we must quickly make a twofold distinction.

First, in the tradition of illumination there entails a philosophical meaning, grounded in medieval Augustinianism. Here "illumination" indicates the enlightenment of the human mind by God's light with such archetypal ideas as truth, goodness, and perfection. According to this theory of illumination, finite truth, goodness, or perfection is recognized by means of a *habitus mentis*, or a disposition of the mind, that has been graciously bestowed to human creatures by the illuminating influence of the *rationes*

10. Kant, *Critique of Pure Reason*, A125–26.
11. Webster, "Biblical Reasoning," 124.
12. We briefly touched on the doctrine of illumination above in chapter 3. There we offered a sketch of "illumination" as that loving, regenerating, radiating action of the Holy Spirit on the saint called out of darkness into light. In this sub-section we are much more concerned with detailing the Spirit's work on the human mind in the process of sanctification and as the occasion of the "illumined mind" set to godly service. It is unfortunate that in "historical" investigations of the "doctrine of divine illumination," the theory is usually cast down as archaic and misinformed in view of "modern science." See such conclusions in Marrone, *Light of Thy Countenance*.

aeternae, the eternal ideas. "The mind," Bonaventure clarifies, "is not only formed from without by images, but also by receiving simple forms from above and retaining them in itself."[13] In addition, the indirect knowledge that we have of these forms is the foundation of *cognitio certa*, certain knowledge. Apart from this illumination of the mind, human knowledge must rest on the sensory perception of the finite order where no absolutes are given and where there is, therefore, no *cognitio certa*.

This view of illumination belongs to the Augustinian tradition as "redefined" by Bonaventure in the Middle Ages.[14] In his *Itinerarium mentis in Deum*, for instance, Bonaventure proposes that the "apex of the mind [is] the illumination of the conscience," in which "by a flash of apprehension . . . the mind turns most directly and intensely to the rays of light."[15] The human mind is an "image" or "reflection" of the perfection of God, and thus by turning inward in contemplation is found the ascent to the eternal "rays of light descending from the eternal law."[16] The light of God therefore works together with the human intellectual faculties as a "regulative and moving cause," ensuring that the human mind grasps immutable truth; yet it does not and cannot replace the human intellectual faculties in their proper roles.[17] The infinite extension of God's knowledge is what makes

---

13. Bonaventure, *Itinerarium* 3.2 (*Opera* 5:303): "Ex *secunda* apparet, quod ipsa non solum habet *ab exteriori* formari per phantasmata, verum etiam a *superiori* suscipiendo simplices formas, quae non possunt introire per portas sensuum et sensibilium phantasies." Bonaventure's doctrine of illumination is an expansion of Augustine's remarks on "truth" and "light" in *Conf.* 7.10: "And I entered and with the eye of my soul, such as it was, I saw above that eye of my soul, above my mind, an unchangeable light. . . . *Whoever knows the truth knows this light*." See our brief remarks on Augustine's Platonic use of noetic light in *Gen. litt.* in chapter 1.

14. We say "redefined" here because Bonaventure codified Augustine's thoughts on illumination and, in so doing, may have gone beyond Augustine's theory itself. Recently, Schumacher has done good work to show that Bonaventure may have more differences with the Augustinian theory of illumination than is often realized. As we are using Bonaventure here in a generalized way, we leave it to the reader to consider Schumacher's claims regarding the finer points of this debate in her *Divine Illumination*, ch. 4. Suffice it to say, the underlying realism of this "redefined" Augustinian position made the theory unappealing to more Aristotelian scholastics, namely Aquinas and Scotus. Still, Whidden makes the case that "Aquinas is modulating the theory of illumination that he and his contemporaries inherited from the Augustinian tradition, which held that any kind of knowledge required divine illumination" (*Christ the Light*, 70).

15. Bonaventure, *Itinerarium* 1.6.*prop3* (*Opera* 5:296–7): ". . . et per fulgorem speculationis, qua mens ad radios lucis directissime et intensissime se convertit."

16. Ibid., 3.5–6 (*Opera* 5:303).

17. Bonaventure, *Quaestiones* 4 (*Opera* 5:17).

divine understanding certain, and the *rationes aeternae* are bestowed upon the human mind.

> The intellect is said to comprehend truly the meaning of propositions when it knows with certitude that they are true.... But since our mind itself is changeable, it cannot see that truth shining forth unchangeably except by some light shining without change in any way; and it is impossible that such a light be a mutable creature. Therefore it knows in that light which illuminates every man that comes into this world [John 1:9], which is true light and the Word which in the beginning was with God [John 1:1].[18]

Here Bonaventure makes more precise the Augustinian lineage of illumination, which concerns "true" intellect with the perception of "light."[19] Thus, human knowledge requires divine illumination; and all other features of human knowledge—namely, universals—come from a created cause.[20]

While instructive, the Augustinian notion of illumination will be placed to one side in favor of a second meaning of illumination that will be our guide in the remainder of this section—one that tends to avoid the philosophical use and retain the dogmatic form of the theory as centered on the internal testimony of the Holy Spirit.[21] In other words, the dogmatic *locus* of illumination is found precisely in the work of grace by which we are "illuminated in the Spirit" as he presents himself to our minds through the Word of God.[22] Edwards further highlights this approach:

> A saving belief of the reality and divinity of the things proposed and exhibited to us in the gospel, is from the Spirit of God's enlightening the mind, to have right apprehensions of the nature

---

18. Bonaventure, *Itinerarium* 3.3 (*Opera* 5:304); cf. *Quaestiones* 4.

19. See our thoughts on Pickstock's interpretation of this "perception" in chapter 1.

20. For good guidance on Bonaventure's theory, refer to Crowley, "Illumination and Certitude," 431–48; Cullen, *Bonaventure*, 20–22; and the many helpful sources in Schumacher, *Divine Illumination*, 110–11.

21. Bonaventure's theory is indeed philosophical in nature, as his collations of Augustine's thought were formed in this fashion. For instance, he is at lengths in the *Itinerarium* to emphasize that the "sciences"—that is, metaphysics, logic, rhetoric, mathematics, and so forth—"have certain and infallible rules, like rays of light descending from the eternal law into our minds. And thus our minds, illumined and suffused by such great radiance, unless they be blind, can be led through themselves alone to the contemplation of that eternal light [*contemplandam illam lucem aeternam*]" (3.7; *Opera* 5:305–6).

22. Webster, "Illumination," in *Domain of the Word*, 57.

of those things, and so as it were unveiling things, or revealing them, and enabling the mind to view them and see them as they are.[23]

Illumination is thus the application of the work of grace, which begins with conversion and baptism, but continues through sanctification as the basis of both repentance and assurance in the life of the saint.[24] Regarding the "purification" of the mind in the act of baptism and the subsequent "assurance" of such grace, Gregory beckons us to obediently

> look at and reason upon God and things divine in a manner corresponding to this grace given us. But let us . . . be grounded and purified and so to say made light by fear, and thus be raised to the height. . . . And where there is purifying there is illumination; and illumination is the satisfying of desire to those who long for the greatest things, or the Greatest Thing, or that which surpasses all greatness.[25]

Illumination is therefore intimately connected with the "satisfaction" of the assent to Christian calling: "we are illuminated by the grace of God alone as to the knowledge of the truth," says Calvin, "so that our calling corresponds with our election."[26]

Staying with Calvin, we see that this illumination can further be divided into the external and internal work of the Holy Spirit—the former relating to teaching that prepares the individual for service, and the latter relating to the salvific teaching of the Holy Spirit at conversion. Calvin clarifies this in his comments on 2 Corinthians 4:6, namely that there is:

> a twofold illumination [*Duplicem illuminationem*], which must be carefully observed—the one is that of the gospel, the other is secret, taking place in our hearts. For as God, the Creator of the world, pours forth upon us the brightness of the sun, and gives us eyes to receive it, so, as the Redeemer, in the person of his

---

23. Edwards, "A Spiritual Understanding" (WJE 14:296). Cf. "The foundation of this spiritual knowledge is a regeneration of the heart. 'Tis not the natural man, whose very nature is sin, whose soul is darkness and filthiness, that is capable of this spiritual, bright and pure light. There is an necessity of the removal of the darkness, deadness and stupidity of the soul before it can be thus enlightened" (ibid., 89).

24. Again, see our brief mention of baptism in the "outshining" of the church in chapter 4, which notes the patristic use of "illumination" to mark this "washing."

25. Gregory Nazianzen, *Or.* 39.8 (PG 36:344; NPNF 7:354). See Beeley, *Gregory of Nazianzus*, ch. 1.

26. Calvin, *Comm. Jas.* 1.18 (CO 55:392; CC 22:292): ". . . ita nos mera Dei gratia illuminari in notitiam veritatis: ut vocatio electioni respondeat."

Son, He shines forth, indeed, upon us by His gospel, but, as we are blind, that would be in vain, if He did not at the same time enlighten our understandings by His Spirit. . . . Therefore God has, by His Spirit, opened the eyes of our understandings, so as to make them capable of receiving the light of the gospel.[27]

Being "made capable of receiving the light of the gospel" marks the mind's particular need for illumination. In examining the *ante lapsum* state of human creatures, Calvin comments: "God's image was visible in the light of the mind" and thus the "highest rectitude of [Adam and Eve] was in the mind and will."[28] Even *post lapsum*, "some sparks [of the mind] still gleam"; yet such sparks of the *imago Dei* "cannot come forth effectively" because this "light [is] choked with dense ignorance" that is inherent in the mind's fallen state.[29] We therefore witness the "dullness" of the human mind in the history of sin, wherein human creatures "cannot hold to the right path, but wander through various errors and stumble repeatedly, as if groping in the darkness."[30] The darkness of human cognition is therefore "like a traveler passing through a field at night," Calvin further imagines, "who in a momentary lightening flash sees far and wide, but the sight vanishes so swiftly that he is plunged again into the darkness of the night before he can take even a step—let alone be directed on his way by its help."[31] The great modern project of the autonomous human mind is, ironically, the very sign of its own darkness, ignorance, and fallenness: "Man's keenness of mind is man's blindness as far as the knowledge of God is concerned."[32] Yet this noetic "blindness" and "dullness" is also the precise sphere in which God performs his illuminative work of regeneration:

> Human reason, therefore, neither approaches, nor strives toward, nor even takes straight aim at . . . the understanding of who God is or what sort of God he wishes to be towards us. . . . [T]hus man's mind can become spiritually wise only in so far as God illuminates it.[33]

---

27. Calvin, *Comm. Cor. II* 4.6 (CO 50:53; CC 20:200).
28. Calvin, *Inst.* I.15.4, 8; OS 3:179, 186: "summa rectitudo."
29. Ibid., II.2.12; OS 3:255.
30. Ibid.
31. Ibid., II.2.18; OS 3:261.
32. Ibid., II.2.19; OS 3:261: ". . . quia eius acumen, quantum ad Dei notitiam, mera est caligo."
33. Ibid., II.2.18, 20; OS 3:261–2: ". . . tantum hominis mentem spiritualiter sapere, quantum abs se illustrata fuerit."

This history of human sin and its scattering by God therefore involves the remaking of human creatures as a whole, not merely of what we classify as their "spiritual" feature. The human mind stands before the divine requirement that it be "in the light" as God is "in the light" (1 John 1:7); it stands beneath the requirement that "the light of the knowledge of the glory of God" is found only in "the face of Jesus Christ" (2 Cor 4:6). And the human mind is unable to receive this "light of knowledge" unless it is "illumined by the Spirit of God."[34] Being illumined by God's grace is not a "common endowment of nature," Calvin continues, but a "'gift' of special illumination" in which the Holy Spirit "forms our ears to hear and our minds to understand."[35] Such a gracious gift of special illumination, in which the human mind is formed to understand the wisdom of God, thus turns the human creature to its call. Here, in Calvin's catechetical tone, we find the aim of Christian calling:

> The Holy Spirit . . . illumines us with his light in order that we may learn and plainly recognize what an enormous wealth of divine goodness we possess in Christ. . . . The Holy Spirit kindles our hearts with the fire of love . . . and day by day he boils and burns up the vices of our inordinate desire so that if there are in us any good works, they are the fruits of his grace and excellencies. But our gifts [e.g., understanding], apart from him, are darkness of mind and perversity of heart.[36]

Alongside, and indeed supporting, Calvin's conclusions, we might add several thoughts from Webster regarding illumination and its effect upon the human act of scriptural reading. "Illumination," Webster clarifies, "refers to the ways in which the operation of creaturely intelligence is caused, preserved and directed by divine light, whose radiance makes creatures to

---

34. Ibid., II.2.19; OS 3:261: "Dei Spiritu illuminetur." Cf. "Flesh is not capable of such lofty wisdom [i.e., knowledge of God] as to conceive God and what is God's, unless it be illumined by the Spirit of God" (ibid).

35. Ibid., II.2.20; OS 3:262. Cf. our comments on "gift" and "participation" with regards to Calvin's work in chapter 3.

36. Calvin, *Catechismus (1538)* (CO 5:341): "Per eam agit, sustinet, vegetat, vivificat omnia: per eam nos iustificat, sanctificat, expurgat, ad sese vocat ac trahit, ut-salutem consequamur. Itaque spiritus sanctus, dum in nobis ad hunc modum habitat, is est qui nobis suo lumine illucet, quo discamus et plane agnoscamus, quam ingentem divinae bonitatis opulentiam in Christo possideamus. Qorda nostra incendit ardore caritatis, turn Dei, turn proximi, magisque in dies excoquit et exurit concupiscentiae nostrae vitia, ut, si qua sunt in nobis bona opera, fructus sint gratiae. ipsius ac virtutis. Nostrae vero sine ipso dotes, mentis sunt tenebrae, cordisque perversitas."

know."[37] And in illumination, that is in the Spirit's work of enlightening the church's reading of Scripture, the "regenerate intelligence comes to know the mind of God." Thus, illumination, as a divine movement on the human mind, is the "subjective revelation of the mystery of God" in the "Spirit of revelation";[38] and the notion of illumination therefore necessarily embraces a wide range of works by the Holy Spirit, namely, the church's reading of Holy Scripture, and the regenerating effect of Holy Scripture as the church comes to know God's loving and radiant will. Yet time and again Webster—like Calvin before him—is clear that the language of illumination is to be set in terms of regeneration:

> Our governing affections are corrupt: inclined to vanity, insatiably curious about the surfaces of temporal things, confident in our intellectual powers, nimble in inquiring into what satisfies unregenerate appetite but sluggish in seeking out knowledge of God, in love with falsehood.[39]

The remedy prescribed for this noetic corruption is found in "an objective communication of the divine splendor and a subjective enlightenment of the mind." Webster is therefore right to conclude in his perceptive study that the illuminating action of the Holy Spirit upon the human mind "engages and redirects a range of human rational powers, advancing them to proper objects and ends as it conducts us out of darkness into intellectual day."[40]

Given these clarifications about the dogmatic use of illumination, we might therefore say that theology—as an instance of having our "rational powers" redirected "to proper objects and ends" and being brought into "intellectual day"—is a precise occurrence of the illumination of the human mind. Here, too, we are to outline what happens as the mind is "kindled with the fire of love" by the radiant work of the triune God. Therefore, if the Pauline images of the "enlightening of the eyes of the heart" (Eph 1:18) and the "renewing of the mind" (Rom 12:2) are perceptible, they have to be so in theology, in which the renewed and enlightened human mind is called not to address the natural law, but to "discern what is the will of God," and "what are the riches of his glorious inheritance in the saints, and what is the immeasurable greatness of his power toward us who believe" (Rom 12:2; Eph 1:18–19). Thus, Calvin:

37. Webster, "Illumination," 50.
38. Ibid., 61.
39. Ibid.
40. Ibid., 62.

What kind of renovation is required of us? It is not that of the flesh only . . . but of the mind. [Because] the mind is a most wise queen . . . it is pulled from off its throne, and is reduced to nothing . . . in that it *must be renewed*. . . . Till the Lord opens them, the eyes of our heart are blind. Till the Spirit has become our instructor, all that we know is folly and ignorance. Till the Spirit of God has made it known to us by a secret revelation, the knowledge of our Divine calling *exceeds the capacity of our own minds*.[41]

In view of the fact that God illumines the "eyes of the heart" and "renews the mind" for "the knowledge of our Divine calling," we move to ask, therefore: What is precisely involved in undertaking theology in the presence of the radiant One? How is this call to be expounded?

Theology in the Presence of the Radiant One

The basis of theology, like the church, is the radiant presence of the Father, Son, and Holy Spirit. Such a doctrinal basis is not a matter strictly "delegated to philosophical rather than dogmatic theology";[42] nor is the God who is *light in himself* merely an abstract concept treated by the human mind *in abstracto*. Rather, he is the radiant One, the One whose radiant presence makes the undertaking of theology possible. The One who is theology's beginning and end is the One who "graciously chooses according to his will, of his inexhaustible fullness" to speak his knowledge to "rational creatures."[43] Thus, a theology that suggests it "arise from nature and reason" is ultimately "corrupt, half-blind, obscure; it cannot occupy for us the place of a theology that is sufficient for salvation."[44] Theology conducted in the presence of the radiant One therefore responds to revelation, in which "we do not rely on our own powers," says Luther, "but rely on that which is outside of us."[45] In other words, theology is possible because of the shining forth of God, which must be found by divine revelation, according to Christian proclamation.

---

41. Calvin, *Comm. ep. Rom.* 12.2 (CC 19:453-54); *Comm. ep. Eph.* 1.17 (CC 21:212).

42. Gerrish, *Christian Faith*, 303. Dogmatics, for Gerrish, is theology "within the limits of piety alone" and not Christian theology *in toto*.

43. Polanus, *Synt. Theol.* II.1.4.

44. van Mastricht, *Theoretico-practica theologia*, 1.1.16.

45. Luther, *Galatervorlesung* 4.6 (WA 40.1:589.25): "ut non nitamur viribus . . . sed eo nitamur, quod est extra nos, Hoc est, promissione et veritate Dei, quae fallere non potest."

Theology, as *sacra doctrina*, comes to human creatures "through revelation," which "flows from the fount recognized in the light, . . . namely God's very own which he shares with the blessed."[46] In short, from Aquinas: "Christian theology . . . is pictured in the field of divine revelation."[47] That revelatory, radiant presence grounds both the formative *field* and *object* in which theology undertakes its activity as the illumined mind.

First, what does it mean to say that divine revelation is the formative *field* of theology as an activity of the illumined mind? It means principally that theology conducts its work within the realm of the radiant presence of the God who is *light in himself*. Aquinas again: "Christian theology takes on faith its principles revealed by God in the light of divine revelation."[48] Theology is thus not an instance of bare cognitive triumphalism, a place at which theology assumes a posture of a false theology. Theology does not bracket the event of the "light of divine revelation" and instead enter a "labyrinth of the human mind."[49] Rather, theology is governed by God's radiant presence; it takes place within the formative *field* made perceptible by that radiant presence; and, if it turns away from that radiant presence, then it has merely impatiently collapsed into a disobedient "labyrinth of the human mind." For theology "must always be undertaken as an act of patience and obedience," says Barth. "But this is possible only as it trusts in the uncontrollable presence of its ontic and noetic basis, in the revelation God promised to the Church, and in the power of faith apprehending that promise."[50]

Once again, however, the far-reaching illusions of the modern project have been that the processes of the human mind are safe from the unthinking "cowardice" of so-called "divine presence" over against the "determination and courage to use one's understanding without being guided by another."[51] Against such claims, as the activity of the illumined human mind, theology can never avoid the utterly serious undertaking that "we speak, not to please mortals, but to please God who tests our hearts." (1 Thess 2:4). In theology, the material of human discourse is not a "someone" whom is negated from human cognitive activities. Rather, theology speaks "to please God who tests our hearts." That is, when human creatures begin to speak theologically about God, as we have sought to do in this study, they soon realize that the

46. Aquinas, ST 1a.q1.1ad2; 1a.q1.2*resp*.
47. Ibid., 1a.q1.3ad.2.
48. Ibid., 1a.q1.2*resp*.: ". . . sacra doctrina credit principia revelata a Deo."
49. Calvin, *Inst*. I.13.21; OS 3:137.
50. Barth, CD I.1:22; cf. KD I.1:21.
51. Kant, "Was ist Aufklärung?" 169.

setting is upended; it is not theology who tests God and so makes him an object of clever discourse, but quite the contrary: God "tests our hearts" in order to "give an account to God for the way in which we speak."[52] That testing itself is the formative *field* of the illumined mind—among other contexts in the cognitive task of theology. This "fallible human work," which is "no more than human talk about God," is subservient to the principal testing from God.[53]

Second, the radiant presence of the Trinity also forms the *object* of a theology of divine light. For, as the activity of the illumined human mind, theology's *object* is granted to it by the radiant presence of God, which is the basis for the church's proclamation. A trinitarian theology is therefore a "true science."[54] That is, it travels along a given "path of knowledge" towards a given "object of knowledge."[55] That given "object of knowledge" we have already described as the radiant presence of God as Father, Son, and Holy Spirit.[56] Yet to talk of this as the *principium obiectum* of theology may deceive some into thinking that theology's subject is simply another set of topics that the human mind calls before itself in an act of "synthetic construction."[57] Theology's *object* is continually its *subject*: the utterly radiant shining forth of God. Thus:

> all things are dealt with in holy teaching under the aspect of God, either because they are God himself or because they refer to God as their beginning and end. Hence, it follows that God is truly the subject of this science.[58]

Theology's position before its object—with God as "truly the subject of this science"—is therefore the humble stance before its given subject as a student "under the aspect of God," for this posture before the given "light of the

---

52. Barth, CD I.1:3.

53. Ibid., 4; KD I.1:2: "Theologie begleitet die Rede der Kirche, sofern sie selbst nichts anderes ist als menschliche 'Rede von Gott.'"

54. Ibid., 9. Barth's point here is precisely what we're after in this section: "If theology allows itself to be called, or calls itself, a science, it cannot in so doing accept the obligation of submission to standards valid for other sciences [given divine revelation as the object of knowledge]" (ibid., 10).

55. Ibid., 7–8; KD I.1:6.

56. See chapter 2.

57. Barth, KD I.1:8; CD I.1:10. Moreover, we would do well in this section to keep before us Barth's caution that theology ought not to be reduced to *doctrina revelata* itself (cf. ibid., 13).

58. Aquinas, ST 1a.q1.7resp.: "Unde sequitur quod Deus vere sit subjectum hujus scientiae."

gospel" is the place where the theological task may find its beginning and end.

When theology thus seeks to talk positively of the light of God, its undertaking of theological speaking and thinking is not "to interpret [religious symbols] according to theological principles and methods."[59] Rather, if it conducts its task in a positive manner, then theology is nothing less than an endeavor to follow the radiant identity of God as he reveals himself to be: "I am the light of the world. Whoever follows me will not walk in darkness, but will have the light of life" (John 8:12). Theology is therefore not in the trade of granting identity to God, still less of forming whatever symbols and metaphors for the divine life that may be deemed noetically constitutive, culturally expedient, or prepatory for receiving the "divine truth all around us."[60] Rather, theology is "reason following God's perfect knowledge of himself and of all things."[61]

This is not to deny that theology has to develop various words and concepts, which has been much of the aim of our very study. Nor is it to deny that, in conducting that work, theology has to appropriate such words and concepts from elsewhere and alter them. But in theology the activity of the human mind is an activity that is illumined. Theology, as the activity of the illumined human mind, recalls that in speaking and thinking of God's light it must not be a hypothetical or contingent activity, but rather learn to be a speaking and thinking that receives its subject from the radiant One. The human mind is therefore called before the radiant presence of God: the presence, in all its radiance, that founds both the *field* in which the illumined mind works, and the *object* to which it must always and ever turn.

Claritas Scripturae

Yet how is this presence of the radiant One manifest? The radiant presence of God, we might say, is revealed clearly in Holy Scripture by the Holy Spirit, for Holy Scripture is that "human expression" inspired and chosen by God

---

59. Tillich, *Systematic Theology*, 1:266; cf. the "theological circle" in ibid.,12.

60. See Brown, *God and Mystery in Words*, esp. 56. We might register a further concern with much of Brown's insistence that symbols and metaphors create a "new knowledge" or have intrinsic access to God. For Brown, theological predication may convey divine reality due to *our* ascent to truth. And while this position is indebted to, say, Aquinas's notion of ascent to faith, the entire conception seems lacking, particularly in its omission of the other side of Aquinas's theory, namely, God's gracious elevation of language *beyond* its incapacities.

61. Webster, "Principles of Systematic Theology," 135.

to attend his shining forth.⁶² And in "speaking to creatures by the Spirit," Webster further clarifies, God "takes creaturely words into his service, ensuring their adequacy, checking the distortions introduced by fallenness, and restoring their function as a sign of God's glory."⁶³ More precisely, these "sacred writings" are "inspired by God" (2 Tim 3:15–16) as the product of a divine undertaking. Holy Scripture is thus generated not merely by human impulse but by the power of the Holy Spirit. That power so orders these human, textual acts of being "inspired" that they may properly serve the declaration of the knowledge of God, "their function as a sign of God's glory." For our present purposes, then, this means that the illumined human mind is situated within the act of exegesis, that is, the human mind led by and towards the reading of Holy Scripture that is "regulated by the revelation of [God's] will."⁶⁴

In virtue of its relation to the radiant One, Holy Scripture is therefore clear—that is, *claritas* or *perspicuitas*. More precisely: because of the "Spirit of illumination," the "things necessary for salvation" in the Scriptures are "anywhere revealed . . . so that the believer can by close meditation ascertain their truth."⁶⁵ The setting of *claritas Scripturae* is thus the "*effective illuminating presence of God the revealer who is in himself light.*"⁶⁶ The clarity of Scripture is a function of its position in the divine communication, and of the Holy Spirit's action of illuminating the human mind—the internal testimony of the reader—and so guiding it to *sacra doctrina*. *Claritas* is not a natural property of the text abstractly pondered; nor is Holy Scripture's perspicuity mere verbal clarity, that is, the clarity of "the meaning of a word sequence," which, in turn, "depends on our ability to relate it to a historical author."⁶⁷ Summoning textual perspicuity in this manner is a rather triumphalist assertion that "what we know from the Bible can, in fact, be known

---

62. Barth, CD I.2:473. See Barth's points on Scripture as *the* "witness to divine revelation" or *the* "human expression of God's revelation" (ibid., 457–71). However, Barth makes it plain that "Scripture [as *the* witness] does not violate the dignity and significance of the other signs and witnesses of revelation [i.e., proclamation and sacrament]" (ibid., 501).

63. Webster, "Illumination," 59.

64. Owen, *Christologia* (*Works,* 1:45).

65. Turretin, *Inst.* II.q17.11.

66. Webster, "On the Clarity of Holy Scripture," 39–40 (emphasis original).

67. Vanhoozer, *Is There a Meaning in the Text?* 109. Vanhoozer may miss the mark when he states: "clarity means that the Bible is sufficiently unambiguous in the main for any well-intentioned person with Christian faith to interpret each part with relative adequacy" (ibid., 315).

simply by reading it."[68] Rather, Scripture is clear because through the Holy Spirit the text serves "*the radiant presence of God who through Scripture sheds abroad the light of the knowledge of his reconciling works and ways.*"[69] Berkouwer continues this thought:

> It becomes increasingly clear that the *confessed* perspicuity is not a mere notation of a "quality" of Scripture in the manner in which we attribute certain qualities to other things, after which we can relax. This confession of the church will only be meaningful if it includes an insight into the power of the *Spirit's* way through the world and to men's hearts as the great witness through the Word. . . . In the gospel we are dealing with . . . the *illuminating character of the message*, . . . with its interrelations, depths, and perspectives. This is a light that does not blind but opens eyes to the joy of the gospel's mystery.[70]

Holy Scripture's clarity is therefore neither an intrinsic quality of the text nor simply the consequence of exegetical endeavor, "after which we can relax." Rather, it is that which the text "*becomes* as it functions in the Spirit-governed encounter between the self-presenting saviour and the faithful reader."[71] And to read in "the economy of grace is not *poiesis*," Webster clarifies, "but intelligence directed by and towards God's self-interpreting, perspicuous Word."[72] To read, therefore, is to be caught up in "spiritual illumination," says Owen, "whereby we are enabled to discern and understand the mind of God in the Scripture."[73] To speak of *claritas Scripturae* is to confess that Scripture is perspicuous in God's work of "opening the eyes to the joy of the gospel's mystery."[74] And it does so, Turretin reiterates, because of Scripture's "efficient cause (viz., God, the Father of men, who cannot be said either to be unwilling or unable to speak plainly without impugning his perfect goodness and wisdom)."[75]

---

68. Sailhamer, *Christian Theology*, 16. See James Callahan's critique of several evangelical renderings of *claritas Scripturae* in his *Clarity of Scripture*, ch. 1.

69. Webster, "On the Clarity of Holy Scripture," 38 (emphasis original).

70. Berkouwer, *Holy Scripture*, 296 (emphasis mine).

71. Webster, *Holy Scripture*, 95.

72. Ibid., 91–92.

73. Owen, *Pneumatologia*, (*Works*, 3:13).

74. Berkouwer, *Holy Scripture*, 296.

75. Turretin, *Inst.* II.q17.11. Cf. Turretin's additional statement that the *form* of Scripture is perspicuous because it is "to us in place of a testament, contract of a covenant or edict of a king, which ought to be perspicuous and not obscure" (ibid.).

There are two results here for the activity of the illumined human mind. *First*, because Holy Scripture has "no lack of clarity," the illumined mind finds there its "common rule."[76] The clarity of Scripture for the illumined human mind is Scripture's Spirit-imparted "common rule" to quicken theology to truthful thought and speech—in short, for "training in righteousness" (2 Tim 3:16). And "training in righteousness" follows that which is "useful for teaching, for reproof, for correction," and thus shapes the activity of the human mind; perspicuity is effective because it bears witness to the truth of this teaching. Hence *claritas Scripturae* is a matter for the church's outshining of proclamation, no matter how "disturbing" it may appear.[77] It is the confession that serves "as a reminder of our need to be constantly evaluating our understanding by God's word," and a "call to seriousness—before God."[78] It is a confession—that is, an acknowledgement of divine instruction—that takes its rise not from a "cursory and careless reading" but in the fact that Holy Scripture is "so wonderfully accommodated by the Lord that the believer (who has the eyes of his mind open) by attentively reading may understand these mysteries sufficiently for salvation"[79] Clarity cannot therefore be bestowed on Holy Scripture by the church or by its theology, but only acknowledged as that which is the "common rule" for the illumined human mind. As such, Holy Scripture's clarity is not at all theoretical; it is a feature of Holy Scripture's witness to the radiant presence of God that assists the church in its witness to, exegesis of, and presupposition that: "Scripture is clear in itself as God's Word; otherwise it will at once disintegrate."[80]

How does this "common rule" function? If it acts in accord with this given "common rule," the work of theology must exhibit—as we saw with the church—the biblical notion of "walking in the light." That is, it must be indicated above all by obedience to the truth of the "light of the gospel" that

---

76. Vermigli, *Loci communes*, 1.6.2. Cf. "Neque deest sanctae Scripturae, quod fideles et pios animos, claritas, et ut Graeci dicunt Neque deest sanctae Scripturae, quod fideles et pios animos, claritas. . . . Quandoquidem omnia quae disputantur a sanioribus theologis . . . semper terminant ad testimonia Scripturarum, tanquam illa sint *axiōmata* Christianis notissima, de quibus fas nemini sit ambigere."

77. Cf. Berkouwer, *Holy Scripture*, 288: "No confession concerning Scripture is more disturbing to the church than the confession of its perspicuity." Berkouwer is stating this in light of Scripture's being the "voice of the Shepherd and not the stranger," which thus renders any human fatalism and subjectivity in reading Scripture illegitimate.

78. Callahan, *Clarity of Scripture*, 272.

79. Turretin, *Inst.* II.q17.2.

80. Barth, CD I.2:712; KD I.2:799: "Schrift als Gottes Wort in sich selber klar ist; sie würde ohne das sofort in sich selbst zusammenbrechen."

is announced in Holy Scripture. That obedient "walking" can be conveyed in many ways for theology: by a rejection of the unbridled speculation of human "sense and reason";[81] by the refusal to exegete Scripture as anything less than in the light of its "objective perspicuity";[82] and by the joy and humility with which the illumined human mind turns itself to the interpretive activity of reading Scripture, not as its judge but as judged, in order to understand the "majesty of the subject."[83] All this is included in speaking of Holy Scripture as the clear "common rule" of the illumined human mind.

Second, because Holy Scripture is clear, the illumined human mind finds there its sole principle. The clarity of Holy Scripture is a vital result of its authority as the inspired witness or servant of the Word of God.[84] It could therefore be said that when a sense of *claritas Scripturae* is absent, one may doubt whether assent has been given to Holy Scripture's authority. Indeed, such a view is observed in a recent proposal by Christian Smith, namely in his argument against an evangelical "biblicist" view that naïvely holds to Holy Scripture's "authority, infallibility, perspicuity [and] self-sufficiency" over against a "more truly evangelical" position that strikes these notions from the text and learns to "live with textual ambiguity."[85] Yet Smith's various proposals attend several contradictions, notably his insistence that a "biblicists" position posits various attributes of Holy Scripture in order to "produce cognitive and emotional security in a very insecure world"; and at the same moment Smith states that Holy Scripture speaks clearly, particularly on the "pervasive, clear, straightforward, obvious, and simple" features of the Christian life and of the gospel.[86] Moreover, it is striking to observe Smith's disregard for the historical context of *claritas Scripturae* in his critical account. This seems the precise point of the older dogmaticians of the seventeenth century, who noted that Holy Scripture is not *equally* clear in every matter, but in matters of dogmatics, Scripture explains Scripture (i.e.,

---

81. See Vermigli, *Loci communes*, 1.6.2: "Caeterum non est haec evidentia ex lumine humani sensus ac nostrae rationis pretenda, sed a luce fidei."

82. Barth, CD I.2:712.

83. Luther, *De serv.* (WA 18:606.22–4).

84. See, again, Berkouwer, *Holy Scripture*, 298. See also Webster's clarification that "These notions . . . do not eliminate the necessity of reading, making exegesis a purely 'pneumatic' activity which bypasses the processes by which written materials are appropriated. Rather, they set those acts within the domain of God's self-explication" (*Holy Scripture*, 93). See also Webster's thoughts on Scripture as "servant" of the Word (idem.).

85. Smith, *Bible Made Impossible*, viii, xi, 146.

86. See ibid., 95, 132, 144.

Scripturam ex Scriptura explicandam esse).[87] One classical notion, for instance, is found in Turretin's comments on whether or not "the scriptures are so perspicuous in things necessary to salvation." He proceeds:

> The question does not concern the perspicuity or the obscurity of the subject or persons. For we do not deny that the Scriptures are obscure to unbelievers and the unrenewed. . . . Also we hold that the Spirit of illumination is necessary to make them intelligible to believers. Rather the question concerns the obscurity or perspicuity of the object of the Scriptures (i.e., whether they are so obscure that the believer cannot apprehend them for salvation without the authority and judgment of the church—which we deny).[88]

Over against Smith's rather confusing claims, we might echo Turretin by stating that such an approach ignores the Spirit's work in the notion of Scripture's perspicuity, assuming that "clarity" can be understood simply as a textual property without the "Spirit of illumination." What sets in motion human understanding of the gospel is the radiant presence of God himself: the revelatory activity of God, attended by the text, in the realm of the Spirit's action. That is to say, *claritas* does not refer to single passages of Scripture, *pace* Smith's view, but to "the single heads of Christian doctrine necessary to faith and the worship of God."[89] Therefore, "if you speak of external clarity," Luther states, "nothing at all is left obscure or ambiguous, but everything there is in the scriptures has been brought out by the Word into the most definite light, and published to all the world."[90] Holy Scripture is clear for its purpose, which is the publication of the saving knowledge of God. The illumined human mind therefore finds in Holy Scripture its sole principle—that is, the limit of human concern.

---

87. See Muller, *Post-Reformation Reformed Dogmatics*, 2:324–40; and see the various *Belegstellen* in Heppe, *Dogmatik*, 12–13, 26–27.

88. Turretin, *Inst.* II.q17.2.

89. Polanus, *Synt. theol.* 1.1.44.

90. Luther, *De serv.* (WA 18:609.4–9, 11–14). The thrust of Luther's passage is to contrast between the oppressive interpretative tradition and the clarity of "direct," unmediated hermeneutics. For Luther, to speak of God as necessary for understanding Scripture is to oppose the idolatrous effect of self-derived, autonomous wisdom. For a succinct account of Luther's double view of clarity (internal-external), see Berkouwer, *Holy Scripture*, 277. Regarding the historical context on the debate between Erasmus and Luther, see Thompson, *Clear and Present Word*, 143–50; Webster, "On the Clarity of Holy Scripture," 43–6; Hermann, "Von der Klarheit der Heiligen Schrift," 170–255; and Beisser, *Claritas scripturae*, esp. 75–130.

This limit of the illumined human mind, namely Holy Scripture as the sole principle, requires that the activity of theology exhibit a singular focus. In other words, talk of *claritas Scripturae* is a caution against allowing theology's work to be lured into "exploring and reflecting imaginatively" on all types of sources of "enchantment."[91] No matter how inspirational such fascinations may appear to be, in the end they almost always distort proper focus. Theology cannot say everything; yet when theology does endeavor to relate itself to all types of other fields of intellectual and cultural desiderata, then—however much it may do so with the "delight in the unexpected"[92]—it risks losing its originality and, what Luther called, its ability to "repeat" the promise of the one Word of God.[93] Rather, Luther continues, the theological task is to portray itself captive to the Word of God, in order that it may

> simply cling to the Word and follow . . . and allow reason to be blinded and taken captive. So, not as hairsplitting sophistry dictates but as God says them for us, we must *repeat* these words after him and hold them.[94]

Theology thus finds its hand led, not by its authoritative "hairsplitting" before the watching world, but by the sheer proclamation that theology indeed *needs*, in light of its creaturely failings, to be led by the *viva vox Dei*. This confession seems to be contrary to what is found in much modern theological endeavors, namely an active "dismantling—the muzzling of the challenge of God to the idolatrous world."[95] The illumined human mind will therefore respectfully reject the so-called "creative potential" of the dissuaders, and refuse the persistent invitations to join the great "rediscovery" of

---

91. Brown, *God and Mystery*, 14. Much of Brown's work is set on the conviction that "revealed religion builds on natural religion" (ibid., 1).

92. Ibid., 15.

93. Luther maintains that in the church's "repeating" it does not substitute its own words for God's words: "Denn wir werden gewislich feylen, wo wir nicht einfeltiglich yhm nach sprechen, wie er uns fur spricht gleich wie ein iung kind seym Vater den glauben odder Vater unser nach spricht" ("Vom Abendmahl Christi, Bekenntnis" [WA 26:439.40–440.3]). The verb "nachsprechen" (repeat) is used intentionally by Luther to suggest the frailty of the creaturely intellect in matters of faith. Luther's concept of the clarity of Scripture serves as a barrier for human speculation: nothing beyond the *deus revelatus* is of any concern to human creatures. This concept also guarantees that creaturely intellect be defined as soteriologically ineffective: it is not required to possess the spiritual meaning of the outer word, which would be just one more *sensus proprius*, but to accept that *res significata extra re* given by God. See Hendel, "'No Salvation Outside the Church,'" 248–57.

94. Luther, "Vom Abendmahl Christi, Bekenntnis" (WA 26:439.31–36).

95. Wright, *Last Word*, 103.

the "less wooden approaches" to its work.[96] Instead, theology will simply set about its work and call: giving itself steadfastly to training "saints for the work of ministry, for building up the body of Christ" (Eph 4:12).

The Call of the Illumined Mind

We have been considering the assertion that, as an outworking of the illumined human mind, theology has both its *field* and its *object* in the radiant presence of the triune God as announced clearly in Holy Scripture, and that Holy Scripture thus operates as a sole principle and as theology's "common rule." As we move to conclude this final chapter, we look more closely at how the illumined human mind assumes its position under the divine call. Three things are to be observed as we conclude this final chapter: first, the primary act of the illumined mind is prayer for the aid of the Holy Spirit who illumines the human mind itself; second, the realm of the illumined mind is the communion of the saints in light; and third, the conduct of the illumined human mind is found in its making a "good confession" before the radiant presence of God.

Theology and Prayer

First, as the activity of the illumined human mind, theology is a task begun in prayer. The illumined mind, we have noted, is a human action conducted in God's radiant presence. The human mind does not turn away from that presence, experiencing arbitrary freedom from God. To the contrary: if the illumined mind is to realize its location and to work to "give an account to God,"[97] then it must be reconciled to God out of the darkness of ignorance and sin. This work of reconciliation is, however, God's work, for the human mind's estrangement from and blindness to the truth occasions the human mind's incapacity. Estranged from and blind to the reality of God's truth and rejecting its calling as God's human creature, the mind undermines that relation to the God who is light which is the necessary sphere for knowledge of the truth. As Paul says to the church at Rome:

> for though they knew God, they did not honor him as God or give thanks to him, but they became futile in their thinking, and their senseless minds were darkened. Claiming to be wise, they

---

96. Brown, *God and Mystery*, 8.

97. Barth, CD I.1:3; KD I.1:1: ". . . daß sie für ihr Reden Gott Rechenschaft schuldig ist."

> became fools; and they exchanged the glory of the immortal God for images resembling a mortal human being or birds or four-footed animals or reptiles. (Rom 1:21–23)

Out of the vainness of the human mind in darkness is born idolatry, that ominous interchange of "the truth about God for a lie" (Rom 1:25), and the giving up of "the glory of the immortal God" for a "debased mind and to things that should not be done" (Rom 1:28). Barth comments further on this interchange:

> The light in us is darkness. . . . Dark, blind, uncritical, given to chance, mankind becomes an entity unto himself. Heartless, conceiving without contemplation and therefore empty, is our thought: thoughtless, contemplating without conceiving and therefore blind, is our heart. Other-worldly [*weltfremd*] is the soul in this world and soulless is the world, when man does not find himself within the sphere of the knowledge of the unknown God, when he evades the true God in whom he himself and the world must lose themselves, in order that both may be restored.[98]

From such "uncritical" and "evasive" blindness, emptiness, and darkness, God alone can restore us: "this relation can thus be re-established only by the ('reasonably perceived') memory of eternity breaking in upon our minds and hearts."[99] This "breaking in" on the mind and heart is achieved through the work of God's Holy Spirit. The Spirit is the one who illumines and renews the human mind to the end that it may once more realize its calling, "giving thanks to him" and "honoring him as God." Through the Holy Spirit, God's light is conveyed to the operation of the human mind; indeed, through the "knowledge of the Eternal Spirit is the joyful discovery that God is omnipresent: the One Light accompanies, illumines, and manifests the entire world to the creature."[100]

As we saw specifically in chapter 2, *God is light in himself*, and *from himself God shines forth his light*. Thus, God sets apart human creatures for the service of his glory. God's light as "quickening" is done in the Holy Spirit's loving work of illumination.[101] And such work can be extended into a portrayal of the work of the human mind, and so of theology. Such a por-

---

98. Barth, *Römerbrief (1922)*, 23–24.

99. Ibid.: "Diese Beziehung aber müßte hergestellt werden dadurch, daß unser Denken und unser Herz (durch 'vernünftiges Schauen') gebrochen wird durch die Erinnerung der Ewigkeit."

100. Sonderegger, *Systematic Theology*, 1:427.

101. See, again, chapter 3.

trayal does not, of course, involve a dismissal of the creatureliness of human intellectual undertakings. What it does is identify what *kind* of human undertaking we are concerned with when we do the human work of theology in the presence of the radiant One.

The *kind* of human undertaking we are involved in is best explained, again, as being "called out of darkness into [God's] marvelous light." Thus, theology in the presence of the radiant One is at the same time theology in the presence of the crucified one. It is human thinking placed under the judgment of God that was accomplished once for all at the cross of the Son of God, the one in whose dying God scattered darkness, defeated sin and ignorance, and "made foolish the wisdom of the world" (1 Cor 1:20). And the illumined human mind continues to live out this accomplishment as it carries the death of Jesus within itself—that is, as the Holy Spirit illumines the mind's idolatry, arrogance, and ambition, and in its place is taught the truth of "the light of the gospel." The illumined human mind is the quickened mind. If it is exposed to the Spirit's conviction as Lord, it is no less exposed to the same Spirit's illuminative work as the giver of life. Through the light- and life-giving Spirit, the human mind is given its aim, and thus directed to its fitting destiny, which is the knowledge of the God who is light. And through the Holy Spirit, the human mind is made competent: its calling renewed, the human mind is taught and endowed by the Holy Spirit. And, through this illuminating work of the Spirit, the human mind *becomes* illumined, called out of darkness and confusion by God so that it may assume the ministry for which it was called.

This is why the undertaking of theology can only be begun in prayer, trusting in the "factual certainty of his presence and action."[102] Thus, the "subject-matter of Christian theology is the triune God," says Wood, "its generative condition is the healing and illuminating presence of Christ . . . its proximate rule is Holy Scripture; its characteristic disposition is humility; its starting-point is prayer."[103] Because theological work is always a humble process conducted in "the illuminating presence of Christ," at its heart is the act of beseeching God for direction:

> O send out your light and your truth;
> let them lead me;
> let them bring me to your holy hill
> and to your dwelling!" (Ps 43:3).

---

102. Barth, CD IV.4:209; KD IV.4:232.
103. Wood, "Maker of Heaven and Earth," 383–84.

Such prayer is not a secondary matter in theology; it is the "starting-point" of theology. In prayer, the human mind turns to God, confessing its incompetence, confessing that it needs to be "led" by the Spirit's "light and truth" to the dwelling place of God. Thus, the task of theology begins and ends with something similar to Anselm's *credo*:

> Let me look up at your light, whether from afar or in the depths. ... I am not trying to scale your heights, Lord; my understanding is in no way equal to that. But I do long to understand your truth in some way, your truth which my heart believes and loves. For I do not seek to understand in order to believe; but I believe in order to understand.[104]

To speak in this way of intellectual work may sound odd, even absurd: can such a description be anything other than a desperately fanciful interpretation of the rational events that make up the human task of theology? And faced with this misgiving, might it not be less humiliating to make an easier statement—about, say, the virtuous character of the theologian? But talk of theology as the activity of the illumined human mind is not just talk of the particular backdrop to the theologian's emotions; nor is it merely a coy use of metaphor. In the final analysis, illumination is not psychological jargon; it is not the deployment of linguistic smoke and mirrors; nor does it give itself "promiscuously to whatever sources of fascination present themselves, particularly if they are novel."[105] The illumined human mind is such because God *himself* acts upon the human mind, preventing its fall into darkness and freeing it from its slavery to ignorant human opposition to God—namely, the domain of darkness. And to define theological work as an activity of the illumined human mind is to say that, without talk of this God and his work of illumination, we cannot describe the work of the theologian: "For I do not seek to understand in order to believe; but I believe in order to understand."

Theology in Communion

Second, as the illumined human mind theology is an activity in the communion of the saints in light, assisting the proclamation of the church. Again, *God is light in himself*, and *from himself God shines forth his light*. The light of God, which is confessed in the Christian tradition as the light of the triune

---

104. Anselm, *Proslogion* 1 (PL 158:227b–c): "Neque enim quaero intelligere, ut credam; sed credo, ut intelligam."

105. Webster, "What Makes Theology Theological?" 26.

God—the same God who graciously turns to creation as the One who elects, reconciles, and illuminates—is a light that "gathers" a community and "scatters" the darkness of sin in order that there be a human reflection of his "radiant event of love." And theology is an undertaking of the saints in the light, the mind appointed to serve the church's proclamation of the triune God.

Because of this, theology is *primarily* an endeavor undertaken within the saints in light, namely, those "in communion with the blessed Comforter."[106] Theology shares in the same endeavor of "outshining" as does the church.[107] It listens to the same gracious call to the light of the gospel; it bears witness to the world sitting in darkness; it is illumined by the same Holy Spirit; it guides itself by the same proclamation of the "excellencies" of the One who alone is light; it is rescued from the darkness which is ignorant of God's radiant identity; and it is a participant in the same prayer and praise of God's radiant identity. Though the academic milieu of contemporary theology has often made it hard to see any of these points, theology as an activity of the illumined human mind is churchly science—a knowing and inquiring that takes place not within "systematic" schemes but *within* the gathered and illumined and pastoral church.[108] Of course, modernity denies the label "science" to any such endeavor, just as it denies the acknowledgment of the "illumined mind" to those intellectual acts that take their rise in the proclamation of the light of the gospel. Indeed, Rowan Williams worries, "If theology is understood primarily as a 'science' in the common understanding of that term, it will assume that its job is to clarify, perhaps to explain, . . . it will be interested in whether or not there are good reasons for saying this or that."[109] But such a worry tells us more about modernity than it does about science or the human mind, and a responsible theology in the presence of the radiant One will not be over anxious about this, but simply take up its work with integrity to the call of God in the communion of the saints in light.[110]

---

106. Owen, *Commuinon with God* (*Works*, 2:261).

107. See chapter 4.

108. This echoes Ellen Charry's call for a renewal of "sapiental theology"—that is, the quest to know God in order to know ourselves—in which theologians once again see themselves as pastors who help people "find their identity in God." See *By The Renewing of Your Minds*, 235, 239.

109. Williams, *On Christian Theology*, 13.

110. I use "integrity" to offer the positive definition that Rowan Williams has in mind: "Having integrity [in theology] is being able to speak in a way which allows for answers" (ibid., 5).

Theology is *secondarily* a practice of communion with the saints in light. As it does its work in the gathered church, theology offers its aid to the saints in light to which it belongs. Its specific ministry is to aid in the edification of the church, building up the church's corporate life, and so attending to the proclamation of the gospel. Theology does this purely by offering a description of the evangel as that to which all speech, thought, and action in the church must obey. "For it is time for judgment to begin at the household of God; and if it begins with us, what will be the outcome for those who do not obey the gospel of God?" (1 Pet 4:17). In the work of the illumined human mind, the saints in light present their lives to the gospel's judgment, testing its apprehensions of God by considering them against the backdrop of the "common rule" of all truth, God's radiant presence as Word. As it conducts its theology, the church questions whether it really speaks, thinks, and acts as the communion of the saints in light; whether the light and the call of the gospel has truly been seen and heard; whether in their proclamation of the gospel the elect of God are truly "walking in the light as he himself is in the light."

Critically, however, theology does not achieve this task as the church's magistrate. The church only has one authority, the radiant One himself, whose position theology cannot claim for itself. Rather, theology's work is begun by submission to the gospel—by theology itself standing "under the Word and therefore under Holy Scripture."[111] And by the fact that the church exists by the Word of God, theology works by overseeing its speech and thought in light of the gospel, and by turning to God, recognizing that, like all things in the life of the church, theology is hopeless unless God *himself* makes it possible and "aretegenic."[112] Only in this manner, humbly confessing that "I am not trying to scale your heights, Lord,"[113] can the illumined mind stand in communion with the saints in light and thus serve their proclamation of God's "excellencies."

Theology as a "Good Confession" before God

Third, and final, we turn to look at theology as being a "good confession" performed in the presence of the radiant One. Theology occurs under the same condition as all other activity in the life of faith, namely, that it is done in the presence of the radiant One who comes to us "in the brightness of his

---

111. Barth, CD I.2:586; KD I.2:653.
112. Charry, *By the Renewing of Your Minds*, 19.
113. Anselm, *Proslogion* 1.

infinite majesty."[114] Because the glory of human creatures is God, to encounter him is to be encountered by that which we can never control, which can never become a particular arrangement of words or a set of "shared experience" that we can possess and examine at will. Rather, as Peter van Mastricht says, all we can do is have a "recognition of that majesty."[115] The majestic God is utterly free; even in his shining forth to human creatures in which he elects and illuminates a people for himself, he is not a disposable article, an object that can become part of the religious furniture of his people. For

> The LORD is God,
> and *he* has made *his* light to shine upon *us*. . . .
> You are my God, and I will give thanks to you;
> you are my God; I will extol you."
> (Ps. 118:27-8 ESV)

This reaction to God's causing "*his* light to shine upon *us*"—that is, the reaction of thanks and praise—is in many ways *the* reaction of theology. The human mind can only be illumined if it opposes its own capacity for idolatry, which is, as Basil tells us, the mind's "imagining that the ornament of glory is attained through itself."[116] Rather: "The LORD is God; *he* has made *his* light to shine upon *us*; *he* is our God; we give thanks to *him*; and we will extol *him*." Christian theology before the presence of the radiant One, therefore, will be properly suspicious of its own grasp of its subject, aware that much of what it says and thinks about such "an intractable object" is ultimately handled with "inadequate means."[117]

God's light means that theology stands under the divine restriction: "unapproachable" (1 Tim 6:16). Consequently, theology will be marked less by confidence and authority, and much more by a sense of "incompleteness of its own knowing and . . . speaking"[118] about the One who is "the blessed and only Sovereign, the King of kings and Lord of lords, who alone has immortality" (1 Tim 6:15-16). Still, this restriction of "unapproachable" is not an absolute occurrence by which the human mind is wholly incapacitated. Next to the restriction of "unapproachable" stands with equal weight an affirmation to speak: "a good servant of Christ Jesus" is the one who,

114. Van Mastricht, *Theoretico-practica theologia* 2.22: "infinitae eminentiae fulgor."

115. Ibid.: ". . . agnitio istius eminentiae."

116. Basil, *De hum.* 1 (PG 31:526; PPS 47:108).

117. Barth, CD I.1:23; KD I.1:22: ". . . untauglichen Objekt und mit ungenügenden Mitteln vorzuliegen."

118. Ibid., I.2:586; KD I.2:653: "Unabgeschlossenheit ihres eigenen Erkennens, Handelns und Redens."

"nourished on the words of the faith," makes a " good confession in the presence of many witnesses," because "Christ Jesus . . . in his testimony before Pontius Pilate made *the* good confession" (1 Tim 4:6; 6:12–13). The sanction to speak a "good confession" is also a promise—that God will take in his hands the good servant's "good confession" and allow it to serve the gospel's truth, the "words of faith." And in such "good confessions," the illumined mind gives voice to the church's proclamation of the light of the gospel.

Conclusion

What, then, is the destiny of theology as the illumined human mind? It is what Mastricht calls the "*celebration* . . . of his majesty recognized through its brightness, which is more properly called *glorification*."[119] The "celebration" and "glorification" of God is, as we saw in the conclusion to our previous chapter, the fundamental end of all the works of the gathering of the saints in light:

> Hail, gladdening Light, of his pure glory poured
>   Who is the immortal Father, heavenly, blest,
>   Holiest of Holies, Jesus Christ our Lord!
> Now we are at the sun's hour of rest,
>   The lights of evening round us shine,
>   We hymn the Father, Son, and Holy Spirit divine!
> Worthiest art thou at all times to be sung
>   With undefiled tongue,
>   Son of our God, giver of life, alone:
>   Therefore in all the world thy glories, Lord, they own.

Praise, celebration, and glorification add nothing to God; they do not or cannot intensify God's light, which is inexhaustibly and unassailably resplendent and "Worthiest . . . at all times to be sung." They are simply a proclamation, a witness to the slain Lamb and true light of life.

To talk of the destiny of the illumined human mind in these terms is once again to refuse to isolate intellectual activity from the "outshining" of the church—namely the call to prayer, proclamation, and praise. The illumined human mind is a practice in the life of the gathering of the saints in light; thus, it participates in the "outshining" of the church, sharing its origin and contributing to its work. To separate the illumined mind from that outshining is to obstruct its course. And not only that, to turn theology away from its destiny in the praise of God nearly always comprises its

---

119. Van Mastricht, *Theoretico-practica theologia* 2.22: "celebration . . . quae magis proprie glorificatio" (emphasis mine).

replacement by other means, the elevation of "natural knowledge" and its aprioristic detachment from the repentant service of God.

Yet theology is not the summons of the gospel; it is not a *sacramentum regenerationis*; it does not have the authority of the teaching office of the church. Theology in the presence of the radiant One is not a means of grace, but the human work of thinking and speaking "to please God." Because it is continually a human work, it shares in the weaknesses of its human age, namely, as it is "an intellectual activity with ends which derive from our nature."[120] Nevertheless, in its particular human atmosphere, theology can be the human mind illumined. It can be an outworking of what happens when our "nature is caught up in the history of creation, revelation, and redemption."[121] Theology can attend to the radiant One and the human "circumference" that gathers around its "radiant center," Christ Jesus. And in falling to their knees as a "sudden light flashes from heaven," theologians may arise dazed and dazzled by the majesty of the triune God, and thus be led by the hand as they make their proclamation with the church:

> For once [we] were darkness, but now in the Lord [we] are light.
> ... Therefore ... "Sleeper, awake! Rise from the dead, and Christ will shine on you." ... For with you is the fountain of life; in your light we see light. (Eph 5:8–14; Ps 36:9)

---

120. Webster, "What Makes Theology Theological?" 23.
121. Ibid.

Conclusion

THE THEOLOGICAL REFLECTIONS OFFERED IN OUR STUDY SOUGHT TO articulate several proposals regarding the declaration that "God is light."

The *first proposal* made in the course of the earlier discussions concerned the content of a trinitarian theology of God's light founded on the witness of Holy Scripture and supplemented by the historical, dogmatic use of the concept of light through which the church has sought to express the reality of the triune God's radiant self-revelation. We thus explored two avenues of thought: light that is proper to the Holy Trinity (i.e., *God is light in himself*); and the gathering of saints in God's light (i.e., *from himself God shines forth his light*). The joining of this content derives from the confession that, as Father, Son, and Holy Spirit, God's light is a way of pointing to God's radiant identity. And this identity has to further be understood by way of the divine decree for communion. Thus, talk of God's light is a conceptual attempt to point to God's radiant identity that is seen in God's shining forth towards his human creatures as the One who elects, reconciles, and illuminates. God's light is therefore God's relation to his human creatures sitting in the darkness of sin and ignorance and death: as Father electing the creature in his "radiant event of love," as Son scattering the darkness of sin on the cross and in his state of exaltation, and as Holy Spirit as the terminus of this movement by illuminating those called out of the darkness into God's "marvelous light." Thus, the church *in* the light is grounded in the work of the Trinity, in a people who are the covenant partners of God. The light of the church is always an external light: reflective, not original. It is, moreover, an "outshining" light in the primary act of the church, which is proclamation—that is, the confession of the radiant love and luminous grace of God. The light of the church is not self-achieved but a witness to the reality of the God who is light. Its primary "outshinings" are hearing and obeying the call of the light of the gospel, witnessing to the light before the world in the domain of darkness, and prayer and praise to the glory of God.

The *second proposal* of this study was that a trinitarian theology of divine light is itself an activity of the illumined human mind. Theological thinking and speaking, if it is to take place in the midst of the gathering of the saints in light, is not autonomous rational inquiry, but an attempt to follow the identity of the One who is light in himself. The human mind illumined is therefore thinking called out of the darkness of sin by God and renewed so that God's radiant presence as Father, Son, and Holy Spirit can be known. Both the formative *field* and the foundational *object* of Christian theology derive from revelation; and so such a theology is not strictly "imaginative" or "participatory," but one of proclamation. It finds its "common rule" and its sole principle in Holy Scripture as the clear, human instrument through which God shines forth himself. Consequently, it tries to read Holy Scripture as a clear witness to God's self-revelation, and is unconcerned with "ambiguous" interpretations. Thus, as the human mind illumined, theology will appropriately display the marks of being renewed by the Holy Spirit for humble attention to the "light of the gospel." Theology's work is its activity in serving the communion of the saints in light in its humble and prayerful position before the triune God.

Yet a *confessio* might be registered here at the end of our study. We note that our proposals regarding the confession that "God is light" will find foreign soil within the landscape of contemporary systematic theology. But perhaps in this *confessio* might be found one final challenge to the reader: a trinitarian theology of divine light is simply incompatible with any *dysteleological* notion of human life. However, an implicit result of our study forces the reader to say that the destiny of the human creature is not of its own making, but rather the undertaking to "walk in the light" of the One who is in himself light. This "visible" action of faith is, indeed, the fulfilling of the human call in history. That is, we *become* "light in the Lord" (Eph 5:8); we *become* "a child of light . . . following, obeying and corresponding to the light of the world."[1] But this *becoming* is not mere mystical contemplation of our own making; nor is it our creation of a human "narrative" or "aesthetics," but rather the outworking of the human call: "walk in the light, as he himself is in the light" (1 John 1:7). Indeed, Barth's quotation at the beginning of our study has particular potency here:

> The light or revelation of God is not just a declaration and interpretation of His being and action, His judgment and grace, His endowing, directing, promising and commanding presence and action. In making Himself known, God acts on the whole man.

---

1. Barth, CD IV.3.2:902; cf. "dem 'Licht der Welt' . . . folgend, gehorsam und entsprechend ein 'Kind des Lichtes'" (KD IV.3:1003).

> Hence the knowledge of God given to man through his illumination is no mere apprehension and understanding of God's being and action, nor as such a kind of intuitive contemplation. It is the claiming not only of his thinking but also of his willing and work, of the whole man, for God. It is his refashioning to be a theatre, witness and instrument of His acts. Its subject and content, which is also its origin, makes it an active knowledge, in which there are affirmation and negation, volition and decision, action and inaction, and in which man leaves certain old courses and enters and pursues new ones. As the work of God becomes clear to him, its reflection lights up his own heart and self and whole existence through the One whom he may know on the basis of His own self-declaration. Illumination and therefore vocation is the total alteration of the one whom it befalls.[2]

Such assertions about the illumination of "the whole man" might appear deeply naïve. Yet it should be noted that the history of God's shining forth to human creatures is a "dynamic teleology,"[3] and its ontology is organized around the fact that it is ever the "true light . . . coming into the world" (John 1:9). It is those who have been "given light" from this "true light," not the enthusiasts of the domain of darkness, who ought to be acquainted with their own "*total* alteration."

Becoming "light in the Lord" is therefore of supreme importance, for the destiny of the human creature will involve not only the world's "*total* alteration," but also the "*total* alteration" of the church by the "light of the gospel." Reflecting on this reality has been the endeavor of our study. The specific accomplishment of this reality, however, resides solely in the gracious realm of God, and so it is a matter for thanksgiving, praise, and proclamation: "At one time you were darkness, but now you are light in the Lord" (Eph 5:8).

In lumine tuo videbimus lumen.

---

2. Ibid., 510; KD IV.3:586.
3. Ibid., 168.

Bibliography

Ambrose. *De officiis. Vol. 2: Commentary*. Edited and Translated by Ivor J. Davidson. Oxford: Oxford University Press, 2001.
Anatolios, Khaled. *Retrieving Nicaea: The Development and Meaning of Trinitarian Doctrine*. Grand Rapids: Baker, 2011.
Anselm. *Monologion and Proslogion with the Replies of Gaunilo and Anselm*. Translated by Thomas Williams. Indianapolis: Hackett, 1995.
Aquinas, Thomas. *Opera omnia iussu impensaque Leonis XIII P. M. edita. Summae Theologiae*. Vols. 4–12. Rome: Ex Typographia Polyglotta S. C. de Propaganda Fide, 1888–1906.
———. *Summa Contra Gentiles*. 5 vols. Reprint. Notre Dame: University of Notre Dame Press, 2012.
———. *Summa Theologiæ* [ST]. Edited by Thomas Gilby and T. C. O'Brien. 60 vols. Reprint. Cambridge: Cambridge University Press, 2006.
Augustine of Hippo. *The Literal Meaning of Genesis*. 2 vols. Translated by J. H. Taylor. Vols. 41 and 42 of *Ancient Christian Writers*. New York: Paulist, 1986.
Ayres, Lewis. *Nicaea and Its Legacy: An Approach to Fourth-Century Trinitarian Theology*. Oxford: Oxford University Press, 2004.
Badcock, Gary. "The Church as 'Sacrament.'" In *The Community of the Word: Toward and Evangelical Ecclesiology*, edited by Mark Husbands and Daniel J. Treier, 188–200. Downers Grove, IL: IVP, 2005.
Baehr, Jason. *The Inquiring Mind: On Intellectual Virtues and Virtue Epistemology*. Oxford: Oxford University Press, 2011.
Balthasar, Hans Urs von. *Mysterium Paschale: The Mystery of Easter*. Translated by Aidan Nichols. San Francisco: Ignatius, 2005.
———. *Theo-drama: Theological Dramatic Theory*. Vols. 3 and 4. Translated by Graham Harrison. San Francisco: Ignatius, 1990, 1994.
———. *Theology: The New Covenant*. Vol. 7 of *The Glory of the Lord: A Theological Aesthetics*. Translated by Brian McNeill. Edited by John Riches. San Francisco: Ignatius, 1989.
Barclay, John G. M. "The Resurrection in Contemporary New Testament Scholarship." In *Resurrection Reconsidered*, edited by Gavin D'Costa, 13–30. Oxford: Oneworld, 1996.
Barth, Karl. *Church Dogmatics* [CD]. 4 vols. Edited by G. W. Bromiley and T. F. Torrance. Edinburgh: T. & T. Clark, 1956–75.
———. *Credo: Die Hauptprobleme der Dogmatik, dargestellt im Anschluß an das Apostolische Glaubensbekenntnis*. Zollikon-Zürich: Evangelischer Verlag, 1948.

---. *Erklärung des Johannesevangeliums*. In *Karl Barth Gesamtausgabe* II.9. Edited by W. Fürst. Zürich: Theologischer Verlag, 1999.

---. *Die kirchliche Dogmatik [KD]*. 4 vols. Munich: Chr. Kaiser, 1932; Zürich: Evangelischer Verlag, 1938–67.

---. *Der Römerbrief (1922)*. Zollikon-Zürich: Evangelischer Verlag, 1940.

---. *Die Theologie Calvins 1922*. In *Karl Barth Gesamtausgabe* II.23. Edited by Hans Scholl. Zürich: Theologischer Verlag, 1993.

---. *The Theology of John Calvin*. Translated by G. W. Bromiley. Grand Rapids: Eerdmans, 1995.

Bäumer, Suitbert. *Histoire du bréviaire*, vol. 1. Paris: Letouzey, 1962.

Beach, J. Mark. *Christ and the Covenant: Francis Turretin's Federal Theology as a Defense of the Doctrine of Grace*. Göttingen: Vandenhoeck & Ruprecht, 2007.

Beeley, Christopher A. *Gregory of Nazianzus on the Trinity and the Knowledge of God: In Your Light We Shall see Light*. Oxford: Oxford University Press, 2008.

---. *The Unity of Christ: Continuity and Conflict in Patristic Tradition*. New Haven: Yale University Press, 2012.

Begbie, Jeremy. "Natural Theology and Music." In *The Oxford Handbook to Natural Theology*, edited by Russell Re Manning, 566–80. Oxford: Oxford University Press, 2013.

Behr, John, et al., eds. *The Popular Patristics Series [PPS]*. 52 vols. Crestwood, NY: St. Vladimir's Seminary Press, 1996–.

Beisser, Friedrich. *Claritas scripturae bei Martin Luther*. Göttingen: Vandenhoeck & Ruprecht, 1966.

Bentham, Jeremy. *The Principles of Morals and Legislation*. New York: Hafner, 1948.

Berkof, Hendrickus, and Han-Joachim Kraus, eds. *Karl Barths Lichterlehre*. Theologische Studien 123. Zürich: Theologischer Verlag, 1978.

Berkouwer, G.C. *The Church*. Studies in Dogmatics. Translated by J. E. Davison. Grand Rapids: Eerdmans, 1976.

---. *Divine Election*. Studies in Dogmatics. Translated by Hugo Bekker. Grand Rapids: Eerdmans, 1960.

---. *Holy Scripture*. Studies in Dogmatics. Translated by J. B. Rodgers. Grand Rapids: Eerdmans, 1975.

---. *The Work of Christ*. Studies in Dogmatics. Translated by Cornelius Lambregste. Grand Rapids: Eerdmans, 1965.

Billings, J. Todd. *Calvin, Participation, and the Gift: The Activity of Believers in Union with Christ*. Oxford: Oxford University Press, 2009.

---. "Union with Christ and the Double Grace: Calvin's Theology and Its Early Reception." In *Calvin's Theology and Its Reception: Disputes, Developments, and New Possibilities*, edited by J. Todd Billings and I. J. Hesselink, 49–71. Louisville, KY: Westminster John Knox, 2012.

Blocher, Henri. *Original Sin: Illuminating the Riddle*. NSBT 5. Leicester, UK: Apollos, 1997.

Bock, Darrell L. *Luke*. Vol. 1. BECNT. Grand Rapids: Baker, 1994.

---. "Scripture and Realization of God's Promise." In *Witness to the Gospel: The Theology of Acts*, edited by I. Howard Marshall and David Peterson, 41–62. Grand Rapids: Eerdmans, 1998.

Bonaventure. *Opera Omnia ad Clarus Aquas (Quaracchi)*. Vol. 5. Florence: Collegio s. Bonaventura, 1891.

Bonhoeffer, Dietrich. *Christ the Center*. Translated by Edwin Robertson. New York: HarperOne, 1978.

———. *Dietrich Bonhoeffer Werke*. Vol. 4. Edited by Martin Kuske and Ilse Tödt. Munich: Chr. Kaiser Verlag, 1989.

Borgen, Peder. *Logos Was the True Light: And Other Essays on the Gospel of John*. Trondheim, Norway: Tapir, 1983.

Bradshaw, Paul F. *The Search for the Origins of Christian Worship: Sources and Methods for the Study of Early Liturgy*. 2nd ed. London: SPCK, 2002.

Braun, Johannes. *Doctrina foederum, sive systema theologica didacticae et elencticae*. Amsterdam: Abraham van Someren, 1691.

Brink, Gijsbert van den. "Social Trinitarianism: A Discussion of Some Recent Theological Criticisms," *International Journal of Systematic Theology* 16, no. 3 (2014) 331–50.

Brown, David. "The Darkness and Light Are Both Alike to Thee: Light as a Symbol and Its Transformations." In *Light from Light: Scientists and Theologians in Dialogue*, edited by Gerald O'Collins SJ and Mary Ann Meyers, 160–82. Grand Rapids: Eerdmans, 2012.

———. *God and Mystery in Words: Experience in Metaphor and Drama*. Oxford: Oxford University Press, 2008.

———. "Trinity, Personhood and Individuality." In *Trinity, Incarnation, and Atonement*, edited by R. J. Feenstra and Cornelius Plantinga Jr., 21–47. Notre Dame, IN: University of Notre Dame Press, 1989.

Brown, Raymond. *The Gospel according to John I–XII*. London: Doubleday, 1971.

Brueggeman, Walter. *Genesis*. Interpretation. Louisville, KY: Westminster John Knox, 1982.

Brunner, Emil. *Dogmatics. Vol. 1: The Christian Doctrine of God*. Translated by Olive Wyon. London: Lutterworth, 1949.

Bucanus, Gulielmus. *Institutiones Theologicae seu Locorum communium Christianae Religionis ex Dei Verbo et praestantissimorum theologorum orthodoxo concensu expositorum Analysis*. Geneva: Esaïas le Preux, 1612.

Bultmann, Rudolf. *Die drei Johannesbriefe*, 2nd ed. Kritisch-Exegetischer Kommentar über das Nueu Testament. Edited by H. A. W. Meyer. Göttingen: Vandenhoeck & Ruprecht, 1967.

———. *The Gospel of John: A Commentary*. Translated by G. R. Beasley-Murray. Oxford: Blackwell, 1971.

———. *History of the Synoptic Tradition*. New York: Harper and Row, 1976.

———. *The Johannine Epistles: A Commentary on the Johannine Epistles*. Translated by R. Philip O'Hara, Lane McGaughty, and Robert Funk. Minneapolis: Fortress, 1973.

———. "Der religionsgeschichtliche Hintergrund des Prologs zum Johannesevangelium." In *Eucharisterion*, edited by Herman Gunkel, 2–26. Göttingen: Vandenhoeck & Ruprecht, 1923.

Butin, Philip. *Revelation, Redemption, and Response: Calvin's Trinitarian Understanding of the Divine-Human Relationship*. New York: Oxford University Press, 1995.

Callahan, James. *The Clarity of Scripture: History, Theology, and Contemporary Literary Studies*. Downers Grove, IL: IVP, 2001.

Calvin, John. *Calvin's Commentaries [CC]*. Edited by the Calvin Translation Society. 22 vols. Reprint. Grand Rapids: Baker, 2009.

———. *Institutes of the Christian Religion (1559)* [*Inst.*]. Translated by F. L. Battles. Edited by John T. McNeill. Vols. 20–21 of Library of Christian Classics. Philadelphia: Westminster John Knox, 1960.

———. *Ioannis Calvini opera quae supersunt Omnia* [*CO* 1–59]. In vols. 29–87 of *Corpus Reformatorum*. Edited by Johann W. Baum, August E. Cunitz, and Edward Ruess. Brunswick: Schwetschke, 1863–1900.

———. *Ioannis Calvini opera selecta* [*OS*]. Reprint. Edited by P. Barth and G. Niesel. Vols. 3 and 4. Eugene, OR: Wipf & Stock, 2010.

———. *Theological Treatises*. Reprint. Translated by J. K. S. Reid. Louisville, KY: Westminster John Knox, 2006.

Canlis, Julie. *Calvin's Ladder: A Spiritual Theology of Ascent and Ascension*. Grand Rapids: Eerdmans, 2010.

Carpenter, Craig. "A Question of Union with Christ? Calvin and Trent on Justification." *Westminster Theological Journal* 64 (2002) 363–86.

Charry, Ellen. *By The Renewing of Your Minds: The Pastoral Function of Christian Doctrine*. Oxford: Oxford University Press, 1997.

Coakley, Sarah. "Can God be Experienced as Trinity?" *Modern Churchman* 28, no. 2 (1986) 11–23.

———. *God, Sexuality, and the Self: An Essay "On the Trinity."* Oxford: Oxford University Press, 2013.

———. "'Persons' in the 'Social' Doctrine of the Trinity: A Critique of Current Analytic Discussion." In *The Trinity: An Interdisciplinary Symposium on the Trinity*, edited by Stephen T. Davis, Daniel Kendall SJ, and Gerald O'Collins SJ, 123–44. Oxford: Oxford University Press, 2002.

Coccejus, Johannes. *Summa theologiae ex Scripturis repetita*. 2nd ed. Geneva: Widerhold, 1665.

Collins, Adela. "Rulers, Divine Men, and Walking on the Water." In *Religious Propaganda and Missionary Competition in the New Testament World*, edited by Lukas Bormann, Kelly Del Tredici, and Angela Standhartinger, 202–27. Leiden: Brill, 1994.

Combs, William. "The Meaning of Fellowship in 1 John." *Detroit Baptist Seminary Journal* 13 (2008) 3–16.

Crowley, Thoedore. "Illumination and Certitude." In *Sanctus Bonaventura 1274–1974*, vol. 2, 421–48. Grottaferrata: Collegio s. Bonaventura, 1973.

Cullen, Christopher. *Bonaventure*. Oxford: Oxford University Press, 2006.

Davidson, Ivor J. *The Birth of the Church: From Jesus to Constantine, AD 30–312*. The Monarch History of the Church. Vol. 1. Oxford: Monarch Books, 2005.

———. "Divine Light: Some Reflections After Barth." In *Trinitarian Theology After Barth*, edited by Myk Habets and Philip Tolliday, 48–69. Eugene, OR: Pickwick, 2011.

———. "Salvation's Destiny: Heirs of God." In *God of Salvation: Soteriology in Theological Perspective*, edited by Ivor J. Davidson and Murray A. Rae, 155–76. Farnham, UK: Ashgate, 2011.

Descartes, René. *Meditationes de prima Philosophia*. Amsterdam: Iohannem Blaev, 1644.

Dionysius the Areopagite. *The Complete Works*. Translated by Colm Luibheid. New York: Paulist, 1987.

Doctorum et Professorum in Academia Leidensi, et al. *Synopsis purioris Theologiae*. 6th ed. Leiden, 1652.
Dorrien, Gary. *Kantian Reason and Hegelian Spirit: The Idealistic Logic of Modern Theology*. Oxford: Wiley-Blackwell, 2015.
Dupré, Louis. *The Enlightenment and the Intellectual Foundations of Modern Culture*. New Haven: Yale University Press, 2004.
Edwards, Jonathan. *The Works of Jonathan Edwards* [WJE]. 26 vols. New Haven: Yale University Press, 1957–2008.
Edwards, Mark. *Catholicity and Heresy in the Early Church*. Farnham, UK: Ashgate, 2009.
Ensminger, Sven. *Karl Barth's Theology as a Resource for a Christian Theology of Religions*. Edinburgh: T. & T. Clark, 2014.
Evans, Craig. *Matthew*. NCBC. Cambridge: Cambridge University Press, 2010.
Ewart, Paul. "The Physical Sciences and Natural Theology." In *Oxford Handbook to Natural Theology*, edited by Russell Re Manning, 419–33. Oxford: Oxford University Press, 2013.
Feil, Ernst. *Die Theologie Dietrich Bonhoeffers. Hermeneutik, Christologie, Weltverständnis*. Munich: Gütersloher Verlagshaus, 2005.
Ferguson, Everett. *Baptism in the Early Church: History, Theology, and Liturgy in the First Five Centuries*. Grand Rapids: Eerdmans, 2009.
Fleming, David. *The Legacy of Israel in Judah's Bible: History, Politics, and the Reinscribing of Tradition*. Cambridge: Cambridge University Press, 2012.
Forrest, Peter. "Divine Fission: A New Way of Moderating Social Trinitarianism." In *Oxford Readings in Philosophical Theology*, vol. 1: *Trinity, Incarnation, Atonement*, edited by Michael Rea, 44–60. Oxford: Oxford University Press, 2009.
Frame, John M. *A History of Western Philosophy and Theology*. Phillipsburg: P. & R., 2015.
France, R. T. *The Gospel of Matthew*. NIGTC. Grand Rapids: Eerdmans, 2007.
Francis I. *Encyclical Letter* Lumen Fidei *of the Supreme Pontiff Francis: To the Bishops, Priests and Deacons, Consecrated Persons, and the Lay Faithful on Earth*. 29 June 2013. Online: http://w2.vatican.va/content/francesco/en/encyclicals/documents/papa-francesco_20130629_enciclica-lumen-fidei.html.
Franke, John R. "God Is Love: The Social Trinity and the Mission of God." In *Trinitarian Theology for the Church: Scripture, Community, Worship*, edited by Daniel Treier and David Lauber, 105–19. Downers Grove, IL: IVP, 2009.
Funk, Franz Xavier von, ed. *Didascalia et Constitutiones Apostolorum V*. Paderbornae, Germany: Ferdinandi Schoeningh, 1905.
Furry, Timothy J. "Analogous analogies? Thomas Aquinas and Karl Barth." *Scottish Journal of Theology* 63, no. 3 (2010) 318–30.
Gathercole, Simon. *The Preexistent Son: Recovering the Christologies of Matthew, Mark, and Luke*. Grand Rapids: Eerdmans, 2006.
Geary, Patrick. *Readings in Medieval History*. 4th ed. Toronto: University of Toronto Press, 2010.
Gerard, Johannis. *Loci theologici: cum pro adstruenda veritate tum pro destruenda quorumvis contradicentium falsitate per theses nervose solide et solide et copiose explicatit*. Tübingen: Georgii Cottae, 1764.
Gerrish, B. A. *Christian Faith: Dogmatics in Outline*. Louisville, KY: Westminster John Knox, 2015.

Giule, Dragoș. *Pre-Nicene Christology in Paschal Contexts: The Case of the Divine Noetic Anthropos*. Leiden: Brill, 2014.

Green-McCreight, Kathryn. *Feminist Reconstructions of Christian Doctrine: Narrative Analysis and Appraisal*. New York: Oxford University Press, 2000.

Grenz, Stanley, and John Franke. *Beyond Foundationalism: Shaping Theology in a Postmodern Context*. Louisville, KY: Westminster John Knox, 2001.

Grudem, Wayne. *Systematic Theology: An Introduction to Biblical Doctrine*. Grand Rapids: Zondervan, 1994.

Gunton, Colin. *The Triune Creator: A Historical and Systematic Study*. Edinburgh: Edinburgh University Press, 1998.

Hanby, Michael. *Augustine and Modernity*. New York: Routledge, 2003.

Hauerwas, Stanley, and William H. Willimon. *Resident Aliens: Life in the Christian Colony*. Nashville: Abingdon, 1989.

Heidegger, Johann Heinrich. *Corpus theologiae Christianae*. Zürich: Typis Joh. Henrici Bodmeri, 1700.

Hendel, Kurt K. "'No Salvation Outside the Church' in Light of Luther's Dialectic of the Hidden and Revealed God." *Currents in Theology and Mission* 35, no. 4 (2008) 248–57.

Heppe, Heinrich. *Die Dogmatik der evangelisch-reformierten Kirche*. Elberfeld: Friderichs, 1861.

Hermann, Rudolf. "Von der Klarheit der Heiligen Schrift. Untersuchungen und Erorterungen über Luthers Lehre von der Schrift in '*De servo arbitrio*.'" In *Studien zur Theologie Luthers und des Luthertums. Gesammelte und nachgelassene Werke*, vol. 2, edited by Horst Beintker, 170–255. Göttingen: Vandenhoeck & Ruprecht, 1981.

Heron, Alasdair. "*Homoousios* with the Father." In *The Incarnation: Ecumenical Studies in the Nicene-Constantinopolitan Creed A.D. 381*, edited by T. F. Torrance, 58–87. Edinburgh: Handsel, 1981.

Holmes, Christopher R. J. "God's Attributes as God's Clarities: Wolf Krötke's Doctrine of the Divine Attributes." *International Journal for Systematic Theology* 10, no. 1 (2008) 54–72.

———. *The Holy Spirit*. Grand Rapids: Zondervan, 2015.

Huijgen, Arnold. *Divine Accommodation in John Calvin's Theology*. Göttingen: Vandenhoeck & Ruprecht, 2011.

Hume, David. *A Treatise Of Human Nature: Being An Attempt to Introduce the Experimental Method of Reasoning into Moral Subjects*. Vol. 1. London: John Noon, 1739.

Hunt, Hannah. "Byzantine Christianity." In *The Blackwell Companion to Early Christianity*, edited by Ken Parry, 73–93. Oxford: Blackwell, 2010.

Hütter, Reinhard. "The Knowledge of the Triune God: Practices, Doctrine, Theology." In *Knowing the Triune God: The Work of the Spirit in the Practices of the Church*, edited by James Buckley and David Yeago, 23–48. Grand Rapids: Eerdmans, 2001.

Jobes, Karen H. *1, 2, and 3 John*. ZECNT. Grand Rapids: Zondervan, 2014.

Johnson, Luke T. *Hebrews: A Commentary*. NTL. Louisville, KY: Westminster John Knox, 2006.

Jowers, Dennis, and H. Wayne House, eds. *The New Evangelical Subordinationism? Perspectives on the Equality of God the Father and God the Son*. Eugene, OR: Wipf & Stock, 2012.

Jüngel, Eberhard. *Gott als Geheimnis der Welt. Zur Begründung der Theologie des Gekreuzigten im Streit zwischen Theismus und Atheismus*. Tübingen: Mohr Siebeck, 2010.

———. *Gottes Sein ist im Werdern. Verantwortliche Rede vom Sein Gottes bei Karl Barth. Eine Paraphrase*. Tübingen: Mohr Siebeck, 1986

———. *Theological Essays I*. Translated and edited by John Webster. London: Bloomsbury T. & T. Clark, 2014.

Kannengiesser, Charles, ed. *Handbook of Patristic Exegesis: The Bible in Ancient Christianity*. Vol. 2. Leiden: Brill, 2004.

Kant, Immanuel. *Critique of Pure Reason*. Translated by Paul Guyer and A. W. Wood. Cambridge: Cambridge University Press, 1998.

———. *Immanuel Kants Werke. Schriften von 1783–88*. Vol. 4. Edited by A. Buchenau and E. Cassirer. Berlin: Cassirer, 1913.

Käsemann, Ernst. "Aufhau und Anliegen des Johanneischen Prologs." *Liberias Christiana* (1957) 75–99.

Keener, Craig S. *Acts: An Exegetical Commentary*. Vol. 4. Grand Rapids: Baker, 2015.

———. *A Commentary on the Gospel of Matthew*. Grand Rapids: Eerdmans, 1999.

———. *The Gospel of John: A Commentary*. 2 vols. Peabody, MA: Hendrickson, 2003.

Kilby, Karen. "Perichoresis and Projection: Problems with Social Doctrines of the Trinity." *New Blackfriars* 81, no. 957 (2000) 432–45.

Kittel, Gerhard, and Gerhard Friedrich. *Theological Dictionary of the New Testament*. 10 vols. Translated by G. W. Bromiley. Grand Rapids: Eerdmans, 1964–74.

Köstenberger, Andreas. *John*. BECNT. Grand Rapids: Baker, 2004.

Kovach, Steven, and Peter Schemm, Jr. "A Defense of the Doctrine of the Eternal Subordination of the Son." *Journal of the Evangelical Theological Society* 42 (1999) 461–76.

Krötke, Wolf. *Gottes Klarheiten. Eine Neuinterpretation der Lehre von den "Eigenschaften Gottes."* Tübingen: Mohr Siebeck, 2001.

Kruse, Colin. *Paul's Letter to the Romans*. PNTC. Grand Rapids: Eerdmans, 2012.

Lackey, Jennifer. "Why We Don't Deserve Credit for Everything We Know." *Synthese* 158, no. 3 (2007) 345–61.

LaCugna, Catherine Mowry. *God for Us: The Trinity and Christian Life*. San Francisco: HarperSanFrancisco, 1991.

Lee, Simon S. *Jesus' Transfiguration and the Believers' Transfiguration*. Tübingen: Mohr Siebeck, 2009.

Leith, John H., ed. *Creeds of the Church: A Reader in Christian Doctrine from the Bible to the Present*. 3rd ed. Louisville, KY: Westminster John Knox, 1983.

Locke, John. *An Essay concerning Human Understanding: In Four Books*. Vol. 1. New ed. Edinburgh: J. Dickson and C. Elliot, 1777.

Louth, Andrew. *Denys the Areopagite*. London: Continuum, 2001.

———. "Light, Vision, and Religious Experience in Byzantium." In *The Presence of Light: Divine Radiance and Religious Experience*, edited by Matthew Kapstein, 85–103. Chicago: University of Chicago Press, 2004.

———. *The Origins of the Christian Mystical Tradition: From Plato to Denys*. 2nd ed. Oxford: Oxford University Press, 2007.

Luther, Martin. *D. Martin Luthers Werke. Kritische Gesamtausgabe* [WA]. 120 vols. Weimar: Böhlaus Nachfolger, 1883–2009.

Mackenzie, Iain M. *The 'Obscurism' of Light: A Theological Study into the Nature of Light.* Norwich, UK: Canterbury, 1996.

Macky, Peter. *The Centrality of Metaphors to Biblical Thought: A Method for Interpreting the Bible.* Studies in the Bible and Early Christianity. Lewiston, NY: Mellen, 1990.

Marrone, Steven P. *The Light of Thy Countenance: Science and Knowledge of God in the Thirteenth Century.* Vol. 2. Leiden: Brill, 2001.

Marshall, I. Howard. *The Epistles of John.* NICNT. Grand Rapids: Eerdmans, 1978.

———. *The Gospel of Luke: A Commentary from the Greek Text.* NIGTC. Grand Rapids: Eerdmans, 1978.

Mastricht, Peter van. *Theoretico-practica theologia, qua, per singula capita theologica, pars exegetica, dogmatica, elenchtica et practica, perpetua successione conjugantur.* New ed. Utrecht: Apud W. van de Water, 1724.

McCarter, Jr., P. Kyle. "Dualism in Antiquity." In *Light Against Darkness: Dualism in Ancient Mediterranean Religion and the Contemporary World*, Journal of Ancient Judaism Supplements, vol. 2, edited by Armin Lange, B. Levinson, and V. Noam, 19–35. Göttingen: Vandenhoeck & Ruprecht, 2011.

McGuckin, John A. "Christ: The Apostolic Fathers to the Third Century." In *The Routledge Companion to Early Christian Thought*, edited by D. Jeffery Bingham, 256–70. Abingdon: Routledge, 2010.

———. "'Perceiving Light from Light in Light' (*Oration* 31.3): The Trinitarian Theology of Saint Gregory the Theologian." *The Greek Orthodox Theological Review* 39, no. 1 (1994) 7–32.

———. *St. Gregory of Nazianzus: An Intellectual Biography.* New York: St. Vladimir's Seminary Press, 2001.

———. *The Transfiguration of Christ in Scripture and Tradition.* New York: Mellen, 1986.

Meyendorff, John. *Byzantine Theology: Historical Trends and Doctrinal Themes.* New York: Fordham University Press, 1979.

———. *St. Gregory Palamas and Orthodox Spirituality.* New York: St. Vladimir's Seminary Press, 1974.

Migne, J. -P., ed. *Patrologia graeca* [PG]. 161 vols. Paris: Garnier, 1857–66.

———. *Patrologia latina* [PL]. 221 vols. Paris: Garnier, 1844–55.

Miller, Ed L. *Salvation-History in the Prologue of John: The Significance of John 1:3/4.* Supplements to Novum Testamentum 60. Leiden: Brill, 1989.

Minear, Paul. *Images of the Church in the New Testament.* Philadelphia: Westminster, 1977.

Molnar, Paul D. "Natural Theology Revisited: A Comparison of T. F. Torrance and Karl Barth." *Zeitschrift für dialektische Theologie* 20 (2005) 53–83.

Moltmann, Jürgen. "God in the World—the World in God: Perichoresis in Trinity and Eschatology." In *Gospel of John and Christian Theology*, edited by Richard Baukham and Carl Mosser, 369–81. Grand Rapids: Eerdmans, 2008.

———. *The Trinity and the Kingdom: The Doctrine of God.* Translated by Margaret Kohl. San Francisco: HarperCollins, 1991.

———. *The Way of Jesus Christ: Christology in Messianic Dimensions.* Translated by Margaret Kohl. London: SCM, 1999.

Montagnes, Bernard. *La doctrine de l'analogie de l'être d'après Saint Thomas d'Aquin*, Philosophes médiévaux 6. Paris: Béatrice-Nauwelaerts, 1963.

Moreland, J. P., and William Lane Craig. "The Trinity." In *Trinity, Incarnation, Atonement*, edited by Michael Rea, 21–43. Oxford: Oxford University Press, 2009.
Morgan, Richard. *The Imagery of Light in St. Ambrose's Theology*. Melbourne: Carmelite Monestary, 1998.
Muller, Richard A. *Calvin and the Reformed Tradition: On the Work of Christ and the Order of Salvation*. Grand Rapids: Baker, 2012.
———. *Christ and the Decree: Christology and Predestination in Reformed Theology from Calvin to Perkins*. Reprint. Grand Rapids: Baker, 2008.
———. *Post-Reformation Reformed Dogmatics: The Rise and Development of Reformed Orthodoxy, ca. 1520 to ca. 1725*. 4 vols. Grand Rapids: Baker Academic, 2003.
———. "Toward the *Pactum Salutis*: Locating the Origins of a Concept." *MidAmerica Journal of Theology* 18 (2007) 11–65.
O'Brien, Peter T. *The Letter to the Hebrews*. PNTC. Grand Rapids: Eerdmans, 2010.
Olevian, Caspar. *De substantia foederis gratuiti inter Deum et electos, itemque de mediis quibus ea ipsa substantia nobis communicator II*. Geneva: Eustache Vignon, 1585.
Olson, Roger E. *The Journey of Modern Theology: From Reconstruction to Deconstruction*. Downers Grove, IL: IVP Academic, 2013.
Owen, John. *The Works of John Owen*. 16 vols. Edited by William H. Goold. Reprint. Edinburgh: Banner of Truth, 2013.
Painter, John. *The Quest for the Messiah: The History, Literature, and Theology of the Johannine Community*. 2nd ed. Edinburgh: T. & T. Clark, 1993.
Palamas, Gregory. *The Triads*. Edited by John Meyendorff. Translated by Nicholas Gendle. Mahwah, NJ: Paulist, 1983.
Palmer, G. E. H., P. Sherrard, and Kallistos Ware. *The Philokalia*. Vol. 4. London: Faber & Faber, 1995.
Pannenberg, Wolfhart. *Systematic Theology*. 3 Vols. Translated by G. W. Bromiley. Grand Rapids: Eerdmans, 1998.
Pickstock, Catherine. "What Shines Between: The *Metaxu* of Light." In *Between System and Poetics: William Desmond and Philosophy after Dialectic*, edited by Thomas A. F. Kelley, 107–22. Aldershot, UK: Routledge, 2016.
Plantinga Jr., Cornelius. "Social Trinity and Tritheism." In *Trinity, Incarnation, and Atonement*, edited by Michael Rea, 21–47. Oxford: Oxford University Press, 2009.
Plato. *Meno and Other Dialogues*. Translated by Robin Waterfield. New York: Oxford University Press, 2005.
———. *The Republic*. Edited by G. R. F. Ferrari. Translated by Thomas Griffith. Cambridge: Cambridge University Press, 2000.
———. *Symposium*. Translated by Richard Hunter. Oxford: Oxford University Press, 2004.
Polanus, Amandus. *Syntagma theologiae christianae*. 2 Vols. Hanover: Abrii, 1609–10.
Polkinghorn, John. "Some Light from Physics." In *Light from Light: Scientists and Theologians in Dialogue*, edited by Gerald O'Collins SJ and Mary Ann Meyers, 17–27. Grand Rapids: Eerdmans, 2012.
Rad, Gerhard von. *Das erste Buch Mose: Genesis*. Göttingen: Vandenhoeck & Ruprect, 1981.
Rahner, Karl. *Foundations of Christian Faith: An Introduction to the Idea of Christianity*. London: Darton, Longman & Todd, 1978.
Ramsey, Arthur Michael. *The Glory of God and the Transfiguration of Christ*. Reprint. Eugene, OR: Wipf & Stock, 2009.

Reno, R. R. *Genesis*. BTCB. Grand Rapids: Brazos, 2010.
Roberts, Alexander, and James Donaldson, eds. *The Ante-Nicene Fathers [ANF]*. 10 vols. Reprint. Peabody, MA: Hendrickson, 1994.
Rogers, Eugene. *Thomas Aquinas and Karl Barth: Sacred Doctrine and the Natural Knowledge of God*. Notre Dame, IN: University of Notre Dame, 1995.
Rutherford, Samuel. *The Covenant of Life Opened; or, A Treatise of the Covenant of Grace*. Edinburgh: A. Anderson, 1655.
Sailhamer, John. *Christian Theology*. Grand Rapids: Zondervan, 1998.
Schaff, Philip, ed. *The Nicene and Post-Nicene Fathers [NPNF]*. 2 series. 28 vols. Reprint. Peabody, MA: Hendrickson, 1994.
Schleiermacher, Friedrich. *The Christian Faith*. Edited by H. R. Mackintosh and J. S. Stewart. Reprint. Edinburgh: T. & T. Clark, 2004.
———. *On Religion: Speeches to Its Cultured Despisers*. Translated by Richard Crouter. New York: Cambridge University Press, 1993.
Schnackenburg, Rudolf. *The Gospel According to St. John*. Vol. 2. New York: Crossroad, 1990.
———. "Logos—Hymnus und johanneischer Prolog." *Biblische Zeitschrift* 1 (1957) 76–82.
Schumacher, Lydia. *Divine Illumination: The History and Future of Augustine's Theory of Knowledge*. Oxford: Wiley-Blackwell, 2011.
Silvas, Anna, tr. *Gregory of Nyssa: The Letters Introduction, Translation and Commentary*. Supplements to Vigiliae Christianae 83. Leiden: Brill, 2007.
Smart, Christopher. *Jubilate Agnu*. Cambridge: Harvard University Press, 1954.
Smith, Christian. *The Bible Made Impossible: Why Biblicism is Not a Truly Evangelical Reading of Scripture*. Grand Rapids: Brazos, 2011.
Sonderegger, Katherine. *Systematic Theology*, vol. 1: *The Doctrine of God*. Minneapolis: Fortress, 2015.
Soskice, Janet. *Metaphor and Religious Language*. Oxford: Clarendon, 1987.
Spinoza, Benedict. *Ethica ordine geometrico pars prima*. In *Opera, quotquot reperta sunt*. Vol. 1. Hague: Nijhoff, 1895.
Steinmetz, David C. *Calvin in Context*. 2nd ed. Oxford: Oxford University Press, 2010.
Swinburne, Richard. *The Christian God*. Oxford: Oxford University Press, 1994.
Tamburello, Dennis. *Union with Christ; John Calvin and the Mysticism of St. Bernard*. Louisville, KY: Westminster John Knox, 1994.
Tanner, Kathryn. *Christ the Key*. Cambridge: Cambridge University Press, 2010.
———. "The Use of Perceived Properties of Light as a Theological Analogy." In *Light from Light: Scientists and Theologians in Dialogue*, edited by Gerald O'Collins SJ and Mary Ann Meyers, 122–30. Grand Rapids: Eerdmans, 2012.
Thiselton, Anthony C. *Systematic Theology*. Grand Rapids: Eerdmans, 2015.
Thompson, Mark D. *A Clear and Present Word: The Clarity of Scripture*. Downers Grove, IL: IVP, 2006.
Tillich, Paul. *Systematic Theology*. 3 vols. Chicago: Chicago University Press, 1951–63.
Torrance, T. F. *The Christian Doctrine of God: One Being Three Persons*. Edinburgh: Continuum, 1996.
———. *The Ground and Grammar of Theology: Consonance between Theology and Science*. Edinburgh: T. & T. Clark, 2001.
———. "Immortality and Light." *Religious Studies* 17, no. 2 (1981) 147–61.
———. *Theology in Reconstruction*. London: SCM, 1965.

Turretin, Francis. *Institutio theologiae elencticae.* Leiden: Fredericum Haring; Utrecht: Ernestum Voskuyl, 1696.
Turner, Denys. *The Darkness of God: Negativity in Christian Mysticism.* Cambridge: Cambridge University Press, 1995.
Ursinus, Zacharias. *Catechesis religionis christianae, quae traditur in ecclesiis et scholis Palatinus.* Heidelberg: Michael Schirat, 1570.
Vander Lugt, Wesley. *Living Theodrama: Reimagining Theological Ethics.* Farnham, UK: Ashgate, 2014.
Vanhoozer, Kevin J. *The Drama of Doctrine: A Canonical-linguistic Approach to Christian Theology.* Louisville, KY: Westminster John Knox, 2005.
———. *Faith Speaking Understanding: Performing the Drama of Doctrine.* Louisville, KY: Westminster John Knox, 2014.
———. *Is There a Meaning in the Text? The Bible, the Reader, and the Morality of Literary Knowledge.* Grand Rapids: Zondervan, 1998.
Vaux, Kenneth L. "Light and Sight in Interfaith Theology and Ethics." In *The Theology of Light and Sight: An Interfaith Perspective*, edited by Kenneth L. Vaux and K. K. Yeo, 3–30. Eugene, OR: Wipf & Stock, 2011.
Vermès, Géza, tr. *The Complete Dead Sea Scrolls in English.* Harmondsworth, UK: Penguin, 1998.
Vermigli, Peter Martyr. *Loci communes.* London: John Kyngston, 1576.
Vinson, Martha, tr. *Gregory of Nazianzus: Select Orations.* Fathers of the Church, vol. 107. Washington, DC: Catholic University of America Press, 2003.
Voetius, Gisbertus. *Selectarum disputationum theologicarum.* Vol. 2. Utrecht: J. a Waesberge, 1655.
Volf, Miroslav. *After Our Likeness: The Church as the Image of the Trinity.* Grand Rapids: Eerdmans, 1998.
———. "Being as God Is: Trinity and Generosity." In *God's Life in Trinity*, edited by Miroslav Volf and Michael Welker, 3–12. Minneapolis: Fortress, 2006.
———. *Exclusion and Embrace: A Theological Exploration of Identity, Otherness, and Reconciliation.* Nashville: Abingdon, 1996.
Wahlde, Urban von. *The Gospel and Letters of John.* 3 vols. ECC. Grand Rapids: Eerdmans, 2010.
Walton, John. *The Lost World of Genesis One: Ancient Cosmology and the Origins Debate.* Downers Grove, IL: IVP, 2009.
Walton, John, et al. *IVP Background Commentary: Old Testament.* Downers Grove, IL: IVP, 2000.
Ware, Bruce. *Father, Son, and Holy Spirit: Relations, Roles, Relevance.* Wheaton, IL: Crossway, 2006.
Ware, Kallistos. *The Orthodox Church.* Rev. ed. London: Penguin, 1993.
Warfield, B. B. *The Works of Benjamin B. Warfield.* 10 vols. Edited by E. D. Warfield, W. P. Armstrong, and C. W. Hodge. Reprint. Grand Rapids: Baker, 2003.
Webster, John B. *Confessing God: Essays in Christian Dogmatics II.* Edinburgh: T. & T. Clark, 2005.
———. *The Domain of the Word: Scripture and Theological Reason.* London: Bloomsbury T. & T. Clark, 2012.
———. *Holy Scripture: A Dogmatic Sketch.* Cambridge: Cambridge University Press, 2003.

———. "What Makes Theology Theological?" *Journal of Analytic Theology* 3 (2015) 17–28.
Westermann, Claus. *Genesis 1–11: A Continental Commentary*. Vol. 1. Translated by J. J. Scullion. Minneapolis: Fortress, 1994.
Whidden III, David L. *Christ the Light: The Theology of Light and Illumination in Thomas Aquinas*. Minneapolis: Fortress, 2014.
Wigley, Stephen. *Balthasar's Trilogy: A Reader's Guide*. London: Continuum, 2010.
Williams, Daniel. *Ambrose of Milan and the End of the Nicene-Arian Conflicts*. Oxford: Clarendon, 1995.
Williams, Rowan. "Arius and the Melitian Schism." *Theological Studies* 37 (1986) 35–52.
———. *On Christian Theology*. Oxford: Blackwell, 2000.
———. *Resurrection: Interpreting the Easter Gospel*. Reprint. Cleveland, OH: Pilgrim, 2006.
Witherington III, Ben. *John's Wisdom*. Louisville, KY: Westminster John Knox, 1995.
Witsius, Herman. *De Oeconomia Foederum Dei cum homnibus libri quattuor*. 2nd ed. Leeuwarden: J. Hagenaar, 1685.
Wright, N. T. *The Climax of the Covenant: Christ and the Law in Pauline Theology*. Minneapolis: Fortress, 1993.
———. *Jesus and the Victory of God*. London: SPCK, 1996.
———. *The Last Word: Beyond the Bible Wars to a New Understanding of the Authority of Scripture*. New York: HarperCollins, 2005.
———. *Paul and the Faithfulness of God*. 2 vols. London: SPCK, 2013.
Yadin, Yigael, tr. *The Scroll of the War of the Sons of Light against the Sons of Darkness*. London: Oxford University Press, 1962.
Yarbrough, Robert. *1–3 John*. BECNT. Grand Rapids: Baker, 2008.
Yeo, K. K. "Light and New Creation in Genesis and the Gospel of John." In *The Theology of Light and Sight: An Interfaith Perspective*, edited by Kenneth L. Vaux and K. K. Yeo, 39–58. Eugene, OR: Wipf & Stock, 2011.
Zizoulas, John. *Being and Communion: Studies in Personhood and the Church*. London: Darton, Longman and Todd, 1985.

www.ingramcontent.com/pod-product-compliance
Lightning Source LLC
Chambersburg PA
CBHW071232170426
43191CB00032B/1353